OF CARGOES, COLONIES AND KINGS

"The time has come, the
Walrus said, to talk of
many things; of shoes and
ships and sealing wax and
cabbages and kings; and why
the sea is boiling hot and
whether pigs have wings."

Lewis Carroll

OF CARGOES, COLONIES AND KINGS

Diplomatic and Administrative Service from Africa to the Pacific

Andrew Stuart

The Radcliffe Press
LONDON • NEW YORK

Reprinted in 2009 by The Radcliffe Press
6 Salem Road, London W2 4BU
175 Fifth Avenue, New York NY 10010
www.ibtauris.com

In the United States and Canada distributed by St. Martin's Press
175 Fifth Avenue, New York NY10010

First Published in 2001 by The Radcliffe Press

ISBN 978 1 85043 978 3

A full CIP record for this book is available from the British Library
A full CIP record for this book is available from the Library of Congress

Library of Congress catalog card: available

Typeset by The Midlands Book Typesetting Co, Loughborough, Leicestershire
Printed and bound in India by Thomson Press (India) Ltd

Contents

Foreword   vii
Dedication   viii
Disclaimer   ix
Prelude: The Prophet on the Rock   xi

1.	The Naïve and Sentimental Colonialist	1
2.	Settlers in the Glue Pot	7
3.	The Lords of Africa	15
4.	'King Freddie'	26
5.	District Officer	32
6.	Safari	39
7.	Fish and Chips	47
8.	New Flags for Old	58
9.	Amin and After	68
10.	Diplomat: A Minnow in the Whitehall Pond	80
11.	Hong Kong: The Fragrant Harbour	93
12.	Seychelles: The Island of Indecent Coconuts	108
13.	Diego Garcia: A Bet on a Bikini	121
14.	New Hebrides: Condominium in the South Pacific	129
15.	Resident Commissioner	145
16.	The Land of the Holy Spirit	159
17.	Rebellions and Taboos	169
18.	John Frum's Cargoes	178
19.	Prince Philip's Paradis	187
20.	'The Pandemonium'	196
21.	Soldier, Soldier	206
22.	The 'Coconut War'	214
23.	The End of Empire	224
Envoi: Brought to Justice		233

List of Illustrations

1. (above) The Rwenzori Mountains – 'Mountains of the Moon' (author in foreground).
2. (above) 'My own costume was as prescribed in colonial regulations.'
3. (right) George Rukidi, the Omukama of Toro, with his daughter, Princess Elizabeth.
4. (below) The coronation of Kabaka Mutesa of Buganda ('King Freddie') by Bishop Stuart.
5. (above) Milton Obote, the first dictator of Uganda.
6. (right) Idi Amin, the second dictator.
7. (above) The governor and the traditionalists.
8. (below) Jimmy Mancham (right), first President of the Seychelles; Albert René (left), first Prime Minister and later President after the military coup.
9. (left) Andrew Stuart and J-J Robert, joint Resident Commissioners of the New Hebrides.
10. (below) 'Exhausting negotiations' – Walter Lini, first Prime Minister of Vanuatu on right.
11. (above) 'The Pandemonium' – announcing the death of Alexis Yolou.
12. (below) Promulgating the new constitution.
13. (left) Members of the British and French police forces.
14. (below) Contrasting styles of the Condominium.
15. 'The end of empire' – with HRH the Duke of Gloucester on Independence Day.

GENERAL SIR CHARLES GUTHRIE GCB LVO OBE ADC Gen

CHIEF OF THE DEFENCE STAFF

MINISTRY OF DEFENCE
MAIN BUILDING (Room 6173)
WHITEHALL
LONDON SW1A 2HB
Telephone   0171-21-83353
Facsimile   0171-21-86799

FOREWORD

Andrew Stuart has enjoyed an eventful life as a colonial administrator and diplomat and his book apart from recording many of his personal experiences captures the spirit of the times and places in which he served.

Although not long retired he writes of events which already seem to belong to a different age and the like of which are most unlikely ever to be repeated. During his career he witnessed many changes and crises in the countries he served or had dealings with. Decolonisation in Uganda, the lead up to negotiations with China over Hong Kong, revolutions in the Seychelles, war in Bangladesh, agreeing basing rights with the United States in Diego Garcia and bringing to an end, with the French, the New Hebrides Condominium.

In 1980 whilst serving as a Colonel in the Ministry of Defence I was despatched at short notice to the New Hebrides as Andrew's Military Adviser and Commander of the British Forces New Hebrides. I had been briefed that the security situation had deteriorated, but had no idea just how bizarre it had become. That two great European nations, the United Kingdom and France, could be in bitter disagreement about a Melanesian Island on the other side of the world inhabited by a primitive tribe who were engaged in an insurrection was difficult to believe. I had been told that the further from their capitals they were the more French the French became and the more British we became. I think this is true and our interests in the New Hebrides and the South Pacific were different. Having just arrived I was also very well aware that neither Paris nor London really understood, nor wanted to understand, the difficulties Andrew and his French opposite number had on an Island, which most people at home would find difficult to place on the map. They wanted the problem, a relic from our colonial histories, to go away, but to go away on their terms.

The British were fortunate to have Andrew Stuart as their representative. He was experienced, wise, pragmatic and patient. Sometimes I suspect his experience of Idi Amin when in a previous appointment must have seemed simpler to him than his dealings with some of the personalities in the New Hebrides. I was never sure that he really needed a Military Adviser but was glad to have been sent to work for him. The Anglo-French military operations, when launched, succeeded to the satisfaction of both of us. And the Royal Marines, as always, also succeeded admirably in what was, for them, an unfamiliar and often frustrating role.

Andrew Stuart writes with a light touch, but the reader should remember just how varied and difficult many of the problems he was confronted with during a distinguished career were. As a colonial administrator and diplomat his contribution was immense.

Charles Guthrie

For Mr Carruthers, the cynosure and exemplar of Her Majesty's Overseas Civil Service. Did he ever exist, I wonder? Or was he just a figment of our overheated imaginations as we sat by our campfires trying to encompass the minds of our Whitehall masters?

– Also for Pat, who was there beyond a peradventure, and for our long-suffering children, Fiona, James and Charles, who endured boarding schools and rootlessness so that, we could, in the old and cynical description of diplomacy 'lie abroad for the sake of our country'.

Disclaimer

'Old Men Forget', or so my children tell me. Certainly it is true that, as time goes by, the details of our lives begin to blur. After the hundredth repetition we are no longer certain whether this or that detail is absolutely cross-my-heart correct. We begin to gather a bit of moss.

The trick is not to lose control of the dividing line between comfortable accretions and sheer phantasy. Latterly my father used to include in his sermons stories about his aunts that were almost certainly exaggerations. Problems only arose when we began to doubt whether a particular aunt had ever actually existed.

If any of my few friends ever get to read these pages they will all, probably, write me angry letters, 'It wasn't like that, it was different.' 'You have mixed up so-and-so and such-and-such.' 'It really wasn't as funny as all that. In fact it wasn't funny at all.'

My apologies to you all. Some of it is deliberate, to avoid complicating the story and confusing the reader. Occasionally too I have melded two or more incidents or characters together in order to avoid embarrassing individuals.

Nor can I vouch beyond a peradventure for total chronological accuracy. In particular, in the hurly-burly of the New Hebrides the only way I could swear, at this distance, that I have got the order of things completely right, would be to re-read the nightly telegrams which I sent to London after the trauma of each New Hebridean day. But the officials of the Foreign Office won't let me read them. This strikes me as a bit absurd; after all I wrote the things. But it will have to be left to future historians to prove me right or call me a liar.

Nevertheless all of these things did happen. Their improbability springs as much as anything else from the fact that the British colonial experience is today as dead as a dodo. That period is over and will never recur. Few understand it. Fewer still believe in it.

And that, indeed, is a large part of the reason for writing this book. When I was still working for the government of Uganda after Independence, my African colleagues used frequently to be entertained by the diplomats of the British High Commission. I never was, despite the fact that I was about to join the heaven-born myself. After one such party my African counterpart came back perplexed. He had been taken aside by one of the keen young men, fresh out from London with the damp still between his ears. 'Please understand,' he said earnestly, 'We are not like these wicked people who have been oppressing you all these years. We are your Friends.'

Such nonsense. What did he know about it?

'The maintenance of Colonial Situations is incompatible with the United Nations ideal of Universal Peace'.

(UN Resolution)

Prelude

The Prophet on the Rock

'What do I see?
'You see me.'
'And how have you spent the day?'
'Well'
'Yes?'
'Yes'
'What is the news?'
'Good news – and what is your news?'
'Good also.'

Properly handled, the stately Luganda greeting and response can be made to last five minutes or more. Normally we used it to avoid having to stop as two friends passed each other, their voices finally dying away in the distance in a prolonged hum of mutual politeness. But just at the moment I needed it for another and more urgent purpose.

No Muganda, however crazy or impolite, would fail to respond to the stately canon, or would interrupt it, once properly launched. Until it was finished, I could reasonably hope that Kigaanira, the prophet of Mutundwe Hill, would not drop his rock on my head, or prod at me with what looked, to my nervous eyes, a remarkably sharp little spear.

Kigaanira had every reason to feel annoyed with me. Some years before, having levitated to the top of a large tree on the sacred Hill of Mutundwe, he had announced to an over-excited African crowd that he was one of their Lubaale, or ancient tribal gods, and would now tell them a few home truths about the colonial government.

A party of the Uganda Police called upon him to desist, but Kigaanira only sneered at them and suggested to his, by now, wildly ululating followers that they should throw the police to the nearby sacred crocodile. An African police sergeant started to climb the tree to remonstrate with him, but was knocked down and killed; though whether by Kigaanira himself or by his followers was never entirely clear.

This was too much for the authorities to swallow. Kigaanira was de-perched and, after due process of law, sent off for twenty years to forget his divine origins in a prison farm out in the forest.

There for some time, he was a model prisoner; but eventually, when the moon was full, he had a second revelation that bade him continue his mission. This time though, his orders were to choose something more substantial than a tree. According to his own story, he flew out of prison that night on the back of a giant crested crane (Uganda's national bird), and circled Buganda looking for a more suitable and durable pillar on which to land. At last he was guided by the crane to the top of Kkungu rock. There he was spotted next day, dancing happily around the summit, allegedly guarded by a monstrous snake with two heads.

The crested crane must have been a wise old bird. Kkungu was ideally suited for both mythological and tactical defence. A spike of grey granite, a hundred feet high and ten feet across at the top, twenty miles from Kampala, the capital of the British Protectorate of Uganda, it already played a central role in the old Buganda spirit religion. Though the people of Buganda mostly were, and are, sincerely Christian, they also sensibly hold to important ancestral truths and many concurrently believe that Kkungu is the home of important gods. These some Baganda propitiated in those days with food and gifts and occasional rather half-hearted ceremonies, like a meeting of embarrassed Freemasons.

At the foot of the rock lived, at that time in the early sixties, a whiskery old, old man, the self-appointed guardian of the shrine, who normally ate the food and collected the offerings. Now, however, with Kigaanira perched on the top of the rock, he proved invaluable, both in summonsing the congregation to hear his latest revelations and in passing round the hat.

With his help, Kigaanira spent his first morning on Kkungu in increasingly profitable sermonising to the crowd, which soon numbered several thousand. Between services the old man sent up the proceeds, food and money, to the prophet at the top of the rock, allegedly via the two-headed snake, which doubled as a lift.

This went on for a day and a half, with the crowd getting more and more excited, swelled by a number of important gentlemen from Kampala who, having heard that the prophet was loose, drove out in their motor cars to drop a few prudent pennies in the collecting box. But the matter did not come to the notice of the authorities until an enterprising businessman tried to hire a bus for a shuttle service and was referred to the police for the necessary permit. And even when Kigaanira's presence on Kkungu was known, there had to be a pause for head-scratching, while everyone wondered what to do about it.

Relations between the Buganda and Central Governments were difficult at the time. Buganda, led by Kabaka Mutesa II (King Freddie to the British media), had boycotted the recent Uganda-wide general elections on the ground that, although they were the central and most developed Province of Uganda, with over two million inhabitants, the Baganda were surrounded by three million members of other tribes who had no reason to love them much.

Understandably, in view of what has since happened to them in the forty years after the British handed over control (from the deposition and death of the Kabaka, to the murderous regimes of General Idi Amin and Milton Obote), the Baganda feared that Elections followed by Independence under anything else except Buganda's leadership, would see the end of their privileges. They had originally won those privileges for themselves by superior organisation and wit, and had then enjoyed them under sixty years of British overrule. They were determined to keep them.

In short they were in a difficult mood. Kigaanira had chosen his moment well. The last thing that Mike Macoun, the Commissioner of Police, wanted at that particular moment, was riots in Buganda.

Macoun's other problem at Kkungu was practical. He could not leave Kigaanira capering about on the top of his rock while the Police dispersed the crowd down below. The prophet had already fomented one riot from his tree and obviously had every intention of doing so again from Kkungu, on a larger scale if possible. But Mike could not think of any way of getting him down.

Despite his Irish origins, Macoun was inclined to discount the threat posed by the two-headed snake. But the sides of Kkungu are vertical and a first abortive attempt by the Fire Brigade had failed to get a ladder more than half way up. Moreover, as the chosen African fireman rather nervously pointed out, even if his ladder did reach the top, there was no certainty that Kigaanira would allow it to stay there while he climbed it. And he himself was not so certain about the snake story either.

So Mike sent a fellow Irish policeman to try the blarney; but Kigaanira's eloquence proved fully equal to the Irish and was anyway more comprehensible to the Baganda crowd, which started getting restive. The police hastily hung up a banner advising the people to return to their homes and then themselves retired to consider what to do next.

Fortunately there was one fact of which Kigaanira was presumably unaware, though the whiskered guardian could have told him if he had thought about it, since his indignant face had often peered at us round the corner of his hut, as we invaded his sanctuary. Kkungu was a training rock-climb for the Mountain Club of Uganda.

A three-foot crack split the rock from side to side and from top to bottom. Three feet is about the ideal width for the mountaineering technique of chimneying. You put your feet on one side of the gap and your shoulders on the other and hunch yourself up with no great difficulty or damage. The technique is not beyond the capability of an agile and bare-footed African and it was perhaps foolish of Kigaanira to assume that it would be too much for a European, however clumsy and booted.

At the time I was president of the Mountain Club, a magnificent multiracial group of friends who frightened each other weekly on the rocks around Kampala and on longer expeditions to the Ruwenzori, the fabled Mountains of the Moon. I was also, although an Administrative Officer of the British Colonial Service, working temporarily for the police in Kampala. I was therefore fair game for Mike Macoun.

Mike duly sent for me and asked, without telling me why, whether I knew anything about Kkungu. When I said I had climbed it the previous weekend, I was ordered to volunteer to do it again, in working hours, so that I could reason with Kigaanira at the top.

By then it was too late for me to back out, so I rescued my climbing rope from where it was doing duty as the cook's washing line and set off to find someone to hold the other end of it for me. In those pre-technical days of climbing, a second to hold the rope was not much use to the leader on a short climb like Kkungu, since, if he fell off, he was apt to hit the bottom before his second could stop him. But every rock climber feels safer tied on to someone else. Anyway the two I had in mind, John Kelly and John Harrop, were good tough characters to have around and might even, if they allowed themselves to be bounced on, be able to cushion my fall.

As I disentangled the washing line, my wife Pat, who was changing the baby's nappy, poked her head through the window to ask what I was doing. 'I'm just off to get a chap down from a rock', I replied with what I felt was the nonchalance proper to the occasion. 'Will you be late for tea then?' she asked, 'Remember we've got your parents staying with us'. Feeling that the whole situation was beyond me, I promised to try to get back for tea and went off to look for the Johns.

John Kelly took some time to find and by the time we arrived at the bush research station where John Harrop worked, I felt we must hurry if we were to get Kigaanira down before his evening service. I therefore simply leaned out of the window and yelled at John to follow me to Kkungu in his own car, as we had to get someone off it.

This led to a basic confusion in his mind for which he has never since forgiven me. Being the Club's most eligible bachelor, he assumed I would not have called on him unless some girl member was in difficulties on the rock. He therefore followed me to Kkungu rehearsing the rescue and the brave words of comfort, to be followed by a dinner for two in Kampala's discreetest night club. The reality of Kigaanira, still capering indefatigably on his rock, was therefore both a shock and a disappointment to him.

When we arrived at the foot of Kkungu, I went off to try to discover the mood of the crowd from various rubbernecking African friends. Meanwhile the two Johns were rapidly sworn in as Special Constables by the senior policeman present.

Then we were handed police tin helmets and riot batons and urged towards the foot of the cleft, which fortunately was hidden from both Kigaanira and the crowd. The strategy thereafter was that the silver tongued Irish policeman would keep Kigaanira shouting at the other side of the rock until I popped up at the top of the crack like the Old Man of the Sea and started to reason with him at close quarters.

This might have worked and I got to within ten feet of the top without being spotted. But, never having climbed with a police truncheon and a tin hat before, and since the baton was longer than the cleft that I was climbing was wide, I got into a hopeless tangle on the last move and found it impossible to avoid knocking down a large stone. This fell through the cleft with a resounding clatter to the ground, a hundred feet below.

Immediately Kigaanira appeared above, brandishing rocks and abuse. Nervously, because I couldn't think of anything else to say and because it was one's natural reaction on meeting a Muganda, I started on the ritual,

'Osiibyotyanno – How have you spent the day?'

To my astonishment he stopped, with the rock poised above his head and replied courteously, 'Bulungi. Osiibyotyanno? – Well, and how are you?'

'Bulungi' I gabbled foolishly, 'Agafaayo – What is the news?'

'Nnungi – good news'. He inclined his head graciously.

All this time I had been trying to inch myself up the last few feet and when, in the middle of himself asking if I had any news, he noticed what I was doing and dropped his rock with a roar onto where it would have caught me in the stomach if I had still been straddled across the gap, I was able to topple back into a niche on the other side of the cleft. I then scrambled without dignity to the top, while Kigaanira hurried back for more rocks.

This brought us face to face across the cleft. For the moment I was unable to do anything about it. John Kelly, hearing our shouts from below, had tightened the rope as far as possible from his stance part-way up the rock, in the hope that it might bring me up short before I bounced. I was therefore left like a belligerent drunk, roaring to get into battle, but depending for safety on the secure grip of his friends, who have him firmly by the coat-tails.

Kigaanira had no such limitations, but was momentarily restrained by his sense of theatre.

'Shall I smite him?' he shouted to the crowd, jumping stiff legged with both feet in the air, spear brandished above his head, in the classic movement of the Buganda Lion-dance.

'Yes, Yes', roared most of the crowd.

'No, No' wailed my few friends.

'Knock the bastard's block off' yelled the Irishman.

At that moment I felt the rope slacken and leapt forward across the cleft, inside the point of Kigaanira's spear. But I wasn't sure what to do with the baton. Having the traditional public-school distaste for hitting people with things, I settled instead for the schoolboy remedy of a rugger tackle.

Kigaanira seemed unfamiliar with rugby and this took him by surprise. He collapsed below me. The spear clattered out of his hand and went spinning down the rock, nearly impaling the Irishman.

Recovering his wits, Kigaanira felt for my crotch, conveniently placed for his hand as I lay on top of him. There is no prescribed counter-measure for this in the public-school code so, to get his hands out of harm's way, I pushed them out flat against the rock above his head. But this brought my face too close to his and he fixed his large, healthy but rather green teeth firmly in my chin.

By this time the two Johns, hearing the noise of battle, had made their way to the top of the rock and decided to join in. So did the Irishman, who had never climbed anything in his life before, but didn't want to be left out of a good fight.

This seemed again to disconcert Kigaanira. Removing his teeth from my chin, he inquired rather breathlessly whether we were Americans? I have since often wondered about that question. I can only suppose that the sudden display of overwhelming force must have reminded his rather muddled mind of the H-Bomb.

Be that as it may, the battle ended with Kigaanira tied up in the climbing rope and lowered unceremoniously to the ground. The next to be lowered was the Irishman who, having climbed the rock in the heat of the moment, found himself quite unable to get down again.

Seeing their prophet cocooned and the two-headed snake apparently fled, the congregation began to disperse quietly. No doubt they felt like a football crowd that had seen a rattling good match. Not too sure of our reception, however, the two Johns and I stayed on the top until most of them had gone, collecting together the assortment of bric-a-brac and good folding money that had come from Kigaanira's collection bag.

Then it was home to put the baby to bed, after a call at the hospital for an injection against septic prophet's bite, thinking we had heard the last of the whole affair. And so it seemed we had, after a few press headlines, the most insulting of which, from a South African newspaper, was 'Middle-aged Magistrate Captures Convict'.

Some months later, however, there were two sequels. The first came when, as an official prison visitor, I inspected the top security prison at Luzira and was told that a prisoner wished to see me. In came a meek little man in a blue prison uniform who fixed me squarely in the eye and said he wished to complain about the prison authorities.

They had taken away his privileges, he said. Why was he shut up in Luzira like this instead of the nice prison farm where he used to grow sweet potatoes? He had done nothing wrong, but the prison Governor hated him and had made up some cock-and-bull story about an escape.

Fingering the scar on my chin, I peered at his teeth and asked if he recognised me. He said he thought not, but I seemed to speak good Luganda and had an honest face for a European. He was sure I would see that justice was done. There seemed little point in prolonging the discussion, so I told him his complaint would be forwarded through the proper channels and left. And that was the last I saw of Kigaanira.

The second sequel came when I was summoned to the Commissioner of Police's office. The Staff Officer opened the door and I was surprised to see a posse of senior policemen standing self-consciously by the Commissioner's table.

Mike Macoun came forward with a serious expression and an outstretched hand. 'Congratulations', he said in a resonant voice, 'On the award of the Colonial Police Medal for Gallantry'. 'But you can't do that', I exclaimed 'I'm not a policeman'.

Not until then did Mike realise that, unlike the others at Kkungu, I had not been sworn in as a Special Constable. They all thought I had, while I had assumed that I was relying on my inherent magisterial powers of arrest.

It was far too late to do anything. The Queen had approved; the Secretary of State had issued his instructions; and the medal had duly been issued, with 'Special Constable A.C.Stuart' stamped around the edge. There was an awkward pause.

Fortunately, the Senior Assistant Commissioner of Police was equal to the occasion. An enrolment form was hurriedly produced and backdated. My signature was attached and blotted. Once more Mike Macoun advanced with hand outstretched. 'Congratulations', he intoned, 'on the award of the Colonial Police Medal for Gallantry.'

And that is how I come to hold a Police Medal, without ever having been a policeman. I am immensely proud of it. But even then the consequences were not ended. Ten years, a continent and an entirely different profession away, dressed in full diplomatic fig of gold lace, cocked hat and squeaky elastic-sided boots, Pat and I were attending the President's Ball on Finland's national Independence Day. A friendly third world diplomat approached, who prided himself on his knowledge of Britain and the British.

'Tell me, Andrew', he said. 'What is that interesting medal you are wearing? I have never seen it before.'

Usually on these occasions I mutter, 'Oh, it's the CPM', leaving people to assume that it is some sort of equivalent of the normal Diplomat's decoration, the CMG, (or 'Call Me God'). But I was tired of the diplomatic game and thought I would try a little truth for once. 'The Colonial Police Medal' I announced firmly.

My third world friend jumped like a shot rabbit and hurried away to talk to someone less tainted. All this had been observed with amusement by an American colleague.

'Say, Mr. Stuart,' he asked, 'What was it really like to be a Colonialist?'

'That, Mr. Van Oss,' I replied, 'is rather a long story'.

And that is when I began to think about writing this book.

"Our job is to convince the
tribesmen that it isn't
Prince Philip who's God –
it's Giscard."

1

The Naïve and Sentimental Colonialist

Outside the half-open door, the night noises of Africa grew more insistent as the light died – the bulbous croaking of frogs in the swamp below; the ratchet noise of crickets in the forest trees; and over at the back of the township where the elephant grass began, a hyena laughed its maniac's chuckle over an old bone or a newly dead dog. Then, suddenly, high in the sky fifty miles away to the south, the last sun flashed unbelievably off the snows of the Ruwenzori mountains, before the light sank into the deep forests of the Congo.

I had not chosen this remote house, built like a railway carriage, with two rooms side by side, a corrugated iron roof, and a strip of verandah running along the front covered in mosquito netting. I was the junior cadet in the district, indeed in the whole of Uganda, and had to go where I was put. But the sudden parting of the evening clouds, and that rare flash of light on snow, could only be seen from the top of my private hill. I was content with my new home.

As I sat beside the verandah on the broad wooden seat of the bucket latrine, which looked out at the same breathtaking view, I could also keep an eye on Suzy, my golden labrador puppy, and perhaps shame her into similar activity on the strip of grass in front of the house.

Suddenly, as I sat, there was a clatter behind the hut. The metal bucket was whisked from below me, and a cheerful African face appeared beneath my throne. 'Jambo Bwana,' it said, as it deftly emptied and replaced the bucket. And then, before I could recover my dignity, the face was off, whistling cheerfully at the black and stinking oxen, with their tub shaped cart and noisome burden, lit by a rusty black hurricane lamp to warn all sober citizens to keep out of its way.

The night-soil men of Fort Portal township were one of my minor, but more mysterious responsibilities. Little, jet-black men from the depths of the forest on the other side of the Ruwenzori, they kept themselves to themselves in their camp at the far side of the township and were said to be adept at potions and spells.

Not that many people made a habit of visiting them anyway. When I arrived, my predecessor told me that he had arranged for them to dig a new pit for their nightly harvest. They told him they had, but this must have been imagination. The little men had not yet got round to it, or perhaps had forgotten the special pit-digging spells. Following them quietly one night, I found that they were instead making full use of a convenient natural hole twenty yards behind the Provincial Commissioner's house. Fortunately the P.C. was on safari, so I was able to arrange for the evidence to be buried before it was discovered.

Being an earnest young man and anxious to do well, I took my responsibility for the latrine buckets seriously, though it was not what I thought I had come to Africa for. Equally serious was my other main job of removing every inch of rough grass from the right-hand side of the township golf course, at the command of my District Commissioner. The D.C. was a fanatical golfer with an incurable slice, who was determined to reduce his handicap. And if I sometimes thought longingly of my Imperial mission, yet to be fulfilled, yet as I sat on my verandah I was well comforted by the sounds and smells of Africa all around me.

I had been brought up with these sounds, and particularly these smells. The sons of missionaries lived closer to Africa than the pampered children of Government servants in their white ghettoes. Strewn round my parents' home were photographs of two small boys in large white topees, with spine pads hanging down their backs, to keep off the deadly actinic rays of the sun. Bare toes scuffling in the dirt, they are proudly sharing possession of a first bicycle with the equally determined figure of the kitchen boy, whose costume differs from theirs only in that, being African, he was not considered to be in danger from the actinic rays.

The Naïve and Sentimental Colonialist

It is not, however, the photographs which bring back to me the reality of that life, but the strong but friendly smells of Africa. These grew to an overwhelming climax in the packed congregations of the tiny bush churches, gathered to greet my father, the bishop, on his yearly visits. Ten thousand devoted heads a year passed under his confirming hands while the steam rising from the newly dunged floor mingled with the odour of sanctity and the harmonies of the homespun Luganda translations of "Hymns Ancient and Modern", to create an unforgettable cocktail in our young minds.

The other smells that were inextricably associated with the bishop's visitations were of goat, over-excited chicken and very old eggs. Coming back from a safari, the back of our old box body Ford was always like a farmyard. For weeks, or even months, beforehand the congregations had been collecting their produce for the Bishop. One government official, visiting a bush village six weeks before my father, was unable to buy any eggs for his own breakfast. They were being saved, he was told, for the Bishop. The official complained bitterly. So did we, when the six week old eggs burst on the way home. But the gifts of the faithful could never be refused.

I had tried to explain about the smells of Africa to Mr Carruthers of the Colonial Office in Whitehall who had interviewed me when I applied to join the Service. Carruthers had very clear ideas about the Colonies. Words like 'Leadership, trust, justice, firmness and fairness' flowed smoothly off his tongue. But he seemed equally interested in my height. 'Tell me, Mr Stuart' he enquired 'Do you think that being so tall will help you dominate the Natives?'

I made the embarrassed face that is a family failing. When you are six foot seven inches high and practically invisible sideways, such remarks are usually the prelude to feeble jokes about the lack of oxygen at high altitudes.

Mr Carruthers' question may well have been a well-intentioned joke to put me at my ease, but if so I was too naïve to understand it. Instead I untied the portmanteau of my liberal prejudices, and poured them all out into his lap. It was not our business to dominate anybody. Uganda was a Protectorate, not a Colony. We had not conquered the Baganda, but made a treaty with them as equal partners. Independence might be a long way off, but it had to be the eventual aim. We must plan, not just for movement, for process, but for progress; and progress implied a goal. In the

Colonies, progress meant movement towards Independence, just as, in individuals, progress meant movement towards God.

Mr Carruthers looked rather staggered at this sudden introduction of the missionary factor, and hurriedly moved on to ask me about games. Recently I have had access to the old personal files of the Colonial Administrative Service, and have often been tempted to look up the records of that first disastrous interview to see what he really thought of me. I have been held back by the fact that no one really likes to read the truth about himself. I was a gangling, priggish and self-opinionated young man. It does not have to be confirmed in writing. It is enough that Carruthers must have thought he detected some useful qualities among the verbiage. He therefore appointed me as a cadet officer in the Colonial Administrative Service and I was posted for a year's training in London before going back to Uganda.

There I found that I was not alone in my priggishness. The thirty-odd Colonial Service Cadets who gathered in Tavistock Square, London in 1952 for a year's study at the London School of Economics, were on the whole, remarkably serious minded about our Colonial Mission.

Part of the trouble was the London School of Economics itself, then going through one of its more virulent anti-colonialist phases. We were attached to the LSE for lectures on Anthropology, Economics, Colonial History, Law, Language and Race Relations.

The Anthropology lessons were a disaster. The lecturer, a distinguished but decrepid feminist, disliked men, loathed young people of either sex, and hated Colonialists. We were all three. There was an air of unreality about our furious squabbles about the matriarchal society of the Trobriand Islanders.

Our seminars on race relations with a pink politicked clergyman, were equally unreal. We sat in a circle sipping Nescafé and discussing what we should do if we were walking down the road with a racist compatriot and saw an African friend coming towards us. Would we greet him, or pass by on the other side? On the whole we thought we would speak.

Our difficulty was that we knew we were liberals, but all around persisted in regarding us as reactionaries of the deepest dye. Our year at the LSE coincided with the beginnings of the Mau-Mau uprising of the Kikuyu in Kenya. The School as a whole threw itself passionately into the Mau-Mau cause. A Kikuyu lecturer was wildly applauded when he compared Mau-Mau to the coming together of the British people after Dunkirk.

I rose and made an impassioned speech. The Kikuyu, I said, had real grievances over their land, some of the best of which had been lopped off to make European farms. But those grievances did not excuse the barbarities and the mumbo-jumbo of Mau-Mau. Nor could all this talk about helping each other conceal the fact that more Kikuyu than white men were being killed by their fellow tribesmen. This was not the way to peace, brotherhood and independence.

The end of the speech was lost in the hubbub. A resolution was proposed to the effect that Mau-Mau was all the fault of the British imperialists. Four hundred and fifty LSE students voted for the motion. Ten Colonial Service cadets voted against. We left the hall to the jeers of all right thinking men. We were not popular.

Our other problem was that we were all in love, or if we were not, were trying to be. We had read our Somerset Maugham. We knew what it was to be lonely in the tropics. It would start with dressing for a solitary dinner, progress through obsessions about year-old copies of the Times, and end with a revolver in the dark. We were young. We would not be back on leave for three or four years. We needed wives.

Ron had an additional problem. He feared he was going bald. He was an engaging and athletic young man, but could see no prospect of getting a wife when he next came home, hairless and yellow with malaria or blackwater fever.

That gave him our year in London to find one. During that year he proposed to every eligible female within reach. We found it difficult to keep up with him, or to cover his tracks during his frequent changes of course. He could not afford to hang around. The question had to be popped rapidly, and a 'maybe' was as bad as a 'no', since there was no time to let an affair mature. Not surprisingly he came to the end of the course still unmarried. The journey out also failed to resolve his problem, and, when we parted in the capital, Kampala, on posting to our new districts, Ron was in a state of unrelieved gloom.

The rest of us were less desperate, or perhaps less honest. I myself was deeply in love with an Oxford girl and drove down from

London at nights in my 1930 Morris Minor to sit sadly under her window wondering how to persuade her to marry me. But she had a prior attachment to a budding politician, and was also, I think, a bit put off by the thought of marrying someone so oddly shaped.

In the middle of all this we had a visit from a Cabinet Minister. This was before MacMillan's 'Wind of Change' speech. It is odd to think how permanent the Empire then seemed, even after the loss of India, and with Ghana and Nigeria so clearly coming up to the starting line for independence.

'Gentlemen,' said the Minister, 'I have come to thank you for the work you are going to do for Britain. I know that you are all anxious to get into the field, and some of you have told me that you find it hard to have to spend this extra year preparing yourselves. You are all mature men. You have already served your country and gained your degrees. But I assure you that this time in London is not wasted. You will be dealing with weighty affairs of state. It is essential that you be prepared. There is plenty of time. I do not know how much time. But this I can say. If any of you have sons, and if they want to follow in their fathers' footsteps, there will be a career for them in the British Colonial Service.'

Fortified by this stirring speech, we prepared ourselves, bought our safari kit from a tropical outfitter who advised us 'not to buy the low camp beds, Sir. The snakes find it too easy to get at you', and set sail to meet our destinies.

On my verandah, I was fortified by it still, despite the reality of the latrine buckets and the loss of my Oxford girl. The weighty affairs of state I was sure would come. Meanwhile there was the evening glimpse of the snows and the hope that next week John Champion the Senior Assistant District Commissioner would send me on safari as the D.C. had promised.

2

Settlers in the Glue Pot

John Champion kept his word. Early the following week I packed Suzy, my snake-proof camp bed, pressure lamp, mosquito net, water filter, and 12-bore shotgun into the ancient box-body car I had just bought from a policeman, who was relieved to get rid of it. In the back of the car rode Kesi, the gaunt black Mutoro houseboy,[1] who had worked for my father.

As we left the house, Kesi was dressed in his own version of what a budding Administrative Gentleman's gentleman should wear, a flowing white night-gown known as a Kanzu, and beneath it long khaki trousers, which, having been inherited from my father, had turn-ups a good eighteen inches too long, held up by safety pins at each calf.

My own costume was as prescribed in Colonial Regulations. Starting with a flat topee like an inverted pie dish, with the Crested-crane emblem of the Uganda Government on a golden badge pinned to the front, it continued with a starched khaki bush shirt with a row of gilt crested-crane buttons down the front, and dotted about with straps, pockets and badges of meagre rank. Below this came capacious khaki shorts reaching to the knee and long khaki stockings held up by fringed garters such as scouts wear. I thought it looked terrific.

After a final, but futile attempt to persuade Suzy to make proper use of the lawn instead of the inside of the car, we rattled off down

---

1. Describing a fully-grown man as a 'houseboy' grates on the modern ear and even on mine. But that is what they were called, and to employ a euphemism would be an offensive anachronism which would degrade Kesi's fiercely independent character.

the red laterite road of my little hill, came briefly on to the tarmac through the trim gardens of the government officials, full of cannas, bougainvillaea and scarlet flame trees; down again across the river, where the previous week I thought I had broken a leg in the collapse of a bridge I had been trying to build in accordance with the 'Handbook for Colonial Engineers'; and then up the other side into the Indian township of Fort Portal to get petrol for our journey.

The township was not supposed to be reserved exclusively for the Indians, but they were not allowed to live or to buy land anywhere else, so they had little option. For their part, the Africans had no incentive to settle in the town. It was the only place where tiresome things like building rules, sanitary regulations, and licensing laws were enforced. So the Batoro not unnaturally preferred to build where and how they liked outside the township, which they only entered for shopping, drinking and, occasionally, for work.

Thus, against all the good intentions of the government, there came about a de facto apartheid, which few of any colour thought strange or made any real effort to break down.

The Indians in particular, most of whose fathers had come from Bombay at the turn of the century to help build the railway up from the coast, made little or no attempt to widen their horizons or even to learn African languages beyond a bastard kitchen Swahili, enough for house servants and for barter.

So, in little townships scattered at intervals of about twenty miles, they lived the life of a ghetto in their identical shops, known as duukas. These had an open verandah in front, on which stood a clattering, foot-treadle sewing machine, operated by a cheerful African, running up khaki shorts and shirts, or the beautiful flow-ered cotton Basuuti which swathed the dignified Baganda and Batoro women from head to ankle.

Behind the verandah was a one-roomed shop, divided by a wooden counter, over which a shrivelled little brown man sold sugar and tea by the teaspoon, matches by the match, kerosene, pepsi cola, hard yellow or blue-mottled soap, salt, bicycle inner-tubes and sandals made out of old motor car tyres. If he had clothes for sale, apart from the shorts and shirts and basuutis, these included hand-made brassieres of incredible capacity and garish design and, in cold upland areas like Fort Portal, cotton jerseys in mock shetland patterns and blankets that may have started life in an army hut in the second, or even the first, world war.

Behind the shop again was a bare room with a corrugated iron roof. There, on mattresses laid out on the concrete floor under mosquito nets, sat seven or eight little Indian children and a shrill voiced Indian wife dressed in sari and nose ornaments, yelling at a downtrodden African servant, while she prepared violent yellow curries on a roaring primus stove between her feet.

Fort Portal, as befitted the capital of the African kingdom of Toro and the headquarters of Uganda's Western Province, was altogether a bigger and more dignified city than most of these little trading estates. Three or four rows of duukas in permanent materials were separated by noisome sanitary lanes down which my friends the night-soil men padded with their buckets on their heads, since the lanes were too narrow for the ox-cart. There was a garage, a bank, a hardware store, and even a bakery, which was always being closed by the district health inspector for multiple evasions of the health regulations and opened again a day later on the concerted petition of the station wives.

At the end of the main street was an enticing establishment known as the Glue-Pot. This was the main rendezvous for Uganda's few white settlers whenever they came to town. In the station club up the hill the beer was cheaper and colder; but the company was less friendly and the ladies less accommodating than in the Glue-Pot, and few of the settlers felt comfortable in the club. So on Saturdays and Sundays, the Glue-Pot was full, and for a few hours the town throbbed with a different rhythm from the wailing Indian music and high-voiced Hindi of its weekday life.

Toro district was unusual in Uganda in having these few white planters to add variety to the otherwise rather uniform pattern of life in a Protectorate. There were about twenty or thirty of them who, with another handful in the rest of Uganda, had over the years acquired land by one means or another, some freehold, some leasehold and some by no more than a barefaced assertion of squatters' rights.

Most of them were getting on in life and beginning to gather some moss. Some were rich and grew tea. One or two were very poor and grew potatoes. All were picturesque, leathery, and exceedingly self-assured.

9

Their backgrounds were as varied as their characters were awe-inspiring to a self-conscious young administrative cadet. One formidable lady, a great friend of my mother's (who tactfully ignored the irregularity of her friend's temporary liaisons), kept a buffalo as a pet in her house. The house was leased from the mission alongside a local secondary school. The African buffalo is rightly feared as one of the most dangerous and short tempered of animals – worse, even, than the rhinoceros, and much worse than the African elephant. But Toni's buffalo had been brought up by her from a calf. She therefore saw no need to take precautions, other than providing each of her European guests with a frying-pan, and instructions to hit the animal on the nose if it got too pushy.

To the African children at the secondary school, however, a buffalo was a buffalo and under no circumstances to be trusted. Absenteeism at the school rose to unprecedented heights, and the headmaster came to Toni begging her to send it away. In the end the mission had to choose between paying Toni to surrender her lease, or closing the school for lack of pupils. They paid up.

Another pair in Toro were both old Etonians. Allcock was a drifter who by some unexplained bit of chicanery, had secured a Temporary Occupation Licence to a piece of forest land high up on the slopes of the Ruwenzori, and had since defied all attempts to remove him. He had built himself a mud and wattle house with a stream running through the middle of it and, with the help of his African mistress, cultivated a smallholding of potatoes and green vegetables, which he sold to the local Indians, who in return kept him in drink. Allock was a hospitable old fellow, but the recognized and essential passport to his table was a full bottle of Beehive brandy, which then had to be disposed of before the guest could leave.

At times the old man would run short of cash and, to make ends meet, was forced to swallow his Etonian principles and put a few stones at the bottom of a bag of potatoes which he took to the Indians for sale. When this happened the Indians did not reproach him. That would have been against their code of never voluntarily offending a European. Instead they told the other Old-Etonian, a rich tea planter called Brown, who lived in some state in the foot-hills and maintained his own private aeroplane which he flew on business trips to the capital. Brown did not refund the money for the stones. That would merely have encouraged Allcock in his un-Etonian behaviour. Instead he would call on the old fellow and remind him of the duty owed by every O.E. to society. A few days later Allcock would go down to the Indian duukas with a hangdog expression and a handful of potatoes, and the matter would be forgotten until the next time.

All this and more about the curious habits of the white settlers, I had discovered during my first nervous visits to the Glue-Pot. And now I rehearsed it anxiously as I drove out of town. For this, my first safari in Toro, was in fact to be concerned with the white settlers and not with the Africans. The D.C. was not yet ready to risk a confrontation between my half-baked idealism and the realities of African administration – and who should blame him. Instead he sent me to check the poll tax receipts on the European estates, starting at a limestone burning kiln at Muhokya, fifty or sixty miles to the south of Fort Portal down the road leading to the great Queen Elizabeth Game Park.

Leslie's factory was a ramshackle set of buildings set on a knoll away from the road and right on the border of the National Park. When I arrived about three o' clock in the afternoon, Leslie had just finished his lunch, or so he told me, though there was no evidence of anything other than liquid refreshment. He hospitably suggested that we might have a snort before going off to check the tax receipts. His partner, Bunduki, was expected every moment. He had expressed a wish to meet me, and it seemed sensible to wait until he arrived.

At six o' clock we were still there, three quarters of the way down the second bottle of Beehive brandy, of which, fortunately, Leslie had had far more than I. He showed no signs of worry at the continued absence of his partner. While I still had the use of my legs, I therefore suggested that I ought to go and find out what had happened to Bunduki before it got dark. The prospect of checking the tax receipts had retreated hazily into the next day, but I still felt vaguely responsible for the safety of all people in what I was beginning daringly to call My District, and I hoped that Bunduki had come to no harm.

When I found him, however, he was alive and well and very drunk. In the attempt to change his truck into low gear at the

11

bottom of the hill leading up to the factory, he had, as he later explained in an unexpectedly nautical metaphor 'missed stays'. He had moved the gear lever into neutral all right, but had then failed to notice that it had not gone into first. I found him there with a bellowing and almost incandescent engine, furiously complaining about the state of the Government roads, which he said had broken his back axle. When after a quick inspection, I pointed out that his gear lever needed another push, he appeared both pleased and surprised, and ground his way slowly up the hill, boiling furiously, to the level space in front of Leslie's house.

With a final curse at the Government, Bunduki finally emerged from the cab of his truck. He turned out to be a tall, skinny, grey-headed man with turkey-cock jowls and a watery eye, dressed in a sleeveless bush jacket and baggy, vaguely military trousers. The trousers, as he explained, were in memory of the high point of his life, the capture of Gondar during the war against the Italians in Abyssinia in 1942. He had played some glorious part in this engagement which he was always on the point of explaining to me; but we never reached the denouement, as something, usually his insensibility, invariably intervened at the crucial moment. Now, as Bunduki mounted the steps with wavering dignity, Leslie, who was still seated behind the bottle, hospitably suggested that we should have a little drink before dinner, so Bunduki's first attempt to tell me about Gondar was postponed for the more urgent business in hand.

An hour or so later we lost Bunduki again. But when, unable to ignore the calls of nature any longer, I went in search of the pit latrine, I found him seated in solitary state, gloomily, by the light of a solitary candle, thumbing through a mail-order catalogue of female clothes, the torn off pages of which served instead of the more conventional tissues. 'Look at this' he mumbled tearfully, squinting at the picture of a substantial model dressed in outsize underwear. 'Why can't I ever find anything like this except in the pissing lavatory? It's not fair. A man in the prime of life ought to have something exciting for his dinner.'

I wasn't quite sure what he was talking about, but thought it best to agree, and waited hopefully for him to finish the catalogue and come out of the lavatory. At last he seemed to notice me. 'What are you pissing about for?' he inquired, not unkindly, 'Piss off and go and piss on the grass, or go and find your own pissing pictures.'

Alarmed, I did as I was told, and then thought I would scout around in the back quarters to see if there was any hope of dinner. But just as I had prised a reluctant cook away from his own bottle of Beehive brandy and implored him to start cooking something, anything, as long as it was food, an enormous racket started up at the front of the house.

When I got back there a large lady, who appeared to believe that she had some sort of claim on Leslie, was shouting that the elephants were in her cotton shamba, and we must come and shoot them quick. Rousing himself from his lethargy, Leslie introduced her to me as Eseza and then, seizing a rusty looking elephant rifle, bade me get my own gun and follow him at once to the cotton plots at the bottom of the hill.

It was only when I got there, crashing in the darkness over anthills, through cotton plants and round banana trees, that I realised we were now in the National Park, where firearms were strictly forbidden and shooting animals almost a capital offence. In this illegal situation, in pitch darkness and still dressed in my Colonial Regulations uniform, it seemed I was proposing to shoot an elephant with my brand new twelve-bore shotgun, fully cocked and loaded with bird-shot.

Fortunately however, the elephants must have heard us coming – it would have been surprising if they hadn't – for we heard them moving off ahead of us back out into the plain in the middle of the Park. After crashing about for another half hour Leslie Graham suggested we should return, as he had left the bottle back at the house. There, after a final nightcap, I went wearily and supperless to bed, leaving Bunduki, who had slept through all the fracas, still enthroned, with the open catalogue in one hand and a burnt-out candle in the other.

The next morning at about ten o' clock the house was still silent and the kitchen black, cold and empty. Despairing of breakfast I decided the only thing to do was to cut my losses and get away to the Government rest house, where Kesi would be able to cook me something himself. There seemed no possibility of saying good-bye to my host, so I tiptoed out and decided to let the car run down to the bottom of the hill before starting the engine. Just as I got Suzy on board, however, a window opened, and a bleary Leslie stuck his head out into the sunlight. 'Oh Andrew,' he called 'I meant to say to you last night. I know what it's like for you young fellows in the Boma. If you'd like me to send up Eseza for a few nights, you've only to let me know. I'm sure she'd be delighted.'

Muttering my thanks and a promise to come back another day to look at the tax tickets, I fled.

3

The Lords of Africa

On the way back to Fort Portal, unshaven and looking decidedly the worse for wear, I stopped in the Queen Elizabeth Park to try and photograph some Water Buck. As I stood beside my car, a Land Rover drew up alongside me. It had no number plate. Instead it carried a large brass badge with a design of shield and spears. Out of it climbed a massive figure, dressed in safari gear, and surrounded by its usual cheerful aroma of whiskey with beer chasers.

'Come here, my good man' it boomed, in an Oxford accent so exaggerated that it could not possibly be a parody. Intrigued, I wandered across. 'I have to tell you' the owner of the voice announced 'That I am an honorary game warden, and I suspect you of being in the Park without a licence.'

George Rukidi, the Mukama of Toro, who would not have known a game licence from a washing list, was off again.

'Sorry, Rukirabasaija,' I said, 'I'm Andrew Stuart. You probably don't recognize me in this state.' Immediately, he was all affability. 'Ah, Andrew, my boy,' he boomed, 'I'm so sorry. I thought you were one of these shenzi Europeans we're getting round here these days.'[1]

The Mukama of Toro was physically and in many other respects the greatest of the Kings of Uganda, and played the part to the top of his bent, as befitted a man sure of his pedigree of a hundred rulers. In truth, however, George was a parvenu compared with his brother Kings, the Kabaka of Buganda, the Mukama of Bunyoro and the Mugabe of Ankole.

---

1. 'Shenzi' means dirty, unkempt, uncouth or generally lower-class. Lesser breeds might be shenzi, Colonial Administrative Officers never.

It was these tribal kingdoms which made Uganda unique in east and central Africa. Long before any outsiders had penetrated to the Great Lakes, Buganda, Bunyoro and Ankole had been ordered societies, with hierarchies of chiefs under the rule of an absolute monarch. The origins of this system were lost in time. The Kabaka claimed descent in fifty generations from Kintu, the first man. But anthropologists had no doubt that the kings were in fact descended from cattle-owning Hima raiders from Ethiopia who, some time in the unrecorded but historical past, had swept down on the less warlike agriculturalist Bantu and enslaved them. In some areas, particularly Ankole in the south-west, the distinction between the sharp-faced cattle-owning Hima, and their broad-featured Bantu subjects was still clear. But elsewhere, in Bunyoro and particularly in Buganda, where the soil is richer and the rewards of settled agriculture are as great as from nomadic cattle herding, the racial divisions have largely disappeared. Only the tradition of kingship remains.

Toro, the most westerly of the kingdoms on the slopes of the Ruwenzori, had, however, no such historical authenticity. George Rukidi was only the second of his line. His throne was indeed an invention of the British. His father Kasagama had been a minor chief whose kingdom was carved by Lord Lugard out of a recalcitrant Bunyoro and presented to him on a plate. But this did not lessen George's magnificence. He was really something else.

Unfortunately for him, unlike Buganda with its cotton and coffee and Ankole and Bunyoro with their cattle, Toro was a poor kingdom whose only riches were the prospect of royalties from the new copper mine on the slopes of the Ruwenzoris. George was therefore rarely able to pay for his drinks at the local hotel, or for his suite at the Savoy on his frequent ceremonial visits to Britain. His remedy, however, was simple. All creditors were instructed to send the bill to the Protectorate Government.

The Fort Portal hotel had long been resigned to the fact that this meant no payment at all. The manager's only answer was therefore to shut the bar as soon as he saw the Mukama's official limousine turning up the drive. Tradesmen in Britain, however, were less wary. We were still having a furious argument about a bill for cleaning the Kingly robes while the Mukama had been in London for the Queen's Coronation.

16

Personally, however, we were on the best of terms. Like all the Kings, he had been a frequent visitor to my parents' house, where the main problem was to ensure that whichever servant brought in the dinner was not of the same tribe as the ruler who happened to be our guest. Protocol demanded that each King's subjects should fall on their faces in his presence. Not only was this destructive of the plates which they were carrying; it was also damaging to the dinner.

The Mukama himself was no trouble at table. On one occasion in a fit of absence of mind, or perhaps as extra blotting paper for the whiskey, he did reach out for the flowers in the middle and start pensively chewing the stalks. But this was in keeping with the exhilarating surprises of his character.

Soon after I had arrived in Toro, George had decided to celebrate the twenty-fifth anniversary of his accession. He was determined to mark this with a really stupendous celebration to wipe the eye of the Kings of Buganda and Bunyoro. He also, to do him justice, meant it as a gesture of support for the Governor, who had just had to exile the Kabaka of Buganda in one of the interminable wrangles between the Protectorate Government and Buganda that, as we shall see, were to bedevil the last years of the Protectorate.

Preparations for the celebrations took many weeks' work by a special committee. I was a member of this team, with a one-line brief from the D.C., to the effect that George could do anything he liked as long as we didn't have to pay for it.

Traditional ceremonies were given due prominence, with much drumming through the night and the Mukama seated in state in his ancestral costume, including an artificial fringe round the chin fashioned from a Colobus monkey skin that made him look like a benign gorilla.

But he had decreed that pride of place must go to a mammoth church service in the great protestant church beside his palace, followed by a cocktail party for three hundred guests and, the next day, a ceremonial luncheon for a hundred or so. The theme of these events was to be the coming together of all races under the joint patronage of God, of Rukirabasaija the Mukama of Toro, and of His Excellency the Governor of Uganda, in that order.

With this end in view it was ordained that the Church service should be seen to take place within this same triangle of forces,

17

with the Anglican Bishop at the centre, ministering to God at the altar, to the Mukama at the right-hand side of the nave and to the Governor at the left. In accordance with this theme of partnership, the Committee decided that an African should take the collection from the Governor and his entourage, and that I, as the junior European cadet, should do the same for the Mukama, his fellow Kings and the chiefs and leaders of the Batoro.

When the great day arrived, we officials had first to go through the agony of donning our Colonial Service white uniforms. This was virtually impossible for bachelors, since the high starched collar could not be done up by oneself; and, even when this was achieved, and we were arrayed like Lot's wife in white drill, brass buttons, an ornamental but tiresome sword and a mushroom-shaped white helmet, the tight strapping under one's boots made it impossible to bend one's legs and therefore to drive a car. Both operations required a wife who could first strap her husband into his uniform, and then drive him to church, legs stiffly outstretched along the back seat and helmet clasped to his manly chest.

Suzy could not perform any of these functions for me, and although Kesi could help with the collar, he could not drive. I therefore had to hire the town's only taxi which normally doubled as a hearse. The inhabitants of the Glue Pot gathered to cheer as we drove past them at an appropriately funereal rate with an apparently moribund figure recumbent in the back, to all appearances dressed in a shroud. And to crown my humiliation we arrived at the cathedral late, just in front of the Bishop, and to the delight of a crowd of several thousands I was slid horizontally out through the hearse's back door and, coming to my feet, stumbled red faced into the cathedral, still wearing my mushroom helmet, until the D.C. hissed at me to take it off.

When the time came for the collection, I had no trouble with the Mukama and his wife in the first row. With a grand gesture he put a substantial cheque into the collecting bag, first making sure that I had seen how much it was for (though the effect was rather spoiled by the fact that I knew, and he knew that I knew, that it would bounce). Trouble, however, came with the second row of dignitaries, when I had to let go of the bag. It travelled straight along the line and out of the side door and I never saw it again.

18

This put me in something of a dilemma. I could hardly pursue the bag outside, and I had no other available receptacle except my white helmet, which I had left on my seat. However, with a decisiveness of which Mr Carruthers would have been proud, I seized a bag from the D.C.'s interpreter, who was responsible for the side aisle, and carried on, leaving him to sort out his own problem as best he could. I was therefore able, as the service ended, to march with the other collectors to present my offerings to the bishop, to the triumphant strains of 'Here comes the Bride'.

That evening saw the next highlight of the celebrations, for which we had all received cards in rather wobbly gold printing inviting us to a 'Grand Corktail Party' in the local Parliament building. The waiters from the hotel had been hired for the occasion and were standing ready to serve, dressed in spotless white Kanzus, with wide red belts and red fezzes on their heads.

But all was not well with the arrangements. The glasses had not been unpacked from their boxes and the Mukama's Prime Minister and a working party of minor chiefs had to sit to behind the bar, taking the glasses out of their straw and dusting them down with a rather unsavoury looking handkerchief. Even then, all might have been well if the three hundred invited guests had not been grotesquely outnumbered by the horde of gatecrashers. Having invaded the party, the latter were totally unwilling to wait for details like glasses. As soon as the waiters emerged from behind the bar, they had their fezzes bashed round their ears and their bottles removed from their trays. They then retired into a huddle in the corner and took no further part in the proceedings.

The scene that followed was more than a little confused. I felt it my duty to try and get the Governor's wife a drink, but having extracted a glass from the Prime Minister, I had to seize a bottle from a county chief who had got it between himself and a corner, and was drinking from the neck with a satisfactory glugging noise. The Governor's wife thanked me nicely for the tumbler full of neat whiskey, but thought it safer to pour most of it through the open window, where it fell on a latecoming missionary trying to find an easy way in.

Round the bar, proceedings were chaotic. I found one of the starchiest of our protestant pastors, who had asked for a lemonade, staring unbelievingly at a beer mug brimful of sherry, at which he was giving nervous little pecks like a sparrow at a birdbath. At the same time I caught sight of Bunduki, jammed immovably, without a glass, two yards from the bar, within sight of the water hole, but patently dying of thirst. There was nothing I could do to help him.

Only the Mukama seemed immune from the hysteria of the occasion. With a truly regal condescension he held court in the Speaker's room behind the main chamber, served from below table level by the hotel's chief barman, a Mutoro, who had perfected the technique of pouring his King's drinks from underneath.

After an hour or so of this, the visiting dignitaries withdrew, leaving the Batoro to what had all the signs of a most successful party. The dancing and drumming continued all night.

The final State Luncheon had to be held early the next day, as the Governor wanted to get back to Entebbe, where pressing matters of state arising from the Buganda problem awaited his attention. There were once again signs that preparations were not entirely complete as we assembled, the men in light suits and the women in brilliant flowered Basuutis or light summer dresses, inside the long chamber of the Royal Palace. The butler, immaculately dressed in black swallow-tailed coat and striped trousers, but with tennis shoes on his feet and no socks, summoned us to luncheon. We followed him in stately procession in strict order of precedence. We sat down. We examined the menu, erratically printed in the same golden lettering, which promised us soup, fish, meat and pudding. It was very hot. We waited.

Eventually, after about half an hour, the butler whizzed round the table passing out soup plates, each plate containing perhaps half a spoonful of viscous yellow liquid. My neighbour's loudly-voiced suspicion that this was the oil from sardine cans was confirmed by the fish course, which was the sardines.

Then followed the meat course – an antique but acceptable sheep; and then again a long pause. Finally after much whispering one of the schoolmaster guests produced a Scout's knife, the kind with attachments for getting stones out of horses' hooves. It turned out that the caterers had forgotten the tin opener for the fruit salad.

The Governor was a man notorious for his lack of attention to what he was eating. He had once absentmindedly eaten a piece of meat that was an exhibit in a court case that he was supposed to be trying. But even he looked a trifle bilious as he climbed into his official car for the long drive back to Entebbe. As the huge limousine disappeared around the corner, the Union Jack streaming along its bonnet and a cloud of dust obscuring the crown on its number plates, the Mukama turned graciously to the D.C., standing stiffly to attention by his side. 'A magnificent occasion, Dick' he remarked, 'Now we can relax. Come and let's have a drink.'

Rukirabasaija George Rukidi, the Mukama of Toro, is now passed away. But the most redoubtable of his descendants is beyond question his daughter Elizabeth, Princess of Toro, who is very much alive. From her earliest days Elizabeth was a phenomenon. Strikingly beautiful, wayward, articulate, shrewd, elegant, unforgettable, ineffable, inextinguishable; Elizabeth has earned all these epithets and more.

It was clear from her beginning that the worthy but somewhat limited and missionary-dominated girls' schools of Uganda could not hold her. Elizabeth was therefore packed off, in the care of my parents, to Public School in England under my own Aunt Violet, one of the most formidable Headmistresses of her time. Hockey and diligence were the order of the day, and on Sunday evening the whole school stood and sang 'Jesu, Joy of Man's Desiring' with passionate commitment and in an overwhelming odour of sanctity. Elizabeth must have stood out in that goodly fellowship like a butterfly on a steam engine.

After her school days, she took Cambridge by storm and in her stride, was called to the Bar, was photographed on the cover of *Vogue*, and swept through Hollywood like a hurricane. Next, as if this was not enough, she appeared on the podium of the United Nations in the improbable capacity of Foreign Minister to the Dictator Idi Amin, to denounce the British and all their works.

According to those who saw her there, her breathtaking oratory was then more than matched by her skin-tight golden gown, which caused one of them to repeat the old chestnut,

'What keeps that dress up?'
'Gravity'
'What d'you mean, gravity?'
'The gravity of what will happen if it falls down.'

By comparison with the Rukidi family, the other lesser kings of Uganda were pale shadows. Sir Tito Winyi, the Omukama of Bunyoro, was a pillar of rectitude and family values. When I was D.O. of his district, he and his wife used to invite Pat and myself to tea in his modest blue-tiled palace. There we ate thin sandwiches and bilious yellow-cakes from the Indian duuka and conversed politely on indifferent subjects. He was a courteous, stately and altogether delightful man, the kind of person who would not have been out of place in a stained-glass window.

But it had not always been so. His father Kabarega and grandfather Kamrasi were a different matter altogether. When the British first arrived in Uganda, one of the reasons why they were welcomed with open arms by the Baganda was that the latter were about to be overwhelmed by Kabarega's army from Bunyoro. Like the Vikings or the Mongols, the belligerence of Kabarega and his father seems to have been largely prompted by the fact that there was not much else for them to do at home.

Their northern boundary was full of elephants (in what later became the Murchison Falls National Park) and their western boundary was full of fish (The Nile Perch of Lake Albert are among the largest and least interesting fresh-water fish in the world). In between was a large expanse of nothing very much.

Whatever the reason, however, the intransigence of the kings of Bunyoro undoubtedly held up the pacification of Uganda by several years. They paid for it in the end of course, having George Rukidi's kingdom of Toro removed from Bunyoro's sovereignty and losing a couple of counties to Buganda. In those expansive Victorian days it never paid to be on the wrong end of the confident British saying:

'Whatever happens, we have got,
The Maxim gun, and they have not.'

Meanwhile, however, Kabarega and Kamrasi before him had themselves a lot of fun. Kamrasi was also obviously a man of taste. When Sir Samuel Baker, the explorer of the Upper Nile, first penetrated his territory in 1864, the King was much smitten by Lady Baker and tried to persuade her husband to leave her behind to become his wife.

That beautiful Hungarian lady was obviously worth a dalliance or two. Her bearded husband had first found and purchased her in a Turkish slave market. But Florence Baker was nobody's slave and was clearly more than a match for Kamrasi. As soon as she understood what he was proposing, she addressed the Omukama furiously in Arabic, a language which he did not understand, with an expression which, according to her husband, was somewhat less amiable than the Medusa's head.

Kamrasi seems to have got the message. He apologised profusely and said he had not meant to insult anybody and was anyway willing to offer several of his own wives in exchange. Since the suggestion seemed to have been badly received, however, perhaps Sir Samuel would give him his kilt instead, together with his compass? This alternative request indeed seemed to Kamrasi entirely reasonable. After all, he was not asking for the explorer's watch. This despite the fact that the chronometer he had been given by an earlier explorer, Speke, had broken while the King was trying to explain to his courtiers how he thought it worked.

Perhaps amused by this naive estimate of her comparative worth, or perhaps because they were surrounded at the time by Kamrasi's warriors, Florence Baker had the kindly thought of assuaging the King's passion by presenting him instead with several pictures of ladies' fashions, cut from the pages of the 'Illustrated London News'. In default of the real thing, Kamrasi seems to have been satisfied by this, thus proving that he and Bunduki would have had much in common.

All in all, Lady Florence Baker is one of the most attractive figures in the age of the great Victorian explorers and Kamrasi was quite right to yearn after her. More than twenty years younger than her husband, she had when he had found her in the Turkish slave market, been part of the flotsam of the Austro-Hungarian empire. But, despite the fact that her husband neglected for many years to marry her, she entirely outfaced the moralists of the Victorian era (even Queen Victoria herself) as she had done Kamrasi, and eventually emerged with her husband as national heroes, and as a model of courage, beauty and virtue. She must also have been great fun.

The next time she went back to Bunyoro, however, was when Sam went south again in 1868 as a fully fledged Pasha of the

Egyptian government, to open up Egyptian trade with the Kings at the sources of the Nile.

But Kabarega, who had by then succeeded Kamrasi as Omukama after murdering his brother and slaughtering most of his other relations in order to assure the succession, seems to have been less dazzled by the Bakers than his father had been. He first of all tried to poison them and then to burn them out of their camp. Greatly daring I once asked Sir Tito Winyi what he thought of his grandfather. He looked at me sadly as he toyed with a cucumber sandwich and said, 'A great man but perhaps not very civilized.' I had to agree with him.

The ancestors of the remaining one of the three western Uganda Kings, Edward Gayonga, the Mugabe of Ankole, might also have been less impressed by Florence Baker's slim blonde beauty. The Kings of Ankole liked their women fat.

The Hima aristocrats in the cattle country of Ankole had integrated less with their agricultural Bantu subjects than had the other Kings. Their wealth was still in cows, and they had the notion that a really stout milk-fed wife would, like the women of Indian princes hung with gold, be the ideal way of demonstrating that wealth. When the explorers Speke and Grant journeyed north in 1862 in search of the sources of the Nile, they came first to the capital of Rumanika, the King of Karagwe and the Mugabe's relative, Speke described their reception.

'On entering the hut I found the old man and his chief wife sitting side by side on a bench of earth strewed over with grass and partitioned like stalls for sleeping apartments, whilst in front of them were placed numerous wooden pots of milk ... I was struck with no small surprise at the way he received me, as well as with the extraordinary dimensions, yet pleasing beauty, of the immoderately fat fair one, his wife. She could not rise; and so large were her arms that, between the joints, the flesh hung down like large, loose-stuffed puddings. Then in came their children, all models of the Abyssinian type of beauty, and so polite in their manners as thorough-bred gentlemen. They had heard of my picture-books from the King and wished to see them; which they no sooner did, to their infinite delight, especially when they recognized any of the animals, than the subject was turned by my inquiring what they did with so many milk pots. This was easily explained by Wazezeru himself, who, pointing to his wife said, "This is all the product of those pots: from early youth upwards, we keep those pots to their mouths, as it is the fashion at court to have very fat wives.'"

These then were the minor Kings of Uganda. It is not difficult to make fun of them and, still more, of their recent ancestors. But the whole point about Uganda is that, from the beginning of the European invasion less than 100 years before, the Kingdoms had been found by the astonished explorers to be oases of ordered government, settled development and civilized and courtly behaviour. And if the Kings at times behaved like Tudor monarchs, with the same appetites and the same casual cruelty, then before condemning them we need to remember a little of our own blood-stained past.

4

'King Freddie'

I n any case, although the Kings of Western Uganda were interesting, they were small beer, compared with the Kabaka of
Buganda, in whose kingdom Speke finally found the source of
the Nile at the Ripon Falls.

Perhaps the best description of the impact which Buganda must
have made on the early explorers was provided by Winston
Churchill, who visited the country in 1907: 'The Kingdom of
Uganda[1] is a fairy tale' he wrote. 'You climb up a railway instead of
a beanstalk and at the end there is a wonderful new world.' The
scenery is different, the vegetation is different, the climate is
different and most of the people are different from anything else to
be seen in the whole range of Africa.

'In the place of naked, painted savages, clashing their spears and
gibbering in chorus to their tribal chiefs, a complete and elaborate
polity is presented. Under a dynastic king ... an amiable, clothed,
polite and intelligent race dwell together in an organized Monarchy
... An elegance of manners springing from a naive simplicity of
character pervades all classes.'

Churchill was always one to be intoxicated by the exuberance of
his own verbosity. Buganda in his time (and in mine) was very far
from perfect. When in 1862, Speke arrived at Kabaka Mutesa the

---

1. When the early explorers spoke of 'Uganda' they meant in fact the Kingdom of
   Buganda, which is only the central province of the modern Uganda. The root
   word is 'Ganda'. 'U' is a bastardised Swahili version of Buganda (the place). A
   person from Buganda is a Muganda; the people are Baganda; the language is
   Luganda; a Buganda thing is Kiganda; a small thing is Kaganda and a huge one
   is Guganda; and so on ad infinitum and ad delirium.

First's capital on the north-eastern shore of Lake Victoria, he found a 'good-looking, well figured, tall young man of twenty-five, sitting on a red blanket spread upon a square platform of royal grass, scrupulously well dressed in a new Mbugu (bark cloth)', but when Speke presented him with a carbine the King immediately handed it to a page and told him to go and shoot a man in the courtyard to see if it worked. It did.

No man, then or later, dared to approach the Kabaka except flat on his face, uttering as a kind of mantra a chant which Speke called 'Nyanzigging' and which he seemed to find peculiarly hilarious. 'Then twenty naked virgins, the daughters of Wakungu (chiefs), all smeared and shining with grease, each holding a small square of Mbugu (bark cloth) for a fig leaf, marched in line before us, as a fresh addition to the harem, whilst the happy fathers floundered Nyanzigging on the ground, delighted to find their darlings appreciated by the King.' (The Baganda are an excessively polite race. 'Neeyanze, Mukama Wange, Neeyanzize' – (I praise you, oh my lord, I praise you very much) – is apt to accompany or acknowledge the most modest present of a bottle of beer, let alone a virgin.) Faced with such universal self-abasement and anxiety to please, it is no wonder that the Kabaka and his immediate descendants found it a bit difficult not to acquire an inflated view of their own importance.

In my time, however, King Freddie, His Highness Edward William Frederick David Walugembe Mutebi Luwangula Mutesa II, the great-grandson of Mutesa the First had no easy life. And he died a sad death, alone and penniless in London, some said poisoned by the dictators Obote and Idi Amin, who drove him from his throne and extinguished his country from the map.

But even more damaging than these external misfortunes, Mutesa was a man of two worlds, lost between a yearning to be an English gentleman and the demands and expectations of as hard-faced a set of traditionalists as I have ever met.

His personal life was a mess. It seems to be the fate of princes to love one person and marry another. Sarah Kisosonkole was his first love but they quarrelled and he married her sister. Then he went back to Sarah and acknowledged her son as his heir, neglecting his legitimate daughter by his wife Damali. It is all woefully familiar.

27

According to the sad book which he wrote after his final exile, entitled 'King Freddie – The desecration of my Kingdom', he had been happy for the first twenty-five years of his life. Although he succeeded his father Kabaka Daudi Chwa in 1939 and was crowned by my father in 1942, he spent the years from 1945 to 1947 at Cambridge and then had an ecstatic year as an honorary Captain in the Grenadier Guards (where, according to his own account, the only difficulty was to know where his face began and the bearskin ended).

But the clouds were gathering. He married the wrong girl; as we shall see, he was exiled for three years in the fifties for challenging the British government on the future status of his kingdom within Uganda; he came back in triumph in 1955 when the British gave in, but because of the arrogance and bloody mindedness of his Baganda advisers, he blew the chance of the leadership of the whole country on the road to Independence that was his for the asking; he allowed the same advisers to persuade him to boycott the political process and then, when they realised their mistake, made a deal with Obote, his bitterest enemy. This allowed the latter to become the first Prime Minister of Uganda on Independence, with all that followed afterwards.

Through it all Mutesa remained a quiet, rather gentle, exquisitely mannered man whom it was difficult not to like and whose effect on women was said to be even more dramatic. His only really irritating habit was an almost complete inability to get up in the morning. I have sat in the grimly furnished antechamber of his palace until midday for a nine o'clock appointment, drinking warm beer or milky tea, while outside a throng of petitioners, relatives, spectators, prisoners or general hangers-on crouched in the baking sunshine, waiting for Ssabasajja (the Lord of all men), to appear.

Such discourtesies were, however, minor by comparison with what the previous generation had had to endure from Mutesa's grandfather, Mwanga. Mwanga was a pederast who was driven to murderous rage when a number of his 'pages' were converted by the Catholic and Protestant Missionaries and refused any longer to agree to his 'little requests'. Mwanga ordered forty-four of them to be killed by dismemberment, castration, burning, clubbing or spearing and they became the first martyrs of the Church in Uganda.

Still closer to my own family, a witch doctor had warned Mwanga that when whitemen came to his kingdom from the north (rather than south-about round Lake Victoria, like all the earlier explorers), they would 'eat' his kingdom.

Unfortunately Bishop Hannington, who was the first protestant Bishop of Uganda, only 40 years before my father's own arrival, chose to come to Uganda by the more direct route to the north of the Lake. This had become possible after the pacification of the wild Masai tribesmen of Kenya, who had previously blocked the northern route, but it was a fatal mistake for Bishop Hannington. Mwanga sent and had him killed on the borders of Uganda, using as an excuse that his courtier-executioners had unfortunately misunderstood him.

His order, he insisted, had been 'Bamute' (with the 't' lightly accented – meaning 'let them preserve him'). But the Chiefs, he claimed, had misheard him and thought the Kabaka had said 'Bamutte' (with an explosive double 't' – meaning 'Let them kill him'). So they did.

Frederick Mutesa, however, never really believed that story. When he told it to me he grinned slightly and added a Luganda proverb 'Obulimba bwe bweyambi bw'omuto' (a lie helps a child escape), which seemed a fair commentary on the bloody deeds of his ancestor.

In those days we thought we could afford to smile. But, although this is to carry the story forward out of context, within fifteen years of that slightly superior conversation, the skull piles of the Luwero Triangle had dwarfed the numbers of the early martyrs, and Mutesa himself was dead.

The story of Buganda has always seemed like some Greek tragedy of nobility, pride, arrogance, dishonour and death. When King Freddie helped Obote to win the last elections before Independence, in return for the promise that the Kabaka be the first President of the new republic, the Baganda chiefs went around with asinine grins on their faces, 'Nyanzigging' away and proclaiming 'We have won, we have won; the Kabaka is lord of all; our prayers have been answered; oh glory be, we have triumphed.'

However, when Obote, a dark-faced northerner took over the reins of government and, within months after Independence, began to turn the screws on the President, the Baganda realised too late that they had been duped.

The Buganda Lukiiko (parliament) then met in solemn conclave and said in effect, 'thanks very much, we want our ball back'. They gave Obote and his government 14 days to leave Buganda.

This was the same tactic they had tried to use before against the British. It had never worked and no one really expected it to work – the consequences would have been rather like London and the home-counties declaring UDI. But in the end the British had always compromised and the Baganda remained absurdly confident. 'We did not for a moment expect them to leave' wrote the Kabaka in his tragi-comic book 'Our purpose, however, was to bring a case against them for remaining, for we felt that if we could get the matter into court we were certain to win our case.' Alas his faith in the majesty of the law was misplaced.

'Those whom God wishes to destroy, he first makes mad.' The Baganda seemed to forget that they were no longer dealing with the British, who by and large stuck by the rules. Obote's response was to send his army under the equally sinister figure of Brigadier Idi Amin to burn the Kabaka's palace and bring him back alive or dead. They failed only because he jumped over the palace wall and spent the next weeks on the run, sheltered by his people, but with every soldier's hand against him, like Bonny Prince Charlie after Culloden.

Poor King Freddie. He eventually found his way to London, and the British Government gave him asylum of a sort. The last time I saw him, I gave him lunch in a London restaurant which he badly needed, but unfortunately I chose a place too close to the Uganda government's offices and found Obote's new High Commissioner also there. That acutely embarrassed civil servant was also a Muganda and could not prevent himself from beginning a 'Nyan-zigg' which turned instead into an embarrassed cough and a pretence that he had dropped his napkin. I felt for them both, but particularly for King Freddie who was thin and unsteady from drink and, some said, drugs, but still unfailingly polite, with a self-deprecating half smile at his own troubles.

He died a few weeks later and remained in an unquiet grave in Britain until Obote was in turn driven out by Idi Amin. The latter, needing friends to consolidate his power, decided to conciliate the Baganda by allowing them to bring the Kabaka's body home.

'King Freddie'

The entourage that accompanied Mutesa on his last journey was a somewhat mixed bag. Good friends who had given him shelter shared the cargo hold of the Boeing 747 in vigil over his lead-lined coffin with soldiers of the Grenadier Guards, who made a sombre but impressive escort for their Honorary Captain. My father, who had crowned Mutesa thirty years before, and was himself now an old man, returned in the same plane to bury him in the place of his ancestors. My mother, who retains a sharp eye for the incongruous, remembers that my father found it difficult to think of anything to say to some of Mutesa's more raffish friends, but rose magnificently to the occasion at the funeral service in Kampala's great cathedral. 'Goodbye Mutesa', he cried with a loud voice 'Sleep in Peace. We love you'.

5

District Officer

A ll this, however was in the future. Meanwhile I was doing my best to prove myself worthy of Mr Carruthers. Sadly, I had only been in Toro about six months when I was posted away to Mbale on the other side of the Protectorate on the eastern border between Kenya and Uganda. The reason was not my failures with the white settlers or any deficiency in the Mukama's celebrations. The problem lay in the east.

My old friend Ron, who had been posted to Mbale when we first arrived, had found the answer to his impending hairlessness. Within weeks of his arrival, he had run off to Tanganyika with a colleague's wife, had resigned from the Colonial Service, and had found himself a new career as a planter. His Provincial Commissioner was most displeased. In his brief service Ron had shown great promise as an opening batsman, and might well have played cricket for Uganda.

As a tennis player who despised cricket, I was less acceptable to the fiery little Irish P.C., but Ron's departure left a serious gap in the administration of Bugisu, one of the two Districts whose headquarters were in Mbale, and the powers that be had caught wind of my pleas to be relieved of the night-soilmen and to start to be a real administrator at last. So I said goodbye to my railway carriage house on the hillside, packed Kesi, the cook and Suzy into the back of the car, and set off down the two hundred miles of dusty red laterite road to Kampala.

The only tolerable way to drive this bumpy and interminable cart track was in the dark. Though nominally a two-way high road, the only viable method was to stick firmly to the crown of the road. This kept the wheels an acceptable distance from the uncertain

32

edges of swamp, forest or precipice, and avoided the piled up ridge along the middle, a thing of dust, rocks and even substantial bushes. Moreover this outrageous surface could only be taken in any comfort at more than fifty miles an hour. Below this speed, the car pounded unmercifully on the corrugations built up by the fat, slow lorries and the oil-spewing buses. At higher speeds, the car floated along on the crests of these corrugations like a water-skier on the surface of the sea. The result was dangerously fast and uncomfortable, but not lethal.

During the day however it was too risky. For two hundred miles the road twisted and turned round blind forest corners, and over the brows of innumerable steep little hills. The skimming dish technique meant that the car's tyres were only intermittently in contact with the road, and any attempt to pull over to the left involved sliding the right wheels through the centre ridge with the near certainty of a furious skid. In daytime every corner and every hilltop could conceal an oncoming lorry, and many of them did. Piled high with bananas or coffee or fifty shouting Africans, they ground forward, predictable only in their total brakelessness and the uncertain control of their drivers.

The other hazard was two wheeled. Uganda must in those days have had a higher concentration of bicycles than any other country in the world. They had to be Raleighs of a specially reinforced construction. No other make would do, because of a famous advertisement which showed a triumphant African on a Raleigh accelerating away from a frustrated lion, while another on an inferior model was left behind to be eaten. This advertisement must have been worth several million pounds to the Raleigh company throughout east Africa.

To the back of these sturdy machines, village craftsmen welded massive wrought-iron carriers, which were the bicycle's combined rumble-seat and luggage carrier. It was rare indeed to see one man alone on a bicycle. The minimum carrier load was a forty pound stalk of Matooke – the green plantains that were the staple food of the Baganda and Batoro. More usually it carried the massively built figure of the owner's wife, riding side-saddle, swathed in her basuuti and padded with blankets to give the required voluptuousness to the hips. Bound across her back with a wide tight cloth would be the youngest member of the family, its head waggling jerkily with the bicycle's motion. Balanced on the lady's head would be another tight white bundle carrying the family's spare clothes, or maybe the Matooke, for which there was no room on the carrier. If the family had been blessed with other issue they were probably perched on the cross-bar between their father's legs. Or the cross-bar might support a couple of chickens dangling by the legs in squawking discomfort. The whole contraption could easily weigh four or five hundred pounds, propelled very slowly on the gearless bicycle by the father's spindly legs, uncertain in direction and always on the point of falling over.

When a lorry swept onto him round a corner, the cyclist's standard reaction was to make straight for the side of the road and down the embankment, scattering wife, children, matooke, luggage and chickens in dusty confusion. Sometimes, more dangerously, the bicycle fell over before it reached the roadside, leaving the family scattered over the surface. The possibility of involuntary homicide was always hideously present.

At night, however, the cyclists stayed at home, the lorries were fewer and there was always the hope of catching the loom of the badly adjusted headlights from around the corner before a collision became inevitable.

It was therefore in a relatively relaxed frame of mind that, at three o'clock in the morning, I bumped down the road at a steady fifty miles an hour, practising my Luganda verbs to myself, while Kesi, the cook and Suzy snored loudly together on the back seat. Suddenly there was a bang and an ear splitting shriek in front of the car. Steam rose from the bonnet and obscured the windscreen. I stopped hurriedly, thinking I had killed someone, and walked back to where a dark patch of blood or oil lay in the road, shining under the moonlight. A good deal of thrashing about was going on in the tall grass beside the road, accompanied by a human sounding shriek that sounded disturbingly like the cliche of a person squealing like a stuck pig.

Fortunately, however, that turned out to be just what it was. A large wild boar, weighing several hundred pounds, lay on its side on the point of death, and, as I watched, expired.

Relieved that at least I was not about to be had up for manslaughter, I made my way back to the car. It was in a sad mess. The bonnet had caught the pig broadside on. Both lamps were smashed and the radiator dribbled its last onto the road as I arrived. We were at least fifty miles from the nearest garage. Even if I could mend the radiator, there was no water at hand to refill it. We contemplated without enthusiasm the prospect of sleeping on the road under the car. There were beasts about.

However, before we resigned ourselves to this, or to an uncomfortable night in the car, we decided, as a last resort, to try a repair with such substitute materials as we had on hand. The cook, a prudent man, had brought with him the remains of his last night's supper, a tin saucepan half full of maize meal porridge (the Posho that is used throughout East Africa to provide bulk instead of bread). Applied to the car's radiator in a satisfactorily thick blanket this soon set like waterproof cement, leaving one to imagine, and to remember, what miracles of constipation it could perform inside one's own stomach.

Then, having no other liquid, I had regretfully to sacrifice a case of beer to fill up the repaired radiator. This soon gave out a most satisfying aroma of mulled ale; and, with a large torch to light the way, we rolled protestingly down the last 50 miles to Kampala, smelling like a brewery and bouncing heavily in the corrugations which we were now going too slowly to avoid.

When, two days later, after running repairs, we arrived in Mbale, I found a bakingly hot tin-roofed town, sheltering under Nkokonjeru, 'the White Hen', a three thousand foot cliff which was itself an outlier of Mount Elgon, the extinct volcano that dominated the Kenya/Uganda border.

The D.C. greeted me kindly and asked about my tennis. A rubicund Englishman in his middle forties, John was not the brightest star in the Uganda service and got on badly with the irascible Irish P.C., but he was an entirely charming person to know and to work for. He and his wife Bunny had no children and I was still unmarried, so, for the next two years, we were able, with the other ADC, an amused Scot, to dig deep into the life of the district, which circled Mount Elgon from north to south.

Frankly I needed the distraction. My Oxford girl wrote that she had finally decided to marry her politician; Suzy produced puppies from an unnamed and unnamable father; and I contracted typhoid while on safari at the other end of the district and was carried back to Mbale as much dead as alive.

I felt low and remember standing in the African night, banging my fist in frustration on the top of the car and wondering how I was going to get through to the next morning. Mr Carruthers would not have approved, but that is what it is to be young.

To keep the pistol-shot in the night at bay I contracted a decorous and entirely unpassionate relationship with the D.C.'s secretary. But she soon went off me after I drove her in my new car to watch a rugby match in Kampala. This was a hearse-like Chevrolet bought secondhand from the local Bishop. Being a van it had no seats in the back, but I acquired a Victorian velvet-covered chaise longue which doubled as a passenger seat and, I hoped, a site for nameless malpractices, if my affair with the secretary ever got off the ground. She did not see it that way, however, and refused even to sit in the car after I touched a hundred miles an hour on an unmade road and she hit her nose in the roof.

I began to feel that I was not cut out for romance and retreated instead into melancholic male macho-mania, doing things like climbing up and down the 12,000 foot Mount Elgon in a day to prove to myself, if to no-one else, that I was tough and could take it.

In the end, however, it was the mountain itself that began the cure. Anxious colleagues, observing my unbalanced behaviour, had decided to take a hand. They brought a young lady friend, Pat Kelly, down from the capital for a dance. Pat was Kenya born and her family were also long-term residents of Uganda. My friends thought it a good match. Eventually they inserted her into yet another group to climb the Mount Elgon. I, however, thought little of this and decided to burn her off on the initial steep climb through the forest. But by the end of the second day she was still there and after that one thing sort of led to another. Some months later we were married by my father in the great Cathedral at Kampala. King Freddie was one of the guests and gave us an elecroplated teapot.

Whether Pat got a good deal out of all this, then and later, I do not know. I certainly did and it equally certainly saved my sanity. And to tell the truth perhaps we were all a little mad. Soon after my arrival in Mbale the newly arrived but desperately lonely wife of an agricultural officer dressed herself in her wedding dress while her husband was away drinking at the club, and then shot herself with her own hunting rifle.

And the inoffensive D.C. suffered the sort of successive blows that still turn the heart over. He was never going to get far in the service so he took early retirement and left with Bunny to put up his shingle as a lawyer in the beautiful Kenya town of Kitale.

But John was always too trusting. He allowed his Goan clerk to embezzle not only the firm's money, but funds belonging to his clients. To start to pay it all back, Bunny had to come in and try and run the practical side of the business for him. But Bunny herself was not well and shortly afterwards she died, leaving a newly adopted son who turned out to have problems of his own. John then returned to England and finally also killed himself with his own service revolver.

That story is hard to write. It is harder still to remember. It is ridiculous and pandering to the myth of colonialism to talk about being lonely in Africa. It was only possible to feel isolated by ignoring African friends and colleagues and the five million other inhabitants of Uganda with whom our daily lives were interwoven.

And yet, in truth, from time to time we were both isolated and lonely. There were times when I thought that if I could not talk English to someone quite soon I would scream. One got awfully tired of eating old goat, and there were other times when a wash in clean water would have been welcome. And yet none of us would have wanted our lives to be different. We were where we wanted to be, working in a country and with people that we loved. Was this so wrong?

All this, however was in the future. For the meanwhile John gave me the north end of Mount Elgon to look after.

Like virtually all the ex-colonial territories, Uganda at the time of Independence was a country but not a nation. Before the arrival of the imperial powers (and even after it), local loyalties were to the tribe and the clan. Boundaries were inventions of the colonialists and meant nothing at all to the local people.

The classic example of this was, and remains, the boundary between the ex-German state of Tanganyika (now Tanzania) and the ex-British colony of Kenya. The two powers eventually agreed, at the Congress of Berlin in 1881, on the virtual partition of Africa. Under that agreement the boundary between Kenya and Tanganyika ran (and runs to this day) straight in a south-easterly direction from Lake Victoria to the ocean. The exception is at

Mount Kilimanjaro, the highest mountain in Africa, where the boundary takes a large loop to include the whole mass of the volcano in Tanzania.

The reason, so they say, is that the German Kaiser wanted the highest summit in Africa in his territory (so that he could give it the absurd title of 'Kaiser Wilhelm-Franz-Joseph-Spitze') and asked his grandmother Queen Victoria to give it to him for his birthday. The fact that a couple of million Africans were thereby transferred to the rigours of German colonial rule, does not seem to have raised any comment, still less complaint.

Uganda too was like this. There is a total ethnic split across the middle of the country. The Nilotic tribes to the north are, in origin, wild black herdsmen, speaking an entirely distinct group of languages and living mostly on maize meal or, in extreme cases in the north-eastern deserts, on blood mixed with milk in a urine-washed gourd. To the south and west, the Bantu tribes live comfortably on the fertile plains around Lake Victoria, speaking variations of the Bantu language that spreads right down to the southernmost tip of Africa.

Bugisu was on the borderline of this great cultural divide. Most of the inhabitants were agriculturalists, civilised, courtly and wise, whose staple foods were bananas and millet. But to the north of Mount Elgon, where the arid scrubland stretched away into the blue distance, wandered the nomadic cattle-herders – tough, nearly naked men whose main pleasure in life was to steal the cows of their effete neighbours to the south.

And, in between stood, at that time, the nervous figure of the Assistant District Commissioner, adviser to the district government, representative of law-and-order, builder of roads, bridges and schools, tax-collector, magistrate and appointed representative of Mr Carruthers of the Colonial Office.

6

Safari

There were different ways of getting around my District. On one, best-forgotten, occasion I flew. The cattle raiders of Karamoja to the north of Bugisu were, in those days, remarkably law-abiding for a people who, in essence, acknowledged no law. Their D.C. had decreed that each adult male could carry one spear in order to defend himself against lions or rival tribesmen. But two spears meant he was on a cattle raid and had thus put himself outside the law.

In retrospect it is astonishing that, by-and-large, this distinction was observed. The D.C., an eccentric bachelor, had spoken, and the rules of the game required it. Nowadays the cattle raiders of Karamoja, or the neighbouring Turkhana and Somalia are armed with Kalashnikovs and nobody but a lunatic would take them on without overwhelming fire power. But then we would go bounding over the bush, armed with nothing but a stick, trying to catch some decrepid old tribesman with a couple of stolen cows, while a prudent chief, fifteen paces back, yelled 'Leeta bunduki' (bring a gun), in an unconvincing attempt to persuade him that we were armed and he had better surrender forthwith.

None of this, of course, had any effect. We became accustomed to seeing the old man move effortlessly away from us as if he were on wheels, driving the cows before him in a blur of dust and leaving us winded in his wake. The only one who really enjoyed the chase was Suzy, who assured us after her tail-wagging return that she would, for sure, have arrested the miscreant by the seat of his trousers had he only been wearing any.

We thought, on the whole, that honour was satisfied by this, and the local chief, for one, was not going to catch anyone if he could help it. But the powers-that-be were not so pleased.

In an effort to bring technological superiority to bear, where muscle-power had failed, the authorities therefore hired me an aeroplane. The theory was that, by flying at three or four thousand feet above the baking plains, we would be able to detect the great herds of cattle below us. We would then dive to nought feet, to see whether the herdsmen were carrying only one spear (in which case they were about their lawful business) or two (in which case they were on a raid).

I, as the plane's only passenger and hawk-eyed director of the whole operation, would then radio to a police patrol underneath, who would set up blocking positions before the miscreants could scatter into the northern deserts.

The almost unimaginable cost of all this had been specially authorised by Mr Carruthers of the Colonial Office who, we were assured, was 'most displeased' at the continued defiance of his authority by people without trousers.

Carruthers himself, however, can never have tried diving and wheeling in a tiny aircraft above the hot African plain. Nor can he have attempted to count spears, as the plane bucked and rocked in the dust devils set up by a thousand panic-stricken cattle fifty feet below. After the first couple of passes, I was completely gone, emptying my lunch out of one window, which then unfortunately blew back over the pilot who did the same out of his, which duly came back over me; thus, as we agreed later over a shaky beer back at the airstrip, setting up the only example of perpetual motion that had ever been observed in central Africa.

But such febrile excitements were rare. Usually, I walked or went by bicycle, after leaving the box-body car at whatever roadhead was nearest to the sub-county headquarters I wished to visit. The trouble with bicycling was that, above about five miles an hour on any prolonged expedition, Suzy was apt to wear out the pads of her paws on the baking ground. We thought we had solved the problem by getting the chief to strap a large box on the welded carrier of his Raleigh, in which Suzy would sit at her ease as we passed through the cotton fields in stately procession. But the chief's sense of propriety would not allow him to cycle in front of me, and when he was in the rear, Suzy was unable to check on where I was, without craning forward on one side or the other of his ample behind. This led to a succession of violent changes of balance which brought the chief and his bicycle crashing to the ground, with consequent damage to his substantial dignity.

On the whole, therefore, I preferred to walk, the only trouble with this being that Kesi's sense of what was proper for a gentleman's safari equipment, meant that a bizarre line of porters was strung through the bush carrying among other essentials, a cut-glass vase, my hip bath and the gramophone.

The other problem with foot-safaris was that, because the distances we could cover each day were not very great, we usually had to sleep beside a camp-fire at night, en route for the rest-house at the sub-county headquarters. And this too would not have mattered except that the county-chief – an ex-soldier with a strong sense of discipline, felt it essential to post a tribal policeman within two feet of my camp bed. Every time I turned over, this individual, fully in accordance with his orders, presented arms with a rattle of the bolt of his ancient Lee-Enfield and a loud shout of 'ALL CORRECT – SAH!' thus effectively waking us all up until the next time.

The most sybaritic of all safaris, however, were when the Governor himself went on tour. Colonial Governors were a strange breed. Pampered and deferred to almost like gods, they were not thought to be willing to put up with the slightest inconvenience or delay. Government House in Entebbe therefore had two entirely distinct sets of safari equipment, each with its own lorry transport and presiding chefs, laundrymen, personal servants and latrine diggers.

When the Governor went on safari, these two entourages leap-frogged ahead of him. He would therefore leave a rest-house in the morning after a stately council meeting with the local chiefs, and drive at a measured pace to his next destination.

There the alternate safari-camp would already be in residence, with persian carpets rolled out on the rest-house floor. Beneath them the floor itself would be in a somewhat pungent state, its covering of cow-dung having been freshly plastered by an over-enthusiastic chief into a close resemblance to a palpitating khaki-coloured swamp. On the carpets were immaculate white-clothed tables, set with linen napkins, silver cutlery and fine wines, while above the heads of the guests the grass-thatched roof of the rest-house whispered with what the ADC-in-charge (me) nervously hoped were lizards or geckoes, rather than snakes that might fall out into the great one's soup.

This particular Governor was something of an eccentric. He had not risen through the ranks of the Colonial Service, but was one of Mr Carruthers personal henchmen from the Ministry. A massive and would-be democratic presence, he was apt to greet chiefs with excessive bonhomie, which lapsed into silence after about the third sentence, when he totally ran out of small talk, leaving others to pick up the bits as best they could.

On safari he used to rumble like the African elephant he so closely resembled, and was apt to set off on mountain walks for which his physique was manifestly unsuited, leaving it to his under-lings to wonder whether they dared push on the gubernatorial behind at tricky places, (assistance which would, however, have been fiercely resented).

My worst experience with him, his eminently gracious wife and his two ineffable young daughters (he had married late), was when he decided that they would go fishing for trout in a mountain stream on the Uganda/Kenya border of Mount Elgon. The Mau-Mau uprising in Kenya was still rumbling on and we had recently noticed some Kikuyu within ten miles of the Governor's fishing camp.

He, however, inappropriately chose the moment to demonstrate that the Governor of Uganda was no namby-pamby. We were cate-gorically forbidden to organise any security cover for him or his family. They were on holiday and did not want any 'bloody great policemen' trampling around and scaring the fish. Nor was anyone to carry firearms. The Kikuyu were just 'ordinary chaps' after all and if he met any of them, he would disarm them with his usual cheery greeting.

This did not seem to the rest of us a good idea. The thought of the Governor of Uganda marching up to a Mau-Mau forest-fighter with hand outstretched, murmuring 'Delighted to see you old chap, delighted' and then relapsing into a brooding silence as they both tried to think of something else to say, did not on the whole ring true.

The D.C., the chief of police and I therefore conferred and decided that, whatever he wanted, the Governor must be disobeyed. We told a number of policeman to remove their uniforms, dress themselves in blankets and hang around picturesquely, trying to look like peasants, while keeping their shooting hands discreetly on the butts of concealed revolvers.

At first all went well. The fishing was good. One of the Governor's children, to the concealed delight of his Aide de Camp, fell in the river, and then had to be rescued by the Chief of Police. Unfortunately he had forgotten that he too was carrying a revolver and so had to retire miserably behind a bush to clean his water-logged weapon.

Unfortunately too, one of the picturesque peasants went too far. The Governor was impressed by the helpfulness of a blanket-covered but apparently English-speaking villager who offered to carry his day's catch, and graciously asked the man his name (the Governor's only other conversational gambit). Thereupon the dung covered and evil-smelling fool drew himself smartly to attention, saluted with the fish and rapped out 'Three, Five, Four, Two, Seven Sergeant Okello, SIR, Special Branch Mbale'. We were not popular.

Underneath all this, however, the purpose of all this frenetic journeying was not simply to belie the stereotype of a stuffed-shirt government, but to serve a real and serious purpose of local African administration. Colonial governments were often accused of putting the needs of good administration above the demands of freedom, and there is truth in this. But unbiased observers would find it hard to deny that the ordinary African peasant in the villages was better-off, less oppressed, had better schooling, justice, health services, roads and public transport than under the murderous regimes of Milton Obote and Idi Amin that followed so soon after Independence.

A safari in Bugisu went something like this. The morning was devoted to court work, checking the well-kept books of the chief who had the right to imprison offenders for up to six months and settle civil cases worth about £100 (a lot for those days). And the chief himself was no arbitrary despot. In his court work he was guided by assessors, chosen by the local people and there was a right of appeal, often exercised, from his court to the African District Court in Mbale.

If I was at the top end of the district near the Kenya border, the afternoon might then be spent driving a bull-dozer. The road around the mountain had not yet been completed but there was no money to have it professionally built. Instead I was given a roaring yellow monster and a few pounds of dynamite and told to get on with it. The resulting track once lost an official Land Rover, carried away downstream from an imperfectly built bridge. But it was a proud moment when I was able to drive the box-body across the last culvert and join together two parts of the district that had been sundered since the beginning of time.

The evening might be spent doing 'Bulungi Bwansi' ('For the Good of the Country'). This traditional activity of Uganda long pre-dated the arrival of the Europeans, but nevertheless earned us the grave suspicion of the officials of the International Convention on Forced Labour, who were concerned that we were driving the unfortunate inhabitants on with whips, if not scorpions.

Basically the idea derived from the tradition whereby, if a man wanted to make himself a house, he called all his neighbours together, gave them plenty of beer, and had his house built by sunset. When therefore the sub-district council wanted a new dam, or a track to get the coffee out from a particularly remote village (or, I have to admit, a path to allow the Assistant District Commissioner to explore a particularly enticing new rock-face), then they would call out the villagers, feed them (at the ADC's expense, and with shameless padding of the bills), on matooke, beans and (if I was not careful) the violent, and illegal, home-brewed hooch known as waragi.

In the course of the day some work would be done, an enormous amount of energy would be expended in the Bugisu equivalent of Women's Institute chat, and by the end the dam would have inched forward by a foot or two, before being put aside until the following week. It was a wicked, inexcusable and entirely congenial way of achieving nothing very much except a hoot of derision at the ADC when he tried his hand at wielding an African hoe (the chiefs were wisely far too dignified to be caught doing any such thing).

Then, as the light fell with tropical suddenness, there were guinea fowl to be shot in the cotton plots, to the delight of the owners whose fields had been raided. Being no real sportsman, I soon discovered that the most effective use of a cartridge was to wait until the guinea fowl had all come to roost in the gathering darkness in the branches of the nearest tree. A single judicious barrel of the shotgun under the tree then caused it to rain guinea fowl.

Occasionally, when Jim, a friendly policeman, was also on safari we would extend this evening activity to go and shoot duck on a neighbouring dam. Well away from the gaze of the British Field Sports Society, our methods were equally unsporting. Without beaters the only way to approach the birds was to borrow a dugout canoe with a villager to paddle it and creep up on the duck as quietly as we could, while they were still on the water. Then as soon as we had got as close as we dared, we fired all four barrels at once into the brown of the duck and hoped for a satisfactory bag. We comforted ourselves that we were really only copying the techniques of the punt gunners on the Norfolk Broads.

The method was not, however, always as secure as it should have been. The villager had been instructed to approach with his canoe at an angle to the duck. This meant that, with me crouched at the front of the unstable craft and Jim just behind me, we could both fire at once without imperilling each other's safety. Unfortunately the paddler got overcome with the excitement of the chase and, just as we were about to fire, he turned directly towards the duck in order to shorten the range as much as possible. A shattering report from Jim's gun behind me left a colander of holes in the broad brim of my hat.

Nor was that the end of the shocks on that occasion. Every dugout canoe leaks. Essentially it is no more than the trunk of a tree that has been hollowed with fire and an axe. It is impossible to control the gouging out process so closely that it never goes through the outer skin of the hull. On this occasion as on every other, the canoe was patched with bits of tin, wedges of reeds and the steersman's broad flat foot jammed in the largest of the holes to keep the water inflow to a minimum. Inevitably this meant that by the time we had finished collecting the duck, the canoe was half full of water.

As we made for the shore, the duck sloshed around our legs as we knelt in the rapidly sinking craft, trying to keep the guns dry. Looking down at where the helmsman's hole-plugging foot was rapidly disappearing beneath the water, Jim then pointed out the unnerving fact that, where the duck were bumping against what would have been his toes, there were none. Leprosy was then a sadly common disease throughout Africa. We knew it was non-contagious, but when we came to eat the duck around the camp fire that night, we tried not to think too hard about where they had been.

In all this activity, however, we were really acting, not for ourselves, but as supports and agents of the District Council, an elected African body, that many saw as the natural future government of the country. This, frankly, was a mistake by the Colonial government. When the Europeans had first arrived they found, particularly in Buganda, a highly centralised and developed political and administrative system, which they were happy to see continue under the then fashionable doctrine of Indirect Rule.

This of course fooled no-one. Those indirectly ruled could be forgiven for not knowing the difference between that and direct administration. Nevertheless, by a series of enactments as Independence approached, more and more functions were transferred from the centre to the District Councils, in the altogether mistaken belief that this would give local people practice in the art of government, which they would then transfer to the centre, grasping the levers of national power as the British withdrew.

What the well-meaning constitution-makers of course forgot was that, since the districts were broadly defined by tribal boundaries, this decentralisation emphasized even more the authority of the tribe, leaving the infant nation of Uganda to starve for lack of the oxygen of power. As a result, the Bagisu referred to the District Council as 'Gavumenti Eyaffe' (our Government) and to the administration in Kampala as 'Gavumenti Ey'engereza' (The English Government).

The effect of all this in setting one tribe against another and leading to the breakdown of all central democratic authority under the murderous assault of the dictators, was all too soon to be apparent.

7

Fish and Chips

The great he-elephant had been sent out to get things moving. Mr Carruthers believed that the colonial officials on the spot had become complacent. Something more must be done to get Uganda ready for Independence.

Unfortunately, the Governor combined an undoubtedly brilliant mind with an inability to suffer gladly anybody else much, except himself. This included white officials like me, who did not matter. More seriously, it included the local kings and traditionalists, particularly King Freddie of Buganda and the whole gamut of Buganda pride, history and downright bloody mindedness.

To the elephant's logical mind, the way forward was first to bring Uganda into some sort of relationship with the other East African territories of Kenya and Tanganyika. There was sense in this. Uganda's exports of coffee and cotton were cut off from the sea except through Kenya. But the idea of being forcibly joined with the white settlers of Kenya was anathema to the whole African population of Uganda.

It sent the Lukiiko of Buganda into a frenzy of opposition. They were frightened enough by the possibility of Buganda being submerged in a greater Uganda; beyond that, as a tiny part of a great East African Federation, they feared annihilation and probably rightly so. The Governor, always forthright, but unskilled in human relations, sent for King Freddie and informed him that, although closer relations were on his agenda, federation was not and to tell the Lukiiko not to be silly.

The Kabaka could probably have got away with telling the Lukiiko anything. They were all his men. But he put on his best pained expression and spoke with unendurable sorrow (he was a

47

marvellous actor) on the following lines to the smouldering pro-consul before him. 'But, Your Excellency, you know I couldn't possibly do that. I am only the King. They are the representatives of my people. That would not be democratic.'

'Nonsense, nonsense,' thundered the elephant. 'Now go away and tell them, there's a good chap.'

This put the Governor, at a stroke, hopelessly in the wrong. How could he, the great democrat, be seen to order this hopeless anach-ronism of a native king to coerce his democratically elected parliament? In the end he was forced into acting more undemocrat-ically still. He sent the Kabaka into comfortable exile in Tooting Bec and ordered the Lukiiko to choose a new king.

This really set the wasps buzzing. The Lukiiko refused to coop-erate. Instead, just as they tried to do later to Obote, they told the Governor that their fifty-year-old agreement with the Queen was at an end and would he please remove himself and his administration from Buganda forthwith. A state of emergency followed in which, fortunately, all concerned had the good sense not to start beating each other over the head.

At the time I was happy to be away from the cauldron of Buganda politics in the relatively calm backwater of Bugisu. And my relief was redoubled when my father, from his retirement in the home counties, decided to take a hand. In a thunderous letter to the Times he denounced the Governor and all his works, praising the Kabaka's 'statesmanship and wisdom'.

This may have surprised Mutesa a bit. He knew well that my father did not approve of his habit of marrying one girl and then setting up house with her sister. As far as I was concerned, however, it meant that I would have been put in a rather ambiguous position if the government had posted me to Buganda, since the Baganda would have expected me to follow my father's line, while duty and Mr Carruthers would have demanded otherwise. That was fine by me, I was happy to stay were I was.

Two years later, however, all this had changed. Wiser heads had realised that the answer was to patch up a peace with Buganda. A new Agreement was signed as a fig-leaf, providing that the Kabaka would now stay out of politics and therefore could not be blamed for the intransigencies of the Lukiiko. King Freddie returned to enormous acclaim and was graciously received by the same

Governor who had expelled him. It must have been a poignant moment.

Immediately, however, as a most minor consequence of this stately dance, my own personal situation changed for the worse. Hitherto I would have been an embarrassment in Buganda. Now I was an insignificant potential asset.

The Lukiiko, having agreed to resume normal relations with the representatives of the central government, now characteristically proceeded to give those representatives a thoroughly cold shoulder. Government officers on safari were politely told that the rest-house was occupied; that the chiefs were too busy to meet them; that the hens had unfortunately ceased laying eggs and had indeed died of a disease that sadly made them inedible; that the spring had dried up so there was no water and firewood had become unobtainable: furthermore community work on the roads had unfortunately rendered them impassable, so no-one could get to their headquarters.

My bosses calculated not unreasonably that it would be more difficult for the Baganda to take this line with the son of the Bishop who had supported them in their hour of need. For the rest of my time in Bugisu I was therefore under threat of immediate posting to Buganda, there to act as a minor political football between the Government's wish to normalise relations and the determination of the Baganda to stay in a huff. I was not best pleased.

Buganda is the place where I belong, the people that I love and the language that I still spout, like a rusty bicycle, whenever I get the chance. Buganda, in other words, is home. Nevertheless, the Baganda, with their pride, their sense of history and their infuriating arrogance seemed in danger of destroying themselves or allowing others to do it for them. I wanted no part of this. For the moment my attempts to stay out of Buganda were successful, but it could not last. Eventually I was brought back again by a combination of circumstances that I could hardly have predicted.

All governments have their departments of dirty tricks. Some of them are impressive, but most, in my experience, are ludicrously ineffective. Uganda's Special Branch was of the cheap and cheerful variety, run mostly by a clever Pole, by the Irishman who had distracted Kigaanira at Kkungu, and by my mother-in-law.

In the early post-war years they had really only one function. Everyone was terrified of Communism. The Russians were making a dead set at any bright young African who caught their eye, initially with the aim of destabilising the colonial regime and then in the hope of creating agents of influence who would work for them after Independence. Their method was quite simple – offer their target a scholarship at the Patrice Lumumba Friendship University in Moscow, and then sit back and wait for the dividend.

Everyone in Uganda was desperate for education. Once they had struggled their way to the top of the impressive secondary schools, with their extended families scrimping and saving to pay for school fees, books, uniforms and food, the only road to higher education was through the magnificent Makerere University in Kampala, the best in East Africa (some said in the whole of Africa).

But places at Makerere were desperately hard to get. There was only one women's college (named, to this day, after my mother, who was a member of the commission which created the embryo University in the forties). Graduates of Makerere were literally gold dust and apt to regard themselves as such (one graduate engineer whom I flagged down because his truck's motor was boiling drew himself to his full height and remarked 'My dear Andrew, I am not a mechanic, I'm an engineer!'). There was no way that Makerere could meet the demand. Besides, anti-colonialism was and always has been a slogan to catch the attention of the idealistic young. Nobody knew anything about the Soviet Union, and the Russians themselves were debarred from opening a consulate in Uganda. But the word soon got around.

It wasn't just a matter of queuing up for a passport and being presented with a ticket to Moscow by some friendly intermediary. The authorities were reasonably benevolent but not totally naive. They did their best to ensure that potential candidates for Moscow didn't leave the country, though this was not too easy to prevent when there was free access to the whole of the East African area.

Most of the candidates for the Friendship University made their way from Uganda by river steamer down the Nile to the Sudan border at Nimule, then crossed the border on foot and travelled on to the Russian consulate in Khartoum, where the standard bearhug awaited them.

At first this worried the colonial authorities almost to the point of hysteria. Huge efforts were deployed in keeping track of individuals. Files in bizarre colours circulated under Top Secret cover, and we were warned to keep a sharp eye out for the absconders and detain any of them that we found. (We never did. How do you detect which African has got snow on his boots among four hundred packed into a stern-wheel Nile paddle steamer?)

Later, however, we decided we could all relax. The first graduates who came back from the Patrice Lumumba Friendship University in Moscow were so virulently anti-communist that they all joined the British Special Branch as paid informers. It was even suggested that we should close down the British Council scholarships to London, where there were all too many sad tales of racial discrimination and lasting bitterness, and instead encourage the Russians to step up their programme and provide them with an office to promote this.

Soon, however, as Independence approached the police Special Branch found themselves with something more serious to worry about. Politicians conspire; that is the nature of the game and politics in Uganda was a complicated dance of tribes, personalities, opportunists, crooks and genuine idealists.

One of the more delicate quadrilles concerned Buganda. As we have seen, four years before final Independence, the Baganda boycotted the first direct elections for an internally self-governing parliament. Drafted in to try to persuade them otherwise, I became fed up with going from meeting to meeting where the chief got up and, trying to read from a Buganda government prepared brief as if it was his own unaided idea, asked me to imagine a football match where one team (Buganda), had only five players, and the other, (the rest of the country) had ten.

The only way to lighten the atmosphere was then to fire off some totally irrelevant Luganda proverb (they loved proverbs) like 'Atannayita atenda nnyina okufumba' (he who has not travelled praises his mother's cooking) or 'Abuulira omugezi takoowa' (he who speaks to a wise man never gets tired). But at the end they would not listen. The boycott went ahead and the totally predictable result was that Buganda was left out in the cold.

There was, however, one more election scheduled before Independence. As we have seen Milton Obote, the leader of the mainly northern party, the UPC, (later to alternate with Idi Amin in a frenzy of death dealing), decided that the best solution was to do a deal with the Baganda leaders, whom he hated, and so ensure that he was in place as Prime Minister at the time of Independence (after which he would know how to deal with any opposition).

This worried the retiring colonial authorities, not just because Obote was intrinsically an evil man (which he was), but because the Baganda clearly did not know their political base from their constitutional apex and in making a deal with Obote were sowing the seeds of their own destruction.

The new Governor, a tough but subtle Scot, who had by that time succeeded the Elephant, therefore told the police to 'watch these bastards', or words to that effect.

Special Branch, however, only had three ways of doing so. The first was to listen to their targets' telephone calls (using a couple of wires inserted into the manual exchange at dead of night, in the hope that nobody would notice the extra cables leading off in entirely the wrong direction). The other was to raid their Post Office boxes, before the legitimate addressees could get to their letters (this was known as 'Fish and Chips', as in 'I'm just popping down the road to get some fish and chips' – though the fact that there was no chippery in Kampala did not add to the verisimilitude of the cover). And the third was for someone to pretend to be drunk and lie around in bars hoping that somebody else would talk indiscreetly. (There was a fourth method – to bribe people; but since Special Branch had practically no money, this was of limited value.)

The top (and Top Secret) floor of Special Branch headquarters therefore contained two essential items of equipment. One was a kettle for steaming open letters. The other was an antiquated tape machine for recording the indiscreet telephone conversations of Obote, King Freddie and one or two other people adjudged potentially dangerous to the State.

The Branch was therefore fully equipped for surveillance, but there was one other snag. Although by that time there were plenty of local nationals in the Police Force, it was really asking too much of their loyalty to their about-to-depart colonial masters to expect them to listen to the phone calls and study the letters of their King and their about-to-be Prime Minister.

At the same time, not many expatriate policemen spoke the local languages at all fluently. Most police work required a rough and ready grasp of Swahili, the lingua franca, and not much more. There was therefore only one expert in Special Branch headquarters, who was going crazy trying to listen to four different telephone calls at once, and at the same time to decipher letters in spidery writing on inadequate paper in search of seditious material.

I did not want to come to Kampala and I did not want to listen to the telephone calls of the Kabaka, who was a friend (I didn't much mind about Obote on whom three months of spying only went to prove what a thoroughly unpleasant man he was). But it was pointed out to me that Mr Carruthers of the Colonial Office had appointed me for precisely this crucial operation; so we moved lock, stock and daughter to a nasty little box in the Kampala suburbs where we were burgled three times in as many months.

At first my duties seemed relatively undemanding. I learned practically nothing about King Freddie except that he was sleeping with the wife of another friend of mine, which made it somewhat difficult, when we met at dinner the following night, to stop myself asking her whether the Earth had moved for her. Nor did I have much to do with the fish-and-chips, as the other expert was much better at deciphering than I was; and I firmly refused to pretend to be drunk in bars.

Unfortunately, however, I was soon dragged into the middle of a major crisis.

The somewhat rough and ready method of dealing with the fish and chips was for a highly skilled technician to boil the kettle and steam them open. After that the language expert would skim through them and note any passages that ought to be copied and kept on the files. He would then send the fish on, in its original envelope, to the same highly-skilled technician, who had the use of a photocopier, with a request for a copy to be made of a particular section.

The thought-to-be-foolproof method of making such a request was to use a paper clip to attach a note from the expert to the front of the relevant envelope. The request complied with, the technician would then seal the envelope up again and return it to the Post Office, hoping that it did not by that time look so woebegone as to invite suspicion.

Unfortunately, one day, for reasons that were never clarified, the expert did not clip the request for copies on the front of the envelope, but put it inside. The technician, seeing no request, assumed that that particular piece of fish had no smell. He therefore duly sealed up the envelope and sent it on its way.

Fortunately the expert had a sufficiently retentive memory to recall that he had received no photocopy. Panic ensued when it was realised that a letter was on its way to the country's next Prime Minister, containing a note, in English, asking for copies to be made of it.

At first I was inclined to think this was a great joke. It was sometimes difficult to take the cloak-and-dagger histrionics too seriously. But all this changed when I asked what the note actually contained. Unfortunately the technician's name was also Andrew. The paper, which would be on Obote's desk the next morning, therefore read:

'Dear Andrew, three copies please.'

Obote was aware that I was working temporarily for the police. He was also familiar with my first name. I immediately became as insistent as anybody that Something Must Be Done. The problem was, what? The Post Office had already been cleared. The Pole had a somewhat reluctant agent inside the UPC office who was able to confirm that the letter was already there, lying unopened on Obote's desk, waiting for him to come back from up-country. The agent, however, was quite unwilling to extract it. He was understandably more frightened of Obote than he was of the Pole. We had about 24 hours. It was clearly time for the highly-skilled technicians to be called in.

One of them claimed to be an expert lock-picker. He had not in ten years' service been required to demonstrate this skill in action and a single attempt to get into the bar at the sailing club, when the barman had left his keys at home, had ended in failure. However this was clearly time for him to prove himself.

At midnight that night the top brass of Special Branch stood anxiously around the UPC office's front door while the expert fiddled in the light of a shaded lantern. He fiddled and he fiddled and he fiddled, but it was not until he started to kick the door in an excess of frustration that it dawned on the rest of us that something else was going to have to be tried, and quickly.

The Pole was sent off to reconnoitre the outside of the building and came back with the news that a substantial drainpipe led up past the window of Obote's office, which appeared to be partly open.

This was shortly after Kigaanira had been removed from the top of Kkungu rock, and everyone looked at me. I looked at the drainpipe and rather gingerly tested its fastenings. They wobbled perceptibly in the light of the storm lantern. I pointed out that I was at least two stone heavier than the Pole. Moreover I outranked him.

With a resigned expression and an oath or two in Polish, he started to climb. Predictably, when he was about half way up, there was a resounding crash. The whole drainpipe came away from the wall. Limping heavily the Pole was assisted from the scene by the Assistant Commissioner of Police.

We wondered whether Obote would notice that his drainpipe had gone. Fortunately it was the dry season, otherwise the first rainstorm would have swamped his office. But that still lay some months ahead and meanwhile the incriminating letter was still there, waiting to explode in our faces when Obote returned the next morning.

The reluctant agent in the UPC office was now our only hope. The Assistant Commissioner withdrew the whole of the Special Branch bribe fund from the office safe. It wasn't much. Nowadays no self-respecting footballer would agree to throw a goal for ten times as much. But the agent was a poor man. When he was woken in the middle of the night by a limping Pole, flashing dirty notes in his face, his scruples and his fear of Obote were swiftly overcome. The next morning he got to the office as soon as it was open, extracted the letter before Obote arrived and handed it over to the Pole at the back of the law-courts (an appropriate place for skulduggery). We were saved.

By that time my secondment to the Special Branch was drawing to a close. As is too often the case, all this clandestine activity had revealed nothing that was not simultaneously in the local press. Indeed when I had to write the weekly Intelligence Digest, I plagiarised shamelessly from the Luganda-language newspapers, which few of the top-brass could read anyway. It was clear that King Freddy had made his pact with Obote and that the next elections would be fought by a coalition between the UPC and 'Kabaka Yekka' ('The King Alone' – a royal Buganda party invented for the occasion). The Baganda would have to be left to take their chances by themselves.

But before all this happened, Special Branch, and indeed the whole of government, had to take urgent action to deal with a residual problem that is seldom mentioned in the accounts of the end of Empire. The whole archive was awash with secret files about the very people who were about to take power.

Sometimes these files contained accounts of dirty deeds that would have cast doubts on the integrity and honesty of the new leaders. Almost as often, as has more recently been revealed in East Germany, the files would have shown an embarrassing degree of collusion between politicians and the colonial government, that would have damaged the nationalist credentials of the new governors. The files had to be got rid of.

Destroying paper is not, however, as easy as it might seem. Special Branch headquarters had one shredding machine, which drew in papers and spewed them out again like mangled spaghetti. But it would only take one sheet at a time and was anyway subject to fits of the sulks when it refused to disgorge anything except a grinding noise and a slight wisp of smoke.

The only possible method of wholesale destruction was to burn the lot. But whole files do not burn easily. They are apt to char at the edges leaving embarrassing chunks unconsumed. We took a lorry load of secret files, under close police escort, down to a bare place by the lake shore and tried to create an auto-da-fe.

It didn't work. We got extremely hot and covered with soot. Transporting secret files is bad enough; gathering up the remains of half burnt ones and loading them back into a lorry is far worse. Something more drastic had to be done.

The Pole had a bright idea. Why not take the files down to the local sugar factory, which had a massive boiler for refining the raw sugar cane, chuck the lot into the burning fiery furnace like Shadrach, Meshach and Abednego, and forget about them? We drove the forty miles to the sugar factory.

Shovelling the files into the furnace was again hard work. It was extremely hot, but for obvious reasons we had to clear the staff from the furnace house while it was going on and do the stoking work ourselves.

Eventually, however, it was finished. The Pole had thoughtfully brought a case of beer. We sat back to take precautions against dehydration. At that moment, however, an excited sub-inspector burst in. 'Come and look outside' he gasped.

We jammed the door and looked upwards. From the top of the fifty foot chimney of the furnace, loose papers and whole files were belching upwards and scattering themselves over a square mile of the adjoining sugar-cane fields.

8

New Flags for Old

But now it was time for the British to go. Conferences in London and Uganda had produced the usual fudge. The colonial authorities had convinced themselves that they were leaving behind them a viable constitution which all parties could agree to. The Uganda politicians indeed agreed. All they wanted was to be left alone.

First there would be a final round of direct elections; then a new and democratically chosen government would take over, operating the full Westminster system, with wigs and maces, points of order, question-time, ministerial responsibility, Erskine May and equality before the law.

This ignored the fact that much of African society was essentially authoritarian rather than democratic. And the colonial system itself had given a poorish example of participatory democracy, its only real virtue in that respect being that at least it foresaw the possibility of its own supersession.

Supersession, however, was a concept that appealed to few of Uganda's new leaders, especially Milton Obote, who held firmly to the cynic's credo of 'One man, one vote – one election'.

For Obote it was therefore vital to win that final election, and to do that, he was prepared to promise the Kabaka the shirt off his own back.

Since the penultimate elections leading to internal self-government had, as we have seen, been boycotted by the Buganda traditionalists, and since Obote's strength lay outside Buganda, this had meant that Obote's enemies, the mainly Roman Catholic Democratic Party, which did have a base in Buganda, had initially come out on top.

The DP leader, Benedicto Kiwanuka, a roly-poly lawyer, was busy preparing for Independence. Committees were set up to plan all the really important matters. I sat on one such – a panel to decide on a new flag for the independent State of Uganda. Since we were all sycophants at heart, we came up with a blue and green confection that was remarkably similar to the Democratic Party colours. Kiwanuka accepted this with enthusiasm.

Less successful was a competition to select a new National Anthem. The eventual winner was that same distinguished musician who, as a kitchen toto all those years before, had competed with me for the possession of our first bicycle. The sentiments of the chosen anthem were impeccable:

> 'Oh Uganda, thy people praise thee.
> We lay our future in thy hand
> United, free
> For Liberty
> Together we'll always stand.'

The tune too had a pleasing rhythm, rather like 'Onward Christian Soldiers'. But unfortunately the composer had neglected the first rule of unaccompanied singing – if the tune starts too low and ends too high, then a natural tendency to pitch the first note where it is comfortable means that you either have to change key in mid flight, or end the whole thing in a falsetto shriek. Neither is conducive to the dignity of a National Anthem, and the composition's first airing on Independence Day was a disaster.

Nor, as it turned out, was our first choice of a national flag any more successful. When Obote won the final election, he was emphatically not about to let the colours of his political opponents fly at the country's mast-head on Independence Day. The flag committee was brusquely reconvened and told to think again.

The choice of a new colour scheme was again not a great problem. Strangely enough, the design we finally selected was remarkably close to Obote's party colours, primarily red and black, and our only feeble gesture of independence was to design a bird for the flag's central emblem that, as someone unkindly observed, looked less like a crested crane than a spavined chicken.

Our real difficulty was to find a respectable reason for the change. I forget which member of the committee it was who finally hit upon the ingenious explanation that we had consulted the world's greatest experts, who had advised us that, unfortunately, although the colours we had first chosen would make an excellent flag, the dyes were liable to fade in the African sun. We had therefore, we said, been advised to choose something a bit stronger. This we duly did, and Uganda's black-yellow-red-black-yellow-red ensign flies triumphantly to this day.

And triumph Obote most emphatically did. He knew that if he could eliminate the Democratic Party in Buganda and if the rest of the country realised that this was going to happen, then the bandwagon effect would roll his own Uganda People's Congress to the crucial victory.

To achieve this he promised King Freddie that Buganda's representatives in the central Parliament would be chosen, not by direct election, but indirectly through Buganda's own regional parliament, the Lukiiko. The Kabaka fell for this and the British accepted it as a way of getting the Buganda problem off their backs.

Once, of course, those indirectly elected representatives of 'Kabaka Yekka' ('the Kabaka alone'), had arrived in parliament as Obote's allies, then he was confident that the lure of office and his own special blend of blandishments, bribes and intimidation would enable him to detach enough of them to the UPC to make his position impregnable.

And so it proved. At independence the UPC emerged with 34 seats, Kabaka Yekka 21 and the opposition DP only 24. Less than two years later and without new elections, the UPC strength had risen to 58, giving Obote enough votes under the carefully structured British system of checks and balances to revise the constitution in his own favour by the use of his two-thirds majority.

This sounds cynical and indeed it was. As one rhymester recorded:

'For a gift of Mercedes
We'll follow to Hades,
Give us Office as well
And we'll go down to Hell.

For we've children to feed
And relations in need
So don't try to name us
Or shame us, or blame us.
For you'd do it too
If offered to you.'

At the same time, it ill-behoved us, the British Colonialists, to join the cynics. We had after all connived at, indeed to a large extent drawn up the new constitution. We could hardly complain when Obote promptly bent it to his own purposes, especially as we had a shrewd idea from the contents of the Fish and Chips and from my own telephone eavesdropping, that that was precisely what he intended to do.

Nor, though it still had all the elements of a Greek tragedy, complete with stiff-necked pride, royal indecision and idiotic counsellors, was it really possible to blame the Baganda or the common people of Uganda as a whole. My most poignant memory of the election which set the whole dire process going, was of a little old lady who came to cast her vote for the Lukiiko at a polling booth in the depths of the Buganda countryside.

Because such a large proportion of the population was illiterate, we could not ask them to write in the name of their chosen candidate, or even to make a cross on a paper, as in Britain. Instead the African electoral commission decided that each candidate would have a separate box at each polling station with his or her party's symbol on it. The voters would then each be given a ballot paper and told to put it in the box of their choice.

This had meant the construction of a large number of boxes, and a certain amount of difficulty with the parties when it came to choosing their symbols. One of the pictures on offer was a chair, and Kabaka Yekka insisted that it be given to them to signify to the voters that they were to vote for Buganda's throne.

In fact the actual throne of Buganda was at that time in some disrepair, having been partially eaten by white ants after being left in unsuitable storage (thus causing my irreverent mother to remark, perhaps not entirely originally, 'Those who live in grass houses should not store thrones'). But it remained a potent talisman.

The catholic-orientated DP objected that they wanted the same symbol to remind voters of the throne of God, but were eventually pacified by the allocation of a cow, which to a large part of Uganda was a sign of wealth.

The only problem with the multiple box method was that, unless the polling booth was adequately screened, it was all too easy for prying eyes to see into which box a voter had put his or her ballot paper, thus giving rise to fears of intimidation. Some of the local election committees, anxious to do the whole thing properly, then got a bit over-enthusiastic and constructed polling booths which provided privacy all right, but were also hard to get into, almost impossible to get out of and virtually light-proof when you were inside.

As bad luck would have it, at one such polling station, we had invited a distinguished collection of international observers, there to assure the world that the elections were fully and fairly conducted.

In came the old lady, her tightly curled hair a frizzled grey, her face a map of fine black lines radiating out from a puzzled and toothless smile at being asked to take part in this mysterious ritual whose purpose she only vaguely understood.

In both gnarled hands and kneeling submissively on the dung floor she received the precious paper from the polling clerk, who ushered her officiously into the booth and shut the door. There was a long pause. Eventually, hesitatingly and beseechingly through a crack in the side of the door, appeared the voting paper, steered by a trembling hand through the only chink of light that must have been visible to that old and bewildered voter, anxious to do her part in guiding Uganda to Independence, but quite unable in the gloom to see anything but that vague glimmer.

A snort of derision from one of the international observers seemed as deeply offensive as any racist gibe. The simple soul had done her best. She had voted for the light in the only way open to her; the use that the politicians would make of her vote was up to them. It was not her fault that they would surely let her down.

Once the elections were over, the count-down to Independence began. There is nothing like it in the world. The birth of a nation is something that happens only once. Even rebirth, like the restoration of freedom in Eastern Europe after the collapse of the Soviet

Empire was, in a sense, only the re-creation of something that existed before in the memories and hearts of the people.

But Independent Uganda (like Kenya and Tanzania and indeed the rest of Africa) was something new and shining, where anything and everything was possible and all the old barriers were swept away.

Even those who were leaving felt this excitement. Their number was not great. A large part of the civil service was already African. Only the top posts were still held by Europeans, and one of the most heartening things for those of us who were staying on was to see how the departing colonialists worked with those who would be taking over their jobs, to ensure that the hand-over was as smooth as possible.

For the latter it was a dream come true. Experienced African administrators, who for years had had to live with the fact that, no matter how qualified and experienced, they would never climb to the top of the tree, suddenly found themselves responsible for the whole machinery of government.

In those situations people change. The motto of a movement which I became involved with later in life is 'Plus est en vous', (there is more in you than you think). Uganda was the living proof of this.

Only the army stood ominously aloof. Uganda's army was an extraordinary historical accident. When Lord Lugard, the first representative of the Imperial British East Africa Company, arrived in Uganda from the east coast in the last years of the 19th century, he needed soldiers. The Baganda were fighting the Banyoro. Within Buganda, the Protestants were fighting the Catholics and both of them were fighting the Muslims. Lugard had two Maxim guns, but only one of them worked. His camp on Kampala hill seemed likely to be overwhelmed.

By chance, however, in the far north-west of Uganda, he found a tiny group of British-trained African soldiers, living in tents with ordered lines, bugle calls in the morning and ancient Martini-Henry pump action rifles that struck fear into everyone who saw them, including their users.

These soldiers were the last remnant of the southern army of the British General Gordon of Khartoum. When 'Chinese' Gordon's force was surrounded and finally massacred by the Mahdi, his troops in southern Sudan, under a weird German doctor-turned-soldier Emin Pasha, retreated southwards and eventually came to rest in what is now northern Uganda, out of reach of the pursuing Mahdists.

Emin Pasha himself had gone, 'rescued' by Stanley (of Livingstone fame), who by the time he reached Emin's camp was really more in need of rescuing than the man he came to save. The now leaderless troops, known to the locals as Nubians after their original homeland in the Sudan, proved a godsend to Lugard and the backbone of the new Uganda army, encumbered though they were with cohorts of women folk, servants and camp followers.

Very little fighting was done. The Maxim gun, though apt to jam after four or five rounds, usually proved decisive. Members of the 4th (Uganda) battalion, the King's African Rifles then fought bravely and effectively in two world wars, but, by the time of independence they had largely relapsed into somnolent ceremonial under a group of engaging but hardly earth-shaking British Officers.

Unfortunately, because the first soldiers were the black visaged Nubians from the bushiest part of the north, who were despised as barbarians by the sophisticated Bantu from the south, it proved impossible to persuade the Baganda to join the army. We did try. I was instructed to enlist the Kabaka's help, particularly to persuade graduate Baganda to enlist for officer-training (which was why I spent so many weary mornings at his palace waiting for him to get up).

King Freddie too did his best. He would have loved to command a regiment of Baganda guardsmen, complete with bearskins and red tunics, sweltering under the African sun. But his subjects really weren't interested. A handful of potential Baganda officers abandoned the training course before it had well begun. Nor would any of his subjects enlist as ordinary soldiers, to be fed the rations of the maize-eating northerners and get shouted at in Swahili, a language they despised. Nor, to be frank, did we get much help from the British officers. Politically naive, they saw no reason why they should not stay indefinitely in charge, after independence as before, obeying whatever political masters were in power at the time. They seemed to have no concept of the storm that was brewing beneath their lordly noses.

Soon after Independence the troops mutinied. The mutiny started in Tanganyika, but soon spread to Kenya and Uganda. Swallowing their pride, the countries' leaders asked the British to send imperial soldiers (who were still based in Kenya), to calm the mutineers down.

Then followed an embarrassing incident when a group of senior Ugandans went to the airport to greet the arriving British troops. Ignoring the welcoming ceremony, the spearhead platoon brushed past them shouting 'out of the way, you bastards' as they rushed to secure the entirely undefended airport control tower.

It was very soon over, without casualties on either side, and afterwards the British Commanding Officer of the Tanganyika battalion was asked on television if he could account for the mutiny of the troops under his command. 'Absolutely not', he boomed 'As far as we knew the chaps were absolutely loyal. Every month or so we had what we called a "Baraza" (meeting), and we'd sit the chaps down on the ground and we'd say to them "Everything all right, chaps?" and they'd all say "Ndio bwana" (Yes Sir). Quite inexplicable, quite inexplicable.'

All this seemed to indicate a certain lack of sensitivity, as well as some failure in man-management. Not surprisingly the prime ministers of the newly independent countries had had enough. They sacked the British Commanding Officers and instructed their African replacements to get ahead with appointing local officers as quickly as possible.

Unfortunately, however, even this was too late. A small veneer of African junior officers already existed, appointed by the British only months before independence on the insistence of more far sighted people in London who could see what was coming.

I was not privy to the secrets of the promotion board, but the results suggested that its British army members must have decided to appoint African officers who were popular but stupid, assuming that this would meet the political requirement, while they themselves remained ineffably in control. At all events the first batch of promoted Africans included a rough, tough sergeant who had been extremely lucky not to be charged with the murder of a Kikuyu when he had served in Kenya during the Mau-Mau troubles. He was popular because he was the heavy-weight boxing champion of Uganda, and he was most certainly stupid. His name; Idi Amin.

All this, however, was no more than a cloud on the horizon, the size of a man's hand. Meanwhile Independence Day, the 9th of October 1962 came closer and unbelievably closer.

I was in charge of finding accommodation for the official delegations who came from every district in the country to attend the midnight ceremony on the old airfield in Kampala. All the previous day they rolled in, in a weird assortment of buses, trucks, lorries, Mercedes-Benz, bicycles, box-body cars, Land Rovers and over-crowded trains.

Nothing seemed to stem their good humour. There were far more than we bargained for. The available accommodation soon ran out. God knows where they all slept, but clearly that didn't matter, as they had no intention of sleeping that night anyway. None of them was drunk. None of them was disorderly.

My own patience ran out on the arrival of two hundred of my old friends the Batoro, three hours before the ceremony, without tickets, beds or food. But instead of being offended by this officious white man who berated them like children on their great day, they soothed me down, assured me how glad they were to see me again and told me not to worry. They had plenty of friends in town with whom they could stay; this was Independence Night and it did not matter whether or what they ate; and as for being at the ceremony itself, the Kampala airfield was dug into the side of a hill and they could always go and stand on the slope above it. And, if there were too many on the slope for them to be able to see – well they could always climb a tree – just as long as they could have a glimpse of the two flag posts on which, at midnight, the Union Jack would fall for the last time, and the flag of the new Uganda would be raised.

I felt properly and utterly ashamed of myself for my ill humour and told them I would see them later on the hill.

Two hours later, Pat and I were there too, seated at the back of all the official guests, including my parents, whom the new government had flown specially out from London for the occasion. In the front row were the Rulers, dressed in their traditional robes, with George Rukidi, as usual, occupying a chair and a half, forcing the Mukama of Bunyoro to perch nervously on the edge like a sparrow about to take flight. King Freddie would have loved to wear his Grenadier Guards uniform, but had been persuaded that this was hardly the moment for the trappings of Colonialism. In the middle, grimly triumphant in his moment of victory, was Obote and behind him the lowering ranks of his army officers, including Amin.

The Duke of Kent, who was to present the instruments of independence, drove up with the Governor in his Rolls Royce; the band struck up God Save the Queen for the last time; troops marched and countermarched, the dignitaries made official speeches that were as empty of meaning as always, but were nevertheless wildly applauded. The Duchess of Kent, who had the rare knack of making everybody feel that she really cared about them and was in those days quite ravishingly beautiful, had complained to me that afternoon that her feet hurt. Under her ceremonial robe, she kicked off her shoes and was comfortable. It was that sort of night. Everybody was comfortable, everybody was excited, everyone knew that something of rare beauty was about to happen.

At midnight, the sounds of the African night seemed to hold their breath. The bright stars over lake Victoria dimmed briefly as the spotlights focused on the twin flag poles. The Last Post sounded; the Union Jack came down. Then bass voices (the only ones which could get down to the opening notes), took up the new National Anthem.

As the tune climbed, more and more joined in, until the last words ended in a shriek that was not inappropriate, as it seemed like a shout of unity and triumph. Our rainbow flag climbed slowly to the top of its mast. Uganda was free.

9

Amin and After

The first years after independence were exhilarating. Anything and everything seemed possible. The people were there ready to make it happen. Moreover, at that early stage of the worldwide process of decolonisation, the means were there too.

Uganda was not the first British colony in Africa to be free. Nigeria and Ghana in West Africa had got there first. But donor fatigue had not yet set in among the aid-giving countries of the West. And with the cold-war raging, the Soviet Union was still competing fiercely for influence among the newly emerging nations.

We were quite unscrupulous about it. If we needed something we went to the Americans to ask for the cash. They demurred, but we told the Russians that the West was anxious to get ahead of them. Then we went back to the Americans to tell them that unless they got there quickly, the Russians were prepared to take over the whole project, complete with 'technicians,' who would doubtless devote themselves to undermining the whole western position. We usually got what we wanted.

In reality communism had no attractions for Uganda. Nevertheless to maintain this appearance of balance, we were quite prepared to send up smoke signals that confused everybody including ourselves. In the hurly-burly of independence, I found myself temporarily in charge of the Ministry of Information, Broadcasting and Tourism.

My Minister, a cousin of Obote, concerned himself mainly with setting up a television service and was happy to leave the rest to his civil servants. He had been bribed by a pantomime American entrepreneur, who had brought a lot of secondhand TV equipment from a derelict station in Guam (including cameras that would pan, but would not tilt, so that if a speaker in a discussion programme got up to make a point, the camera remained focused on his stomach until somebody fetched a book to put under its front legs).

Obote and his henchmen were fascinated by television. Every ministerial pronouncement was delivered from the TV studio alone, effectively to an audience of about three hundred Indians, who were the only ones rich enough to buy the indifferent black-and-white Japanese TV sets, for which the American had been given a five-year monopoly of importation as part of his deal with the Minister.

As a result, radio, which penetrated to virtually every household in the country and should have been an essential instrument for nation building, was neglected by its new masters. Our only instruction was to ensure 'balance' in its news broadcasts between East and West.

We could not spare the time to write the news bulletins ourselves so we took our instructions to mean that we must broadcast alternate items from Reuters and from the Czech News agency, which, at that time, was peddling only the extreme Moscow line.

This must indeed have been confusing for unsophisticated listeners. It was the time of the Cuban missile crisis. Reuters faithfully recorded the efforts of President Kennedy to persuade Kruschev to withdraw. Two minutes later, the same newsreader (sometimes including me when we were short of staff), would shift gear. 'The Imperialist hyena Kennedy', we would intone, 'supported by his lickspittle lackeys in London' would never be able to destroy the peace-loving Cuban forces, backed up by the Soviet Union, the greatest democratic power that the world had ever known.

Had Mr Carruthers heard the relish which we managed to inject into that 'lickspittle lackeys', he would not, I am sure, have approved. But this was only the froth on the most good humoured and exciting honeymoon period I personally have ever known.

Maybe freedom is always just such a heady cocktail. South Africa's sea-change must have been the same (The New Hebrides, as we shall see was more despairing, but there were special reasons for this).

All I know is that in Uganda, at that time, it would really have been possible to say, with the poet, 'Bliss was it that dawn to be alive, but to be young was very heaven'.

But at the same time the clouds were gathering. The army was becoming more and more arrogant, especially after the mutiny. My boss, Frank Kalimuzo, the head of the Civil Service, who was later murdered by Amin, was on more than one occasion pushed off the platform by Nubian army officers, who lounged in the front seats of parliament in their bemedalled uniforms, or staggered drunkenly out of the Kampala Club with their temporary girl friends under their arms.

Instead of confronting the root causes of this shift of power, we tried to deal with its symptoms. At meetings of the civilian heads of Ministries (by now 95% African) we decided that, to outface the military morons, we must ourselves have uniforms, as the departing colonialists had before us.

Session after session was taken up with deciding on appropriate badges of rank and exactly where they would be placed. An emissary was despatched to Europe and came back with a collection of old German cavalry swords. The government tailor measured us all up for a confection that would not have disgraced the cat-walks of Paris.

When some, including me, demurred at ourselves having to pay for these monstrosities, it was decided that the uniforms themselves would belong to the government, and would be stored at the Prime Minister's office and loaned out to us all for use only on ceremonial occasions.

I never wore mine. By the time the exercise was complete, three years after independence, I was on my way out. Very probably somewhere in the ruined Uganda government offices, there still hangs one Permanent Secretary's uniform, six-foot-seven officer for the use of. I can't imagine it would be much use to anyone else.

Too often this Ruritanian mode was also carried over into what should have been serious moments of nation building. The first anniversary of Independence was a disaster. Far too many people were invited to a ceremonial reception at the new Parliament building. A huge queue formed at the front entrance. An hour after the scheduled opening we were still there.

Finally and very slowly we shuffled sweating into the vestibule, where each was handed an unopened bottle of warm champagne, without a glass. Equally slowly we wound our production line through the building, unable to talk to anyone, to pause or to sit down. Finally we were expelled explosively through the back entrance like corks from the bottles which we still clasped to our bosoms. Drinking hot champagne from the bottle in the African sun is not an experience which many of us would wish to repeat.

There seemed indeed to be a jinx on these annual independence celebrations. By the third year, plots and counter plots had begun to bubble. As Obote's official limousine drew away from the national stadium, a line of machine gun holes ripped into the body work at head height.

Obote, however, was unhurt. He had prudently stayed at home. So too was the Vice-President, who was occupying the limousine in his place. He was lying prone on the back seat, having drunk rather too much in the heat of the day.

Life was getting dangerous. First the Kabaka was driven out of his palace when Obote suspended the constitution and appointed himself life President. Then Idi Amin, who had done Obote's dirty work for him, but was himself about to be arrested for smuggling gold across the Congo border, took advantage of Obote's absence at a Commonwealth Conference in Singapore and mounted a *coup d'état* of his own.

Idi Amin was a phenomenon. A huge rounded figure, against whose backside I had often pushed in the scrum as a fellow member of the Uganda rugby team, he was perhaps the first real primitive to seize power in a modern state. In the West, throughout his six years of absolute rule, he was often made out to be a joke. Certainly he seemed to have no sense of his own absurdity. He allowed himself to be filmed haranguing his cabinet of near-illiterate army officers. 'You must all work hard' he thundered, whereupon the camera focused down to a Minister's note pad, where 'WERK HAD' was printed in wobbly capitals, before the Minister broke off to poke his pencil into his ear to dislodge some troublesome wax.

Commentators attributed this grotesquery to Amin's own lack of education, or even to the effects of syphilis. In truth, however, Amin was no more and no less than a peasant, the descendant of one of Emir Pasha's Sudanese soldiers, with all the cunning, rough humour and cruelty of his kind. Certainly he had enough intelligence to realise that power really does come out of the mouth of a gun, provided it is used ruthlessly enough.

Nobody knows how many people he killed during his reign of terror. The dead were sometimes left where they fell, and the piles of Amin's victims were often confused with the half-buried skulls of the even greater terror that came after him, when Obote came back to take his revenge.

Today the only tangible reminder of Idi Amin in Kampala is a half-finished mosque, built on the hill where Lugard first set up his Maxim gun. Amin did his best to superimpose Islam on mainly Christian Uganda. He murdered the Protestant Archbishop, running him over repeatedly with an army truck until his remains became unrecognisable.

Amin's Islamic fervour stemmed partly from his Sudanese background, but probably owed more to the support given to him by Colonel Ghadaffi of Libya. When Amin first ousted Obote, he had relied very largely on help from Israel, which provided military training to replace the despised British (Amin had by that time appointed himself Field Marshall Idi Amin Dada C.B.E. ('Conqueror of the British Empire')).

Soon, however, he grew tired of the Israelis and toured the middle-east under Ghadaffi's tutelage offering to lead Ugandan troops to dislodge Israel from the Golan Heights. He also planned a memorial to Hitler in Kampala and sent a message to the UN Secretary General saying that Hitler, like Idi Amin himself, was a much maligned man.

The great mosque, rising proudly in the face of the Protestant and Catholic cathedrals, was intended to stand as Amin's memorial for a thousand years. Unfortunately, however, it had to be abandoned when the huge minaret began to sag visibly to one side. Its lopsided profile is now known, appositely enough, as 'Amin's last erection'.

In the end Amin overreached himself. As usually happens with dictators, he found that the only way to keep his subjects happy was to give them someone to hate, like Hitler and the Jews. Amin found this national enemy in the 30,000 Asians who still controlled ninety percent of Uganda's trade and who could plausibly be condemned as the exploiters of Uganda's poor.

In a display of what they believed to be generosity, but was in fact an example of post-colonial arrogance, London had given these Asians British passports, rather than insisting that they become citizens of Uganda, where most of them were born.

No-one dreamed that they would use those passports to come to Britain, or be forced to do so. (This was before the days of mass commonwealth immigration.) The assumption was that their British citizenship would protect them where they stood. No-one, it was implied, would dare to molest the holder of one of those stiff blue booklets in which Her Britannic Majesty 'requested and required all those whom it may concern to allow the bearer to pass freely, without let or hindrance and to afford the bearer such assistance and protection as may be necessary.'

Amin however thought little of such requirements. He and his sinisterly named 'State Research Bureau' (in other words his murder squad) made a speciality of 'letting and hindering' everybody. To him the Indians were an ideal target. They were exploiters; their expropriated businesses could be given to his officers to help them forget that they had not been paid; their expulsion would show the British who was boss.

In London we sat around the Foreign Secretary's table (I had by that time become a British civil servant and a minor cog in the smoothly purring Foreign Office machine) and wondered what to do. The Under Secretary in charge of relations with Africa set the scene for us. 'It is evident' he said with patrician disdain 'that President Amin is not a gentleman. He should not be treated as such.' He could say that again.

The expulsion of the Asians led directly both to the ruin of Uganda and to the collapse of Amin's army. Senior Officers were given the sugar factories, the cotton ginneries, the coffee hulleries, the breweries and the department stores. Junior officers and sergeants got the little bush duukas with their treadle sewing machines.

None of them had the faintest idea how to run a business or interest in doing so. For them the store rooms of their newly acquired businesses were a treasure trove, to eat if it was eatable or drink if it was drinkable, to pass on to relatives if they so desired, or, in the last resort, to be sold and the proceeds used to support the life style to which their new owners wished to become accustomed.

Those who were given the coffee factories and cotton ginneries complained to Amin that their products could neither be eaten nor drunk nor sold within Uganda. His response was to set up the Whiskey Run. The sole remaining Boeing 707 of Uganda Airlines (there had been two, but one landed on a road in Rome by mistake for the airport runway) was pressed into service to carry coffee and cotton to Britain. On return the proceeds were used to buy duty free whiskey and cigarettes, which Amin, in his new guise as an Islamic fundamentalist, pretended he knew nothing about.

The new apostles of conspicuous consumption found that they had little enthusiasm (or perhaps strength and fitness) left for soldiering. It was one thing to round up groups of 'rebels' and beat them to death with pickaxe handles. It was quite another to fight a proper war.

After one false start, a group of Uganda exiles, supported by regular troops of the Tanzanian army, invaded Uganda from the south and, after a short campaign, occupied Kampala. The lamp of freedom flared briefly again.

For the best part of two years, under the disapproving eye of the Tanzanian soldiers, a succession of pantomime figures appeared in quick succession, danced across the stage and disappeared again into the shadows. One short-lasting President was a Muganda lawyer, the son of a well-loved Canon in my father's church. He had once admitted to me that he had taken thirteen years to pass his Bar examinations in London. In those unreconstructed days each stage of the exams could be taken separately as many times as the candidate wished. Godfrey's technique had been to prepare the answers to five possible questions on criminal law, contract, tort or real property, whatever happened to be his current target. He would then present himself at the examination hall and glance briefly at the test paper. If the questions were unfamiliar, he walked out. If he was lucky, Bingo; he was through to the next stage. His technique as President of Uganda was rather the same.

Soon, however, the shadows closed again. A supporter of Milton Obote (who was still hiding in exile in Tanzania) grabbed power. Obote was, of course, no stranger to the gerrymandering of elections. His surrogate was instructed to stage a repeat of the Independence elections of 1962, complete with ballot-boxes, symbols and international observers. When it seemed possible that, despite all precaution, Obote would lose, his henchman took over the counting from the independent commissioners. Obote was reinstalled in the President's palace.

The next five years were grimmer than ever. This time Obote's opponents did not take things lying down. Sporadic fighting continued under a shadowy guerilla leader, Yoweri Museveni, an academic-turned-soldier, who led a rag-tag army of dissident politicians, disaffected soldiers and young orphan boys, most of whose parents had been killed in the last twenty years of fighting.

Obote reacted savagely, as was his wont. A narrow strip of land to the north of Kampala, known as the Luwero Triangle, became a killing ground as desolate as Pol Pot's graveyard in Cambodia. Only a few brave souls clung defiantly to the edges of the triangle. One such was an indomitable lady missionary, headmistress of a girls' school just south of Luwero, where an admirable group of girls learned mathematics, scottish dancing and Christian ethics. This formidable figure entirely outfaced a gaggle of Obote's soldiers up to no good. Faced with her withering tongue, they discharged their rifles into her ceiling and retired frustrated.

During the same bad time, my ninety year-old mother, returning to Uganda to inaugurate a memorial to my father at his cathedral, was stopped at a road block by a drunken northern corporal. Waving his sub-machine gun menacingly across the car he inquired unsteadily, 'Where you come from?' 'From England' replied my mother in her best, 'I am the bishop's wife' tones. 'Uganda much better than England, hey?' challenged the soldier as he fingered his safety catch. 'Well,' said my mother serenely 'It's warmer, I'll give you that,' and before he could work that one out, she waved the driver on with an imperious hand.

During the same visit we were bidden to pay an official call on Obote's wife, a well educated and on the whole sympathetic Muganda lady from the same girls' school at Luwero. As we sat and drank china tea in the drawing room of the former Governor's house, a flock of vultures were tearing at something on the lawn outside. We hoped it was a goat.

Once again, however, Obote overreached himself. Gradually his forces were beaten back by Museveni's encroaching army. For a while complete lawlessness seemed likely to take over.

My former chief clerk, a gentle and harmless old man, who had retired after a lifetime of devoted service to successive governments, was robbed at gun-point, his house burnt down and every piece of clothing, stick of furniture and household utensil either removed or destroyed. I found him sitting on the ground in the ruins. He had nothing, but when I presented him with a Marks & Spencer sweater, he asked us to kneel down and thank God for his goodness.

Pat and I went to stay with the British High Commissioner, in Kampala, looking out over our old home. Automatic rifle firing began in the valley just below us, in pursuit of God knows what vendetta, robbery or revenge. After a while we judged it prudent to get out and under the bed, thus reminding me of a gung-ho member of my service, who had once said that he would not consider his career complete until he could send the Foreign Secretary a telegram saying 'I am dictating this despatch lying on my office floor as the bullets whistle over my head.' He went on to be Governor of the Falkland Islands and got more than he bargained for.

Eventually, however, Museveni took control of the whole country. The attack on Kampala was short but violent. To this day the Ministry of Education building, close to the key strong point of the radio station, has shell holes in its staircase. More innocent people died.

Not that a few shell holes made much difference to Kampala. By that time nothing worked. In the main street the cars drove on the side-walk and the pedestrians kept to the middle of the road. The pot-holes were so deep that if a car had ventured out into the middle it would have grounded. No traffic control was needed, which was just as well as all the traffic lights had been used for target practice. There was virtually no petrol anyway, as Kenya, fed up with not being paid, had imposed a rail embargo.

Well meaning Western aid experts found it difficult to understand, from the security of London or Copenhagen, that you could not telephone anyone in Kampala, as the phone-lines were all down. Nor could you write because no letters were delivered. And even if, by a miracle, a letter reached its destination, no reply could be expected. Civil Servants could not afford to stay at their desks. They had not been paid for months, and even if they had been, it was not a living wage. Nor could a secretary have typed a reply anyway. The typewriters that were not broken had no ribbons, no carbon and no paper.

In our comfortable security, it is hard to realise that the breakdown of civilisation consists as much in the collapse of small everyday amenities as in the great tragedies of life. We went to stay with a friend in Kampala who had had no running water for eight years. He announced proudly that it had been switched on again the previous week. I could have a bath. Unfortunately the electric water heater had been out of commission for a similar period. I foolishly stepped into the water as the hot tap was still running, but then leaped out again with a yell. The water was electrified.

Women students at my mother's Mary Stuart hall at Makerere University lived at the top of a twelve-storey tower block. The lifts had been out of order since their early childhood. There was no water or electric power for cooking. Their families at home could cope in their one-storey shacks with wood-burning stoves. Surrounded by the trappings of civilisation their daughters were helpless. They tried connecting cooking stoves to the lighting circuits and succeeded only in nearly burning the place down. They had not had regular classes for years. Obote regarded students as potential subversives, as indeed they were. The University had been closed for long periods.

Visiting Makerere, or the great government hospital at Mulago, or the formerly trim bungalows of the government servants was a depressing experience for those who remembered how they had been. Some brave souls had soldiered on. Henry, an old friend, belonged to a respected mixed-race family from Buganda and had married Faisi, a delightful teacher from Bugisu. After Amin took over, Henry had escaped and gone to work for the United Nations, where he and his wife and lively family had lived comfortably until, on Obote's return, Henry had been asked to come back and put the civil service together again after Amin had virtually destroyed it.

Throughout the Obote period, Henry had loyally tried to do his job. They had never had enough to live on and two of his four children, for the lack of proper medicines, had succumbed to sickle-cell anaemia and, when Obote was finally expelled, were close to death. Henry's cheerful face was clouded and Faisi was a harder and more bitter person than the bright soul that we remembered.

77

Henry, however, claimed that they were the lucky ones. Benedicto Kiwanuka, the roly-poly lawyer who had been the first Prime Minister of Uganda, was dead. After his party had lost the independence elections he had gone back to the law. Briefly he was Amin's Chief Justice, but soon, when one of his judgements upset the dictator, he was seized in his court room, bundled into the boot of his car by State Research Bureau thugs, taken out into the forest and hacked to death.

Nor was a white skin necessarily a guarantee of safety. During the worst of Amin's terror, two Americans were foolish enough to go to an army barracks to try to verify stories of the killing of soldiers from tribes other than Amin's Nubians. They were not seen again. Allegedly they were tied to drums of gasoline and tracer bullets were fired through them into the drums. When challenged by the American ambassador Amin claimed that they had gone south to Tanganyika, but their car was seen being driven by an army officer. A commission of inquiry, set up at the insistence of the Americans, was forced to drop the case.

All this was Yoweri Museveni's inheritance. The country was in ruins. A huge national debt, left behind by Amin's arms and whiskey-buying sprees and Obote's incompetence, meant that he was totally dependent on reluctant Western aid. His children's army had to be disarmed, disbanded and found other employment. Every petty thief was armed with a Kalashnikov and an endless supply of bullets. With the Indians gone there were few businessmen and entrepreneurs.

Slowly, however, he has rebuilt Uganda, mostly by the sensible expedient of doing nothing. Ten years after his return I revisited the Luwero triangle. Amin's burned-out armoured cars still littered the road. The piles of skulls had been tidied away, but the shells of the houses destroyed in the civil war had mostly been left to rot.

Under the shadow of Kkungu rock, however, a little old lady was hoeing her beautifully-kept banana plot. The garden had belonged to her family for generations. In the attempt to defend it, her husband had been shot by Obote's soldiers. Her son and her daughter were dead from AIDS, the modern scourge of Africa. She was left to look after her three grandchildren who were working behind her with their miniature hoes.

She showed me over her spotless house. A new corrugated iron roof covered the charred walls where the old thatch had burned. Scrawny chickens scratched in the backyard. Even a few defiant Canna lilies lined the path down to a new 'Bulungi Bwansi' road, completed by the villagers the previous week.

She remembered the prophet of Kkungu rock very well. Her husband had been one of the rubber-necking crowd who had gone to listen to his sermons. But she herself had had none of it. 'Such nonsense' she said. 'In those days people were always looking for change. Anyone who promised a bit of excitement would be listened to. Nowadays we know better. I listen to nobody. I just get on with my life and hope that these children grow up healthy.

The enduring strength of Uganda was in that old lady. The land is fertile, the climate benign. If you leave such people alone in such a land, they will pick themselves up, dust-off their lives and start to grow bananas.

It is to President Museveni's credit that he has recognised this latent strength and that he himself is strong enough not to interfere more than he has to. There is plenty to provoke him. He is neither a patient man nor an instinctive democrat. A Constituent Assembly was then trying to draw up a new constitution for Uganda. It was depressing to hear the same old slogans being trotted out by the tribalist zealots.

Museveni has probably favoured development in his own south-western area more than Buganda or the non-Bantu areas of the north. The current shibboleth is therefore 'Federo' (Federation)

'Buganda's money should be spent in Buganda'
'No one should be above the Kabaka'
'How can we take part in a parliament where we are not a majority?'

Oh God, Oh Montreal. Have we really learned nothing?

10

Diplomat: A Minnow in the Whitehall Pond

But by this time Pat and I had moved on. No one threw us out. We were welcome to stay. Until Amin started killing people there was no compelling reason not to go on working in the country where we had spent our lives. The civil servants under Frank Kalimuzo, were mostly new and mostly African. But it never occurred to anyone to count the colour of heads or wonder whether the colonial left-overs were subversives in disguise.

The difficulty was not with colleagues, but with those who hoped to exploit them. An American (or a German, a Russian or a Japanese), would make an appointment to see 'the Permanent Secretary'. But when they found it was me they were manifestly ill-at-ease. 'Is there any chance of seeing the boss?' they would whisper to my indignant African secretary as they left the room. She knew perfectly well what they meant. They hoped to bribe somebody.

If anyone inside Uganda felt uneasy about our staying, it was probably ourselves. The diplomats of the British High Commission were not the only ones who looked askance at the old hands. The dinosaurs felt it too. Unlike the French, who think it perfectly natural to go on holding the levers of power in their ex-colonies, the British are remarkably thin-skinned about the appearance of neo-colonialism. White faces were starting to feel self-conscious.

Besides it was obvious that we couldn't stay forever. Sooner or later, Obote would have us out. And the children were growing up.

80

Soon they would have to go to school. Other former colleagues were making new careers for themselves all over the world.

Some remained peripatetic 'experts' on Africa, a sad and dying breed. Others went off to become academics. One decided to grow water-cress, but made such a mess of it that he had to buy retail from his rivals in order to fulfil his orders. Another remote and powerful figure ended up as a marriage guidance counsellor. He must have terrified his clients out of their wits. He had never before appeared familiar with any human emotion. Some of the best seemed sadly diminished. A much revered boss ended up as an office manager.

One or two joined MI5 or MI6. Meeting them was often a nerve-wracking business. It was unwise to accost a former colleague seen walking slowly down the Mall in London with a newspaper in front of his nose and the remains of a colonial tan. Anyway he was unlikely to answer. Through a small hole in the middle of the paper, he was attempting to maintain surveillance over a 'suspect' on a training course. The fact that he stood out like a light house and was apt to fall over things was apparently not thought to detract from his invisibility.

I personally had a narrow escape. On a visit to my old Cambridge College, the Senior Tutor asked if I had given any thought to what I was going to do next. When I replied that I had sometimes imagined myself as a diplomat, he said that a friend was in charge of recruitment for a specialised branch of the Foreign Office, which he thought I might find interesting. 'Rather like the Diplomatic Service without the cocktail parties', was how he described it.

That seemed fine to me. I was never a great hand at cocktail parties. The difficulty is that, if you are half a metre taller than everyone else in a crowded room, you have very little idea what is going on at chest level. The only way to take part is to straddle your legs like a giraffe at a water hole, or in extreme cases, to kneel down as if it was all a joke and you are pretending to make a passionate proposal to the lady in front of you. On the whole, though, I have found that this does not work, particularly with royalty.

I was therefore happy to attend a series of interviews with an agreeable gentleman in Carlton House Terrace who seemed remarkably well informed about the details of my previous career.

By this time, however, friends had begun to realise that I was being naive and advised me to find out a bit more about what his department actually did. So I asked him.

My interviewer suddenly started to become remarkably vague. 'Well, don't you know' he said 'I'm really not sure, old chap. I'm just the recruiter, you see, and it really is a remarkably *pragmatic* service. I tell you what, though. The final selection board meets next week. Why don't you ask them? I'm sure they'll tell you.'

So the following week I came back to the same building and found myself in front of a panel of amiable gentlemen who chatted gently among themselves about the last week's pheasant shoot.

This gave me the opening I was looking for. At the end of a relaxed and seemingly inconsequential interview, the chairman asked if I had any questions.

'Well, yes,' I said. 'I'm sorry but I don't know very much about what you actually do do. I mean do you shoot anything else except pheasants? Is there any *violence* involved?'

I must have looked an absolute idiot. The chairman raised a bushy eyebrow. The others stared at the ceiling. I was politely ushered to the door. At the end of the week I got a courteous letter saying that although they were impressed by my record, they didn't think I'd be happy in their service.

Whenever thereafter I told that story to tease a member of Secret Intelligence Service (MI6, the so-called 'Friends'), they offered me another drink, or looked at each other with the selfsame expression, as if to say 'we've got a right one here'.

My next try was better directed. The Civil Service Selection Board chooses members of the senior branch of the Diplomatic Service, the Heaven Born. It happened that they were short of middle-grade diplomats that year, and they let it be known that a few selected members of the Colonial Service, the Armed Forces, the professions and the Universities might be considered for what was politely known as 'retreading'. 'Only the very best, of course, old boy' they murmured when I asked if I could apply.

The selection process itself had hardly changed from the wartime War Office Selection Boards, where candidates were sent off to a country-house for three days and watched to see how they handled a knife and fork. Added to this, however, were some formidable individual and group tests of intelligence.

The first was a paper exercise involving the selection of a supposed centre somewhere in the Midlands for a new social service project. We were expected to master a massive file full of conflicting economic, logistical, social and political aspects of the problem. We were given only a limited time to come to a considered solution and to write a recommendation to our imaginary minister, who, we were told, was to present it to Cabinet that same evening.

I made a complete hash of this. In my legal days I had been taught that the one essential was to miss out no relevant piece of evidence, the exclusion of which might give grounds for an appeal. When the deadline arrived on this occasion, I was still trying to master the details and had written no form of recommendation. Had the exercise been for real my master would have gone naked and briefless in front of his colleagues. I had yet to learn that the perfect brief, ready one minute too late to slip into the Minister's hand as he walks into the House of Commons to defend his supposed policy, is worse than no brief at all.

However, when it came in the selection process to oral discussions of practical problems arising from this imaginary project, I did better. Not all our group found this so easy. One academic with a PhD from Göttingen University, was asked to propose the division of a building to be used for this social service project, so that half could be used for girls' courses and half for boys'. He managed so to split the accommodation that, on the girls' side, there were nothing except stand-up urinals. What's more, even when the difficulty was pointed out to him, he failed to see that there was a problem, which made one wonder how he had been spending his time at Göttingen.

Nor did I fall into the trap of one unfortunate young man I met later when, in due course of time, I myself became chairman of the Foreign Office selection board. Candidates were always asked to list their interests and hobbies and there was a temptation to make ourselves sound as interesting as possible.

This unfortunate claimed that his main passion was flying gliders. Having done the same for a large part of my own life, this was a gift for my interview with him.

The Chairman is supposed to be an avuncular figure (unlike the psychologist and the junior civil servant on the panel whose purpose is to test the candidate's emotional and intellectual stability to destruction and beyond). It was always revealing to give nervous young candidates their head in a discussion of things that really turned them on. So I asked him from which gliding club he flew.

He blushed, thought for a bit and said 'Caterham'. I thought this a bit odd. There is no airfield at Caterham. So I probed further. It finally transpired that he had a friend who was a glider pilot and lived in Caterham. The candidate had been offered a flight with him, but had unfortunately never got around to it. As a major passion this seemed a trifle meagre and he was not selected for the Diplomatic Service.

When it was my own turn, however, the Chairman had asked me to explain Idi Amin. This was a gift and he could hardly get a word in edgewise for the rest of the interview. The panel must have concluded that the only way to shut me up was to let me in.

Being turned into a Diplomat, however, was not so easy. In those days it was a painful and often demoralising experience. The few of us who had got through the selection board approached our new career with dewy-eyed hope. Although we had been relatively big fish, we knew that the ponds we came from were small.

We now thought we had made it to the big time. We cherished the naive belief that, albeit we were back again to being minnows, we were approaching the calm centre of the world, where wise decisions were being made by super-intelligent beings, based on the unhurried digestion of the best information and the most comprehensive analysis. In Uganda we had known we were in a mess. In Whitehall we hoped for perfection.

The reality was a shock. The British Foreign Office is full of dark little cubby-holes, disgracefully furnished and still heated, in my early days, by buckets of coal carried up worn stone stairways by creaking servitors. There crouched two or three threadbare secretaries (everyone in the diplomatic service is a 'secretary' of some sort, from the 'Secretary of State' down through the 'Parliamentary Under-Secretary', and the 'Permanent Under-Secretary' the 'Deputy Secretaries', the 'Assistant Under-Secretaries', the 'First, Second and Third Secretaries', to the real secretaries who are curiously called 'Personal Assistants'). From dawn to dusk, they wrestled with the machinery of government, desperately trying to get through on telephones, which no-one answered (because the operators were at lunch), or drafting finely turned phrases which no-one had time to read.

Their deathless prose was then dumped on some unfortunate Minister overnight for him to initial off, and finally telegraphed through creaking hand-cypher machines as instructions to bemused Ambassadors, who were apt to complain that no-one in London had the faintest idea what was going on in the field.

It was difficult after a few years of this not to become cynical. In an idle moment a few of us concocted what we chose to call the 'Stupidity Theory of History' (as an antidote to the 'Conspiracy Theory'). This was based on the assumption that all really important decisions in history were taken by mistake, by harassed and overtired people, on the basis of inadequate information, imperfectly digested. In other words we knew we were still in a mess.

There was plenty of evidence for this. Somewhat later in my career, I was charged with writing daily reports for the British Cabinet on the progress of a war between India and Pakistan, over the creation of the new state of Bangladesh. Not unnaturally this worried our masters because, for the first time, two Commonwealth countries were fighting each other, using the same tactical doctrines and manuals that their respective commanders-in-chief had both imbibed at the same Staff College course in Camberley.

Things were hectic in the Foreign Office. Not only had we to report on the progress of the war, we also had to make arrangements to remove British subjects from out of its path. The Joint Intelligence Committee of civil servants held daily meetings to decide what was going on.

This was difficult. Some of our information, for example on airfields in the sub-continent, came creaking out of the woodwork from old boys who, it later turned out, had not been there since Partition in 1947. Different branches of HMG told us different things, (as indeed happened more damagingly before the Falklands war, when some said that the Argentinians were going to invade – others that they definitely weren't). The Committee somehow had to make sense of all this conflicting advice and even when it was agreed on what was happening, someone had to reduce it all to writing and submit it to our masters before close of play on the same day. One morning having dictated a report on the most recent developments, I was called away without having time to read what the typist had produced. Unfortunately she had misread her short-hand outlines and instead of recording, as I had intended, that there was an 'Indian armoured brigade' in the north of Bangladesh, the version which went unhindered to Ministers, reported that there was an 'Indian armed frigate' in the same position.

When, too late, I noticed the mistake, I cowered under the table waiting for the rockets to fall. The significant fact about my gaffe, however, is that no-one noticed. So, when the British government's papers on the Bangladesh war are eventually released under the 30-year rule, historians will be left to puzzle out how an Indian warship can have been transported a thousand miles overland through enemy territory. Presumably they will conclude that the Ganges floods must have been unusually severe that year.

Our second urgent task, the evacuation of British subjects, we tackled by setting up an emergency centre, full of maps, arrows and evacuation routes, all represented by Foreign Office red tape which showed up well on the television cameras when they came to inter-view us.

There had been a hiccup in the early stages when I attended a briefing session in the great conference chamber of the Ministry of Defence in Whitehall. Seated around the massive pear-shaped table were enough brass hats to sink an aircraft carrier and two shrinking Foreign Office First Secretaries, somewhere near the bottom.

The Air Marshall in charge was handed an impressive wand with which to demonstrate the evacuation routes on a huge wall-map. The idea was that British subjects would be encouraged to congregate at the centres of population in Pakistan and from there be transported by RAF planes and civilian charters away from the battle zone.

All went well while the Air Marshall was describing the proposed evacuations from Karachi and Lahore. When it came to the third congregation point, however, (the new Pakistan capital of Islamabad), there was an embarrassed pause. The wall map had been printed sometime between the partition of India and the move of the Pakistan Government to its new home near the Afghan border. Islamabad was not on it.

For a while, junior brass hats rushed around like the White Rabbit muttering 'Islamabad, Islamabad, Islamabad', for all the world as if they were late for an appointment with the Duchess. Eventually however, the Air Marshall got fed up with moving his wand in aimless circles round the map and boomed down the table 'Perhaps the gentlemen from the Foreign Office would care to assist us?' We felt as if we had won the lottery.

Nor, even within our own oppressed circle, did absolute priority always seem to be given to providing the right information at the right time to achieve the right result. The deputy head of my department (always known as 'The Assistant', as if he worked at Harrods), was a stickler. Long after the fashion had been discarded by most of Whitehall, he was always dressed in a black coat and striped trousers. When he left the Office he carried with him his bowler hat and immaculately furled umbrella, which could never, under any circumstances, be opened. He clearly did not know what to make of the reformed colonialist who was given into his reluctant charge to lick into diplomatic shape.

One day I drafted an Answer to a Parliamentary Question. This is a ritual designed to allow the Minister to answer in the House, with a minimum of information or embarrassment, for the sins of omission or commission which the Opposition of the day wish to father upon him. The PQ usually asks him, or her, to list something, or explain something, or justify or excuse something.

By comparison with Questions for the Prime Minister, other cabinet colleagues have a relatively easy time of it. By convention a large number of the PQs directed at the Prime Minister ask him to list his engagements for next Tuesday week (or whenever).

This is not because MPs wish to hear him say that, with luck, he will be at home with his wife (or even not with his wife). The sting is invariably in the Supplementaries, where, by the same convention, the MP who asks the Question has the right subsequently to demand that the Prime Minister tell the House why, instead of wasting his time at home on Tuesday, he does not plan to visit the shop of a constituent, where a road widening scheme has severely hampered the said constituent in the pursuit of his lawful business.

This is a nightmare for the Civil Servants, who not only have to draft suitable Answers to the Question itself, but also to all possible Supplementaries which the Honourable Member might be preparing to bowl to the PM off the back of his hand. This involves nothing short of a psychological profiling of the Member concerned, to pre-guess what particular bees he might currently have buzzing in his bonnet.

The convention, however, has it that Ministers other than the PM have to be asked rather more straightforward Questions and that Supplementaries have to be at least peripherally relevant. Moreover if the questioner strays outside the departmental responsibilities of the Minister concerned, he can always be referred to 'My Right Hon. Friend the Minister for So-and-so', whereas the Prime Minister is fair game on all topics.

In addition, on occasion, a PQ is not asked by a member of the party in opposition, but is put down in collusion by a supporter of the Minister's own side. This enables the Foreign Secretary to 'thank my honourable Friend for his expression of confidence in Her Majesty's Government's handling of the crisis in Ougadougou'.

In preparing answers to all these questions, however, a vital part of the civil service desk officer's work is to collect together and make copies from Hansard of all previous PQs on similar subjects and attach them to the back of his drafts. The last thing that any Minister wants is to be told that he said something entirely different three months (or three years) ago.

The most satisfying of all Answers is not to answer at all, but to say 'I refer the Honourable Member to the Answer which I gave on the 30th of September 1994.' The implication that the honourable member has not done his homework is usually enough to shut him up, at least until the end of Question Time.

On this occasion I had prepared what I thought was an immaculate Answer. The Honourable Member was referred to 'The Speech by My Rt. Hon. friend the Minister of State' (in which, as it happened, the junior Minister concerned had said no more than that 'The policy of Her Majesty's Government is absolutely clear', meaning that we were waiting on events and had not yet made up our minds).

By way of possible answers to supplementaries I referred to 'the White-heat of the technological revolution' (this was in the days of Harold Wilson's first Labour Government), and derided the fact that the opposition Tories had no policy of their own (*plus ça change, plus c'est la même chose*).

Then, with great care, I attached behind the drafts, all the extracts from Hansard, identified by red slips of card, known as 'flags', which were securely attached to the back of each cutting by standard issue pins. Finally I put the drafts in a black Foreign Office despatch box (red ones were for Ministers only, just as green ink could only be used by Ambassadors), summoned one of the creaking messengers, and sent it off to my boss.

There were still hours to spare before the PQs were due to reach the Parliamentary Unit (whose main task was to put them in a special leather folder, to which the Minister could refer negligently as he stood before the House, pretending that he had just produced the answers out of his own head). I was conscious of a job well done.

I was thus unprepared for the Assistant's lugubrious tones when he called me half an hour later. The telephones happened to be working that day, but this did not brighten his evident mood of ancestral despair.

'This Answer, you know. It's no good – no good at all.'

'I'm sorry' I replied, thinking that I had made some dreadful mistake and referred to 'the Honourable Member' (from the opposite front bench) as 'my Honourable Friend' (a member of the same party as the Minister) or still worse as 'my Right Honourable Friend' (a member of the Privy Council). 'What's the matter? Shall I get it re-typed?'

'No, No, No,' he replied pettishly 'It's the pins. Surely you know how to put pins in the flags?'

A candid reply would have been that I had never previously given the matter any careful thought, but I was still a probationary diplomat and asked, humbly enough, to be shown the true and only way.

'You must always remember' he said, kindly enough, 'that, after you have pushed the pin through the cutting and the flag behind it, the point must then be brought back to the top of both papers and finally buried between the Hansard extract and the flag.'

I brushed aside the thought that the point of this manoeuvre could only be to prevent some senior official from pricking his haemophiliac thumb, and promised that, if he would return the box to me, I would ensure that all pins were removed and replaced shipshape and Bristol-fashion.

This I did, and sent the box off again hoping for the best, with apologies to the ancient messenger, whose arthritis was giving him hell. Ten minutes later, the voice on the telephone sounded extremely tired.

'This is absolutely hopeless I'm afraid. I'm going to have to do it all again myself.'

'Why, what's the matter now?'

'The pins – you're supposed to put them in from right to left. You've pinned them from left to right'.

I began to realise that being incurably left-handed was more of a handicap to the diplomatic life than I had hitherto imagined. It was also evident I still had a lot to learn.

There were of course, compensations. One of the main ones was that, once we got past pin-fetishists and the man-traps of parliamentary nomenclature, my diplomatic colleagues were, if not all Rolls Royce minds, at least something between a Jaguar and a Rover. One or two of them, indeed were Ferraris. Most of them had Oxbridge degrees in languages or history and had come to the Foreign Office straight from University. Occasionally this put them at a technical disadvantage alongside, for example, their German counterparts, who nearly all had post-graduate degrees in law or science, or the Americans, many of whom were Masters of Business Administration and apt coyly to admit, when discussing some minor point of the disarmament negotiations, that they had written a book on it.

But this was not necessarily a disadvantage for the British diplomats. Their fine and flexible minds were often able to go straight to the issue and suggest solutions which met the immediate need, even if they did not do much to solve the underlying problem.

The classic example of this was the famous resolution 242 of the United Nations. The world body was deadlocked on how to tell the Israelis to get out of land which they had seized in the six-day war. The Islamic nations insisted that they give up the lot; Israel's friends knew that it was unreasonable, as well as unrealistic, to insist that they abandon Jerusalem. There was endless wrangling over details.

Finally the British suggested that the resolution call on Israel to leave 'territories' occupied during the war. Not 'The Territories', not 'Some Territories', just 'Territories'.

There was immediate and almost unanimous approval The resolution could be interpreted either way. The fact that it solved nothing was not germane. It enabled the United Nations to present a common front against aggression. There was admiring praise for the copyright owners of that fine and fluid instrument, the English language.

About the only thing that fazed my new colleagues was technical jargon. Quite early on I realised that one of the Foreign Office legal advisers was cheating. These specialist officers mostly wanted to be mainstream diplomats. They were as keen as any to win the political argument. This engaging, though arrogant, young man was quite unashamedly doing so by blinding his colleagues with law-speak.

'Under the rule of Rylands and Fletcher', he would intone 'I am afraid there can be no question of our signing this agreement. It's a case of '*de minimis non curat lex*', old boy.' The fact that neither Rylands and Fletcher nor the Latin tag had anything at all to do with the point at issue was unknown to most of his audience, but they did not choose to admit it and instead nodded sagely and remarked that of course they had known it all along.

Taking a leaf out of his book I started peppering my arguments with references to '*Res Nullius*' and '*Res Communalis*' and I found to my amazement that I was beginning to hold my own.

There was a very clear pecking order within the Foreign Office. Some subjects and some departments mattered. Others did not. The high-flyers graduated naturally to the key jobs.

The highest flyer of all was the Private Secretary to the Secretary of State. The Private Secretaries to other Ministers came next, followed by the Head of Personnel and the middle ranking diplomats in charge of the departments dealing with overall Planning, the European negotiations, NATO, North America, Western Europe and the Soviet Union.

Other departments were for the odds and sods; Cultural Relations, Aviation and Marine Department, Science and Technology, the Commercial Departments and the like. I and the other late entrants were clearly among the sods.

Later on when, by a mixture of bloody-mindedness and Buggins' turn, I became Trade Union representative for the late entrants in the First Division Civil Servants Association, I felt it my duty to present to the Head of Personnel some statistics which suggested that the Retreads were not being given a fair crack of the whip. Instead of being steered towards jobs where they could broaden their diplomatic talents and make use of their often substantial administrative experience, they were being used to fill gaps in the less favoured departments.

One able ex-Permanent Secretary from Uganda had been given three commercial jobs in a row and remained, in his middle forties, at the same rank which direct entrants could expect to achieve when they were thirty.

Receiving my protest, the personnel supremo observed kindly 'What I am about to say of course does not apply to you, my dear Andrew, In many ways, you are almost like one of us. But I have to tell you that on the whole the late entrants have been something of a disappointment. They seem to find it difficult to fit in.' I thanked him humbly for his good opinion, but remained with the uncomfortable feeling that I had been outflanked.

The real bottom of the odds and sods league were the departments dealing with the remaining Dependant Territories. By this time the Colonial Office was dead and Mr Carruthers long retired. There were not many colonies left; apart from Hong Kong, most of them were bits of rock that nobody much wanted and could never sustain themselves – Pitcairn, Tristan da Cunha, Aldabra, Farquhar and Desroches; or they were stubborn little groups of people who, for some reason no-one at the Foreign Office could fathom, seemed to prefer to remain British – Gibraltar, the Falklands, Bermuda and the Turks and Caicos Islands.

The Diplomatic Service found it difficult to staff these remaining outposts of Empire or to man the departments responsible for them. A circular went round Whitehall soliciting volunteers and saying that service in the Dependant Territory Department 'should not be regarded as the diplomatic equivalent of the Siberian salt-mines' (a phrase which clearly betrayed what the person who drafted the paper really thought of them).

The trouble was that most diplomats are unaccustomed to administering anything. Ideas are their stock-in-trade and they are good at them. Building a dam, collecting a tax, judging a case or mending a Land Rover is foreign to them. It makes them dither.

Soon after my interview with the personnel head, therefore, I was unsurprised to find myself moved from my attempts to inform our masters about what was going on in India, Pakistan and Bangladesh, and posted instead to the Hong Kong and Indian Ocean Department.

I did not mind. It was promotion. The 'Indian Ocean' part of my responsibilities included some fascinating corners like Seychelles and the Anglo-American base on Diego Garcia, while Hong Kong was the last great challenge of Britain's Colonial Empire.

11

Hong Kong: The Fragrant Harbour

'One Section, double forward, draw enemy fire and locate their position. Two Section give covering fire. Three Section hold firm. MOVE.'

'AIYAH GURKHALI' yelled eight small brown men, as they charged, Kukris drawn, over the bare brown hillside. Eight others fell forward to the prone position, going through the motions of pouring accurate and sustained fire into the massed ranks of the assumed enemy, who fled back in confusion across the river to safety.

'What on Earth are they doing?' I asked the Brigadier, standing with me on the hill-top.

'Practising platoon attacks.'

'Who against?'

'The Chinese army.'

'What Chinese army?'

'The Chinese army they've just defeated.'

Hong Kong was like that. A pimple on the bum of China, as one of my hosts had elegantly put it, it was founded as an act of rampant colonialism in the 19th century. The British wanted a port. They also wanted to punish the impudent mandarins, who dared to challenge the right of British merchants to flood the Chinese market with Indian opium. Successive defeats forced the Emperor of China to cede to Queen Victoria Hong Kong Island and Kowloon, with their incomparable harbour, and later to agree to a hundred years lease of the New Territories.

For seventy years, Hong Kong had been a standard British Colony, with a Governor in a plumed topee and the usual

93

apparatus of bewigged judges, district officers and the Royal Hong Kong police. Until the second world war the first line of Hong Kong's defence had been the power of the British Fleet. Thereafter it was protected mainly by the prosperity brought by the phenomenal energy of its Chinese inhabitants.

True, there had been a few hiccups. During the second world war, Hong Kong was occupied by the Japanese. The fight had not lasted long, though there were over 2,000 Allied casualties. When the Governor and Commander-in-chief, Sir Mark Young, handed over his authority to Lieutenant General Takashi Sakai of the Imperial Japanese army it was the first time that a British Crown Colony had ever been surrendered to the enemy.

Despite the nominal incorporation of Hong Kong into their Greater East Asia Co-Prosperity Zone, it remained in Japanese military occupation, 'The captured territory of Hong Kong'. In the process the Japanese conquerors treated Hong Kong as badly as they did anywhere else in Asia. The Kempeitei secret police behaved, as always, with senseless cruelty. The British were imprisoned and the Japanese made no attempt to administer the Chinese population fairly, or even efficiently.

Some attempt was made to maintain the trappings of Empire. To this day Government House Hong Kong retains a Japanese tower, built by a 26-year-old army engineer Seichi Fujimora. But the military governor evidently never felt comfortable there, and preferred instead to live in Repulse Bay under the protection of the Kempeitei.

Despite their humiliation, however, the British, as usual, kept their end up by pretending that what had happened had not happened. While Sir Mark Young was interned in Manchuria, his Deputy, Frank Gimson, continued to hold court in Stanley Prison. 'The British Government' he announced, 'is still in being and functioning except where prevented by the Japanese'.

So when, after Hiroshima, the Japanese gave up, Gimson was on hand to ensure that there was no nonsense about implementing the decision of the Allies that territories should be surrendered to those who had liberated them. In Hong Kong's case this could have meant the Chinese, since Chiang Kai-shek was, at least in theory, the Supreme Allied Commander of the Hong Kong War zone. This was not merely a theoretical possibility. Efforts by the French in

Indo-China and by the Dutch in Indonesia to regain control of their ex-colonies proved in the end both bloody and vain.

But Gimson would have none of it. He declared himself Acting Governor and 'representative of His Majesty King George VI in the British Crown Colony of Hong Kong'. So when an exhausted Mark Young returned from his Manchurian prison, Whitehall was able to maintain with a straight face that he had never relinquished his Governorship, but had merely been on 'extended leave'.

And this fiction is sustained to this day. In the great hall of Government House, under the Japanese tower, there hung, at least until the hand-over to China, the pictures of successive 'Governors of Hong Kong'. There was not a Japanese (still less a Chinese) face among them. Instead one pro-consular photograph bears the bland inscription 'Sir Mark Young, Governor of Hong Kong 1941–46', and no nonsense about it.

The Gurkhas, practising their platoon attacks on the bare hills above the Shau Chan river, were carrying on the same tradition. The fact that (as the Brigadier admitted to me in the Mess after-wards) had the Chinese army really crossed the river into Hong Kong, the Gurkhas' only hope would have been to run like hell, and me and the Brigadier with them, was not the point. Nor was it relevant that the five million population of Hong Kong was only half of one percent of the one billion Chinese across the border. The Gurkhas were there to show the world that the British were in Hong Kong and intended to stay.

Occasionally we had complex and highly secret discussions about the size of armed forces that were appropriate for our defence of the Colony. The ultimate risk was that the Chinese government would decide to take over Hong Kong by force. If they had done so, there was very little that we could have done to stop them. The combined weight of the Chinese army would have swept aside any force that we could possibly have put in the field. But equally we could not leave Hong Kong undefended. It was abso-lutely necessary to have a force in being to act as a deterrent, as well as to prevent an uncontrolled influx of refugees and deal with any possible civil disturbances in the Colony.

After prolonged analysis at the Ministry of Defence in London and the Headquarters of the Commander British Forces in Hong Kong (who later became the splendid Field Marshall, Lord

Bramall, the Chief of Mrs Thatcher's defence staff), we decided that the situation required four army battalions, one squadron of RAF helicopters and two naval frigates.

The four battalions I could understand. They were all that the British and Hong Kong Governments between them could afford. But it took me some time to figure out exactly the need for one squadron of helicopters. It seemed to be either too little or too much. I fretted about this unnecessarily until a friend in the Ministry of Defence patiently explained the realities to me.

It seemed that one squadron was laid down as the minimum command of an Air Commodore. The RAF flag officer lived in great comfort on Hong Kong island. Besides, said my friend the whole structure of Service promotions depended on no single brick being removed from the pyramid near the top. To abolish an Air Commodore's post in Hong Kong would unfairly damage the legitimate aspirations of a host of deserving officers. At least one squadron, therefore, it had to be. There was no money for more.

All this made good sense to those who tried to juggle the political, military and economic realities of a complex situation, where fail safe solutions were never available. But it still niggled us that, in terms of men, machines and bullets, the sums just did not add up. Who, exactly, were they designed to fight?

It is the nature of politics to ignore unpalatable facts, but we felt the need of some sort of justification. The Ministry of Defence, however, were happy to duck out of this one. Their job was to provide, train, administer, equip and, if necessary, to fight the armed forces. Scenarios were for diplomats to think about. We scratched our heads.

Then some Sinologist had a bright idea (it was not for nothing that the best of the Heaven Born found their way into the Foreign Office Planning Staff.) In the past China had often broken up into factions under rival barons. Supposing this was to happen again and a Cantonese war-lord in Guangdong (China's southern province) was to cast envious eyes on the riches of Hong Kong on his border? It was true that he would still have sixty million Cantonese under his control against Hong Kong's five. But even this disparity would shorten the odds dramatically by comparison with a billion. And if such a warlord did try to invade Hong Kong, it would surely be in a situation of civil war in his own country. Anyway he would have to keep back the major part of his forces for defence against a possible invasion by a central government in Beijing.

Moreover the land border between Hong Kong and China is only about fifteen miles long. The Cantonese warlord would not have much of a navy. He could not attempt a seaborne landing. Four British battalions would fill the land gap nicely, supported by the helicopter squadron.

The fact that nobody in their senses thought that China was about to fall apart into rival satrapies, was not the issue. Politics is the art of the possible and in our personal, as in our public lives, we often have to survive by finding reasons for what we are going to have to do anyway. Nor is it a new discovery in the age of nuclear deterrence that weapons and armed forces are not actually made to be used – if they have to be, then the cause is lost anyway. Their purpose is to provide enough confidence to maintain the status quo and send clear enough signals to avoid the need for their use.

So, in truth, the Gurkha platoon were doing what was required of them. They were certainly being watched from across the river. Chinese sentries with high-powered binoculars were posted at hundred metre intervals all the way along the frontier. And those sentries too were there for more than one purpose.

Their main function, like the armed forces of most totalitarian powers, was not to keep the enemy out, but to keep their own people in. Not long before, during the Chinese Cultural Revolution of the sixties, a sizeable proportion of the population of Canton had tried to escape from the socialist paradise to the capitalist hell-hole of Hong Kong. The British authorities then operated a 'Touch Base' policy. If a refugee could make it to the urban areas of Hong Kong, then he, or she, was 'home' and could stay. If they were tagged on the way from the border to the town, then, like a grown-up version of 'French and English', they could be sent back where they came from. This was mocked as an example of a British obsession with sport but the underlying truth was that we could not afford the potential unrest of sending snatch squads into the teeming refugee settlements in the city to winkle out newcomers, once they had made it to the bosom of their communities.

Some sort of restrictions had, however, to be imposed on the flow. About half of the whole population of Hong Kong were already refugees from China, living in squatter camps or in horrendous 'Resettlement Housing' blocks, with one room to a family and toilets at the end of the corridor.

A few hundred yards back from the border on the Hong Kong side, the British had built a rudimentary barbed wire barrier known as the Snake Fence. This was intended to provide a back up for the security forces, who could intercept refugees in the Tom Tiddler's ground between the river and the fence, without risking incidents on the border itself.

The area before the snake fence was not a killing ground. Nor was it, as some alleged, a gesture of subservience to China. It was designed simply to control the refugees and prevent Hong Kong from being overwhelmed. Nor was it even particularly successful. Desperate people will find a way around any barrier.

In my time the favourite route was to swim the narrow waters of Hou Hoi Wan (Deep Bay) at the western end of the border, or Taiping Wan (Mirs Bay) to the east. Many Chinese cannot swim, but even that did not deter them. Anything was pressed into service, rafts, boats, inflated lorry tyres, even loose balks of timber. Nor were the refugees deterred by sharks, which occasionally took a limb or even a whole body, still less by Chinese or British patrol boats. They just wanted to get away from China and into the lure of the bright lights.

This attempted mass exodus deeply embarrassed the Chinese authorities. Their guards were vigilant and strangers were discouraged from approaching the border. But even the Red Army can sometimes nod. And those watchful binoculars were not always used as the Chinese authorities intended.

On my first visit to Hong Kong, the police took me to look at the border settlement of Sha Tau Kok. Here the dividing line was not a river, but the village street. The houses on one side of the street were in China, on the other in Hong Kong. The road itself was no-man's-land.

As we crouched on the roof of the Hong Kong police station, we could see across the street a Red Army soldier, gun ready to hand, pointing his binoculars steadily in our direction. But there was something peculiar about his gaze. It seemed to be directed at a point slightly below and to one side of us. We peered over the balcony and realised that what he was really watching was television. An obliging Hong Kong shop keeper had pointed a set across the divide and the defender of the purity of the Chinese empire was engrossed in a capitalist Kung Fu film.

Hong Kong was full of such surprises, some of them pleasant, others less so. The rich Chinese and British Taipans are really very rich indeed. On my first visit, one of them offered to tell me where to buy pearls to take home to Pat at, he said, a very reduced price. These turned out to cost no more than a meagre U.S. $5,000 and I had regretfully to decline the offer.

On the other hand my favourite definition of the good life was, and remains, a lunch party on the luxurious yacht of one of the richest of the shipping tycoons. Our host was geniality itself and asked whether I would like to go water skiing to give myself an appetite for the meal. When I accepted with pleasure, a white-coated steward bent solicitously across my back. 'For your water-skiing boat, Sir' he intoned, 'Would you care for a Johnson or an Evinrude outboard motor?'

I had visions of racks of the things, all custom-built and discarded after each use. I graciously agreed to sample a Johnson.

But underneath this genial surface there were huge problems. One of the most intractable was corruption. Not only were many of the Chinese on the take, not a few of the lordly whites had joined in and were busy making themselves a packet.

A serious problem was in the Royal Hong Kong Police itself, the body on which the whole structure of Hong Kong's law and order depended. The majority of this well trained force were, and remained to the end, admirably disciplined, impartial and impressively effective. But some, and some of the most influential, had undoubtedly succumbed to the money of the drug barons and the pressure of the Chinese Triad gangs.

My Minister, an emotional Welshman with whom I had journeyed out from Britain on his first official visit, found this more than he could stomach. 'Ah no, Andrew boyo' he exclaimed when we were alone after the first day's briefing, 'This goes far too deep. We must do something. I do not at all like what I hear.'

I was a bit surprised that he had heard anything. Overcome with jet lag, he had spent most of the morning's military briefing with his head on my shoulder, fast asleep. At one point in the briefing, General Bramall had switched on the lights and asked if the Minister had any questions. When the Minister replied only with a gentle snore, the general hurriedly switched the lights off again and carried on with his slide show as if nothing had happened. But something in the Governor's description of the newly established Independent Commission Against Corruption (ICAC), must have penetrated the Minister's dream, and he was in a Welsh nonconformist mood of high dudgeon.

The current trouble centred around a British Police Officer who had skipped from Hong Kong just ahead of the Commission's investigators and was now living comfortably and undisturbed in Worthing. He was a middle Fat Cat, not in the leadership of the corrupt faction, which allegedly rested with a group of Chinese police sergeants. But the fact that this European officer was now sitting as a free man in Britain, apparently protected by the authorities, seemed to every Chinese in Hong Kong to prove that ICAC was a paper tiger and that in the end the round eyes would look after their own.

The difficulty was that the crime with which he was accused in Hong Kong was one of having far more money in his bank accounts than he could possibly account for from his official salary. This ignored the general principle of the law that it is up to the Prosecution to prove its case, not the defendant his innocence. But it was defensible in Hong Kong (however much it scandalised the lawyers), because it was almost impossible to get direct evidence of actual corruption. The code of silence among the corrupt would have made a Sicilian Mafia boss feel instantly at home.

But another general legal principle states that if an accused person is to be extradited from one country to another to face trial, then the crime of which he is accused must be an offence both where the trial takes place and in the country where he is found. It seemed unlikely that the British Parliament would pass a special law simply to get our rogue policeman back to Hong Kong. More subtle means were required.

In the end, by a manoeuvre that would have made the legal purists even crosser if they had heard about it, we persuaded another and possibly even more corrupt policeman (who, however, was still in custody in Hong Kong) that it was in his interest to help us. If he broke the code of silence and agreed to testify to specific acts of corruption by his colleague in Worthing, then we would see to it that some of his sins were forgiven him, or at least ignored.

With his help Worthing was duly deprived of one of its leading citizens. He was slipped back to face trial in Hong Kong and the Chinese began to believe that maybe ICAC had some teeth after all.

But even this was not enough for my master. We must do more to clean out this nest of vipers (he had a fine biblical turn of phrase). After much rather irritable telegraphing between Whitehall and Hong Kong, it was agreed that a really tough copper from the London Metropolitan Police would go out to head the Hong Kong Criminal Investigation Department. The Metropolitan Police Commissioner assured us that he had just the man. One of his most respected Police Commanders had already seen service overseas. He was ready to face a new challenge.

I interviewed the gentleman. He looked tough and competent in his neatly pressed Metropolitan Police uniform. I had no hesitation in recommending him to the Governor and in a couple of weeks he was on his way.

Understandably the Royal Hong Kong Police did not much relish the prospect. This was not because they wished to hide the truth. Their top brass were sensible and professional policemen, determined to clean up their stables. But the prospect of a London policeman doing it for them was not palatable. He would have a direct line to Whitehall and his very presence would belie the main tenet of their creed, that to deal with the Chinese you need to know the Chinese, to live with them, to hate them and to love them in the manner of a good policeman on his beat the world over. And undoubtedly, however much the senior policemen may have welcomed the prospect of reform, there were others lower down who had a great deal to hide.

When, therefore, Bob Stokes (not his name) arrived at Kai Tak airport on a Friday afternoon, still shaking with jet lag, he was taken straight to the Hong Kong Police mess and thoroughly cold-shouldered. Then they decanted him at his hotel and left him alone for the weekend.

As far as I was ever able to discover, he went for a walk next morning through the teeming streets of Hong Kong, with their tens of thousands of alien faces and high pitched incomprehensible jabber, the clicking of innumerable Mah Jong counters and the smell of steaming rice. After an hour or two he had had enough, went back to his hotel room and had a nervous breakdown. We had to ship him back to London the next day.

To those who don't know Hong Kong it is not easy to explain the overwhelming impact of that extraordinary place, able to make grown-up policemen break down and cry. Everything conspires to create in the newcomer a sense of disorientation.

Even the first approach to Kai Tak, which was then the only airfield, seems to break every rule. Page one of the Air Pilot's instruction manual says, 'Don't turn low; don't turn slow; don't turn over inhabited areas.' As the Cathay Pacific Tri-star eased down through the mists that shroud the Peak of Hong Kong Island, the first thing that a passenger saw was Chinese washing suspended from a tower-block, apparently higher than the aircraft's wings.

Then a wrenching turn, buffeted by downdraughts from the ridge of mountains above Kowloon, sent the aircraft apparently heading straight for the sea. The Kai Tak runway is built out over the harbour. To the nervous passenger there seemed nothing but water on either side of the aeroplane and nothing in front.

Full of indignation on my first visit. I asked the official who had come to meet me why developers had been allowed to build those tower blocks at the end of the runway. His answer was that the authorities had no say in the matter. Almost the weirdest of Hong Kong's anomalies was the Kowloon Walled City.

For some unfathomable reason, when the Chinese and British Officials had agreed on the lease of the New Territories, they also agreed that a Chinese Magistrate would stay on in the city to exercise the Emperor's residual jurisdiction over his subjects. What that jurisdiction was supposed to be was never defined and the magistrate himself did not stay long in the barbarian city. But for a hundred years successive governments in Peking had insisted that eight acres of land at the end of the Kai Tak runway, belonged to them and to no-one else.

Equally mysteriously the British had never bothered to challenge this assertion and, since the Chinese also never bothered to exercise any sort of control over their eight acres, this meant that there, in the middle of the great city, was an area where there was no law.

No policemen went into the Walled City; no regulations were exercised or enforced there; no one had to ask for a licence to do anything; there were no public utilities, no legal electricity, no water, no drainage and no health services. Or rather there was a health service and an extremely efficient one, but it was entirely unlicensed and unregulated.

The visitor's first overwhelming impression of the Walled City was of huge pink gums and mammoth teeth. Little shops along the outside wall housed Chinese dentists, mostly refugees from Canton. Without a license to practise western medicine they and their equally unlicensed but often highly skilled medical colleagues gravitated to the Walled City, where they advertised their trade with huge plastic dentures, sometimes flashing with electricity illegally connected from the public supply.

To all appearance the Walled City had no exits and no entrances. All the buildings were joined together at the top, so that light and air never penetrated to the tunnels within. Only those who lived at the top, their washing imperilling the jumbo jets' approach, ever saw the sky.

Inside the City was like a glimpse of hell. Alleyways filthy with rubbish and non-existent drainage wound between doors that shut secretively as one approached. A whispering, quite different from the chatter of the open streets seemed to pervade the place. Cables carrying purloined electricity coiled sinisterly overhead. Equally illicit standpipes gushed at alley corners, and overflowed through the slimy green of the stagnant drains.

Few Europeans ventured into the Walled City, and those who did so, mostly wished they were somewhere else. Only one brave evangelist, Jackie Pullinger, lived there permanently. She had felt the call when she got off a boat in Hong Kong a decade before, and had since devoted her life to serving the Walled City's drug addicts, street children, gangsters, pimps and petty criminals.

But though the Walled City was an extreme example of the enigma of Hong Kong, it was not by any means its only manifestation. As far as they were able, the British had imposed their own concepts of morality on an uncomprehending Chinese population. Left to themselves the Chinese had no objection whatever to selling ivory or whale meat, or eating protected scaly ant-eaters or dogs, and could not understand why the Europeans made such a fuss about it all.

Even more incomprehensible to the Chinese was Whitehall's edict that, while the law allowing murderers to be hanged could stay on the colony's statute book, under no circumstances was it ever to be put into effect. The Triad gangs exercised control even inside the maximum security jail at Stanley. They did so by a reign of terror enforced by a regular executioner, who had already been convicted of two murders and reprieved from the gallows and who therefore had nothing further to fear from the courts. Even law abiding Chinese could not understand how this could be. For years the Governor had saved Whitehall's face by finding grounds, after each convicted murderer had been condemned, for exercising the prerogative of mercy on the Queen's behalf. Finally a case arose where it was quite impossible to detect any grounds for clemency. A murder had been committed in horrifying circumstances by a man who undoubtedly knew exactly what he was doing. The Governor asked us in the Foreign Office what to do, and Ministers decided, at last, that the convicted criminal must be allowed to hang.

But a threatened vote of no confidence in the House of Commons led them to reverse themselves. The Governor's decision was publicly overridden and the murderer reprieved by the Queen's prerogative, exercised by her Ministers. A lesser man than Governor Maclehose would have resigned on the spot.

Murray Maclehose (privately, but never to his face known, for obvious reasons, as 'Jock the Sock'), was the last of the great pro-consuls. For ten years, during one of the most crucial periods of Hong Kong's history, he towered, both physically and metaphorically, over the colony.

Unlike his predecessors, who were mostly run-of-the-mill colonial officials, Murray knew exactly where the levers of power lay in London. At an earlier stage in his career he had been Private Secretary to the Secretary of State for Foreign Affairs. He feared no one and always did what he believed to be right. When later I got my own plumed topee, albeit a shabby and motheaten one compared with Hong Kong, I tried always to act like Jock the Sock.

Perhaps Murray's greatest contribution to dispersing the cloud of illusion that shrouded the whole history of Hong Kong, was to reject for ever the myth that 1997 would be just a year like any other. Nobody knew for sure why British Officials in 1897 had settled for a hundred-year lease of the New Territories, rather than a complete cession, like the rest of the colony in Hong Kong Island

and Kowloon. The Chinese would not have been in a position to object to whatever was demanded of them. No rent for the lease was ever requested or paid.

Maybe the negotiators had just had a good lunch, or maybe it was another example of the workings of the Stupidity Theory of history. A hundred years must have seemed like an eternity to those Victorian officials and perhaps they thought that, by 1997, the whole world would be coloured red on the map anyway.

Be that as it may, by the start of the fourth quarter of the 20th century, the end of the New Territories lease was starting to seem uncomfortably close. There was no possibility of hanging on to Hong Kong Island and Kowloon and letting the leased areas of the New Territories revert to China. Although the permanently ceded territory included the harbour, the airport and most of the built-up areas of the city, Hong Kong without the New Territories was just not viable.

One major reason was water. A supreme example of the thrusting capitalism of the colony was the High Island dam. A whole neck of the sea had simply been blocked off. The salt had been pumped out of it and the resulting reservoir filled with fresh water running off the mountain of Tai Mo Shan during the rainy season.

The Hong Kong authorities reasoned that, so long as they controlled directly more than fifty percent of the colony's water supply, they could, if necessary, get by with rationing and the separate salt water system that already flushed the majority of Hong Kong's sewers. But High Island and other reservoirs were in the New Territories, and if they were controlled by a hostile Government in Peking, then there would be no need for the Chinese army to roll across the border. They could simply turn off the water tap.

The trouble was that, as the end of the lease approached, no-one knew what to do about it. In our safe in Whitehall we had a Top Secret file labelled 'The Future of Hong Kong'. Once a year, we took it out, dusted it and, in effect, shuddered and put it away again. So soon after the Cultural Revolution, with Mao Tse Tung still alive and under the influence of his maniac wife, there was no prospect of negotiating a renewal of the lease or of any sensible agreement for safeguarding the future of the five million people for whom we were responsible.

To avoid this conundrum, Murray Maclehose's predecessors had evolved a comfortable theory that merely perpetuated the unreality of Hong Kong's Alice in Wonderland politics. As far as China was concerned, they said, none of the agreements by which they had leased or ceded parts of Hong Kong to Britain had any validity. This was understandable. Successive governments in China had repeatedly denounced the 'Unequal Treaties', which they claimed, with truth, had been extorted from them by force and fraud.

Thus, claimed the apologists for inaction, we were already, from the Chinese point of view, in illegal occupation of Hong Kong and had been so from the beginning. If therefore, we conveniently forgot that the lease of the New Territories was due to expire in 1997 and simply stayed put thereafter, then Peking would have no greater grounds for complaint than they claimed to have already. Q.E.D. The right thing to do was nothing.

Murray Maclehose, however, exposed the hollowness of all this. The Chinese might be able to endure what they regarded as an illegality that they had already suffered for a hundred years. They were certainly not going to accept that we could just ignore the terms of a lease which we ourselves had imposed.

Moreover, like the very existence of the Empire, the whole British position in Hong Kong rested in the last resort on confidence and the political equivalent of the Indian rope trick. The Chinese entrepreneurs of Hong Kong were hugely confident. They were accustomed to investing and getting their money back in ten or even five years. But if, as 1997 approached, nothing whatever had been done to clarify the colony's future, then confidence could simply evaporate and Hong Kong's prosperity with it. Our position would then be untenable. Something had to be done.

By the early 1980s, when the climate in China had relaxed to an extent that made negotiation possible and when Mrs Thatcher was in control in Whitehall, I was long gone from the Hong Kong scene. I have no idea what drove the negotiations then and whether the final 1984 Anglo-Chinese agreement that the whole of Hong Kong would revert to China after 1997 was really the best that could be got.

At first the omens seemed set fair. Deng Xiaoping spoke of 'One Country, two systems' as a guarantee that, after 1997, Hong Kong would remain semi-autonomous as a Special Administrative

Region of China. An independent Commission concluded that in Hong Kong there was an 'overwhelming message of acceptance' of the agreement.

But the massacre in Tiananmen Square in 1989 changed all that. It reversed the confident belief that the changes towards liberalisation in China were unstoppable. With only eight years to go before 1997 there was terrifyingly little time left for China to become accustomed to the idea of a vibrant, democratic, capitalist enclave within its territory.

It was fashionable in the dying months of the Colony to say that the British had betrayed Hong Kong and that the 1984 agreement was a sell-out. But in truth, I don't know what else we could have done. If the option of ignoring, or renegotiating, the deadline of the lease was unavailable, as it was, then some sort of understanding had to be reached, and 1984 was probably about the most favourable moment to do it.

None of us who were involved in the process can be entirely easy in our minds. But maybe we beat our breasts unnecessarily. The Hong Kong Chinese have never been the passive pawns of European diplomacy. There is a wild freedom about them that suggests that, come what may, they will carve out their own destiny.

The last time I was in Hong Kong, I went for a solitary walk around the Peak, high above the city, as the lights began to come on in the harbour and in the shops and hotels of Kowloon across the water. It is one of the most romantic sights in the world, 'A celestial palace in a fairyland' as Wei Yuan, a 19th century Chinese scholar described it.

As the daylight faded over Lantau Island a red deer, disturbed in its own evening stroll, bounded away down through the forest towards Deep Water Bay. Heedless of all the frantic activity and the teeming millions below, the deer was its own master. Such individualism is not characteristic of present day mainland China, but it is of the determined, incredibly hard-working people of Hong Kong. I believe they will survive.

12

Seychelles: The Island of Indecent Coconuts

The Seychelles and Diego Garcia were the other half of my colonial responsibilities in the Hong Kong and Indian Ocean Department. They could not have been more different from the Hong Kong half.

When I went to stay in Government House Hong Kong, I had to watch my step. On one occasion I had left London in a hurry to catch the flight to Kai Tak. My day-old half-eaten sandwiches were still in my briefcase when I arrived at the other side of the world. That evening when I came in to change, I found them laid out in a silver dish on the dressing table, teeth marks and all. They had been elegantly embellished with a thinly cut tomato, a slice of cucumber and a sprig of parsley. Government House Seychelles by contrast had white ants in the walls and a toilet bowl that leaked when you pulled the chain.

The underlying idea was the same – white pillars at the front and a staircase designed for sweeping down, but in my Seychelles guestroom I could hear the Governor turning over in bed, whereas in Hong Kong, when I forgot my handkerchief in the dressing room, it took a five minute walk to get back to it from the Government House dining room.

Both Murray Maclehose in Hong Kong and Bruce Greatbatch in Seychelles had official yachts, but Murray took his guests out into the South China sea for the weekend in the Lady Maureen, a miniature ocean liner, while Bruce had a rotting motor boat which rolled horribly in the Indian Ocean swell.

108

1. (above) The Rwenzori Mountains – 'Mountains of the Moon' (author in foreground).

2. (above) 'My own costume was as prescribed in colonial regulations.'

3. (right) George Rukidi, the Omukama of Toro, with his daughter, Princess Elizabeth.

4. (below) The coronation of Kabaka Mutesa of Buganda ('King Freddie') by Bishop Stuart.

5. (above) Milton Obote, the first dictator of Uganda.
6. (right) Idi Amin, the second dictator.

7. (above) The governor and the traditionalists.

8. (below) Jimmy Mancham (right), first President of the Seychelles; Albert René (left), first Prime Minister and later President after the military coup.

9. (left) Andrew Stuart and J-J Robert, joint Resident Commissioners of the New Hebrides.

10. (below) 'Exhausting negotiations' – Walter Lini, first Prime Minister of Vanuatu on right.

11. (above) 'The Pandemonium' – announcing the death of Alexis Yolou.

12. (below) Promulgating the new constitution.

13. (left) Members of the British and French police forces.

14. (below) Contrasting styles of the Condominium.

15. 'The end of empire' – with HRH the Duke of Gloucester on Independence Day.

The downtown areas of Hong Kong and the Seychelles were both named after Queen Victoria, but they could have been on different planets. In Hong Kong, time and money were everything. Cargo ships unloading in the harbour were turned around faster than anywhere else in Asia. But this was not, at least in those days, because of a superior degree of mechanisation. The ships were unloaded into lighters by frantic coolies who ran down the gangway under fifty kilo loads and then charged back for more.

In Seychelles, time appeared to mean nothing. The main, and only, cross roads in the Seychelles Victoria was adorned with a clock tower proudly, if obscurely, described in the French version of the official Seychelles Guide as a 'Tour de Londres miniature'. In the English version this was translated, into the equally intriguing 'copied from the clock tower in Vauxhall Bridge road, near Victoria Station, London'.

The same official Guide also explained the clock's odd habit of chiming twice, once on the hour and once two minutes later, as being designed 'for those who didn't hear it the first time – but many people don't hear it the second time either'.

Everything in the Guide had to be written in both English and French because, although Seychelles had been British since the end of the Napoleonic wars, it remained obstinately French in its laws, its customs and its religion; and the Seychelles patois was based on French with English add-ons, rather than the other way around.

This persistent francophonie may have owed much to the Governor installed by Napoleon in 1794. Throughout the Napoleonic wars Le Chevalier Quéau de Quinssi kept French and British flags permanently bent to his two flag poles. Six times a British naval squadron appeared and demanded his allegiance. To the earliest arrival de Quinssi gave an impressive document entitled 'The First Capitulation of Seychelles'. He then lowered the Tricolore and hoisted the Union Jack. The squadron commander sailed away satisfied.

As his sails dipped below the horizon, up went the French flag again until the arrival of the next British squadron, whose captain was handed an equally impressive document entitled 'The Second Capitulation of Seychelles'; and so on down to number six.

Even when the Treaty of Paris finally awarded Seychelles to Britain, de Quinssi's ingenuity was not exhausted. He simply changed his name to de Quincy and successfully petitioned London for the continuation of his appointment as commandant; which post he triumphantly retained until his death thirteen years later. I could have done with some of de Quincy's ingenuity later in the Anglo-French condominium of the New Hebrides.

This cheerful confusion of the Seychelles identity was underlined by the Seychellois themselves. A mixture of African, Indian, Chinese, Malaysian, Indonesian and Arab, with a sprinkling of French and English blood, their only settled conviction was that life was made for living and girls for loving. The Official Guide waxed lyrical about the last of these. 'The Seychelloise girl is tender, caressing, ardent, gracious, natural and utterly unvicious. She is French enough to have a good shape, English enough to have good manners, Asian enough to have a touch of the exotic, and African enough to still have the call of the wild in her.' The author would appear to have enjoyed himself.

Fortunately, however, for the peace of mind of their priests, divorce was virtually unknown among the mainly Catholic population. But this was mainly because not too many of the Seychellois bothered to get married in the first place. Their national symbol was a large and incredibly indecent bifurcated nut, known as a Coco de Mer, which grew only on female palm trees in the Vallée de Mai on the island of Praslin. To quote the Official Guide again 'The male tree sports an enormous phallic catkin. It is said that, at midnight the trees march to the sea, bathe and make love with any passing lady before returning to the Vallée de Mai at dawn'. That sounds to me less like a myth than an excuse thought up by Seychellois ladies to explain any small surprises.

When I arrived in Seychelles there was a row going on with London because it was found that, on the 50 Rupee currency notes, designed by a local artist, the palm leaves surrounding the Queen's head intertwined in a way that unmistakably spelled out the word 'Sex'. The notes were hurriedly withdrawn before we could decide who to prosecute for Lèse Majesté.

The Seychellois were mostly the descendants of freed slaves or of the indentured servants of lordly French planters, but their blood-lines had been preserved from more recent dilution by the fact that the islands of Seychelles were incredibly difficult to get to. A thousand miles out in the Indian Ocean from the coasts of Tanzania, the only way of reaching the islands was by the monthly mail steamer. Any tourist who found his way to the Seychelles had no option but to stay there for at least four weeks, and by the end of that, there was a good chance that he or she would have decided to remain indefinitely.

A couple of years before I took over the department, however, all this had changed. Aid funds had been used to build an airstrip on the edge of the coral reef fringing the main Seychelles island of Mahé.

Not too much thought had been given to the consequences of this change. There was a vague idea of developing tourism, but the only clear decision had been to make the tarmac runway of the new airport so narrow that any large jets, other than the British VC10, (which had its four engines conveniently grouped close in to the tail), would have blown stones all over the runway and, hopefully been discouraged from landing again.

An enterprising British company, viewing the new facility and the unparalleled white sands and coral reefs of Mahé, decided that it was the ideal place to build retirement homes for British pensioners. They acquired a whole peninsula and set about erecting a tourist hotel which would be the centre-piece for the pensioners' half-acre bungalows.

They were encouraged in all this by the fact that the vast majority of the Seychellois themselves had absolutely no intention of remaining anything but British. The symbol of the Seychelles Democratic Party, which had won every election, was the Union Jack. Its leader Jimmy Mancham, part Chinese and part African, had married a Scottish girl, and liked nothing better than a stay at the Connaught Hotel in London for a swift tour around the night clubs, preferably paid for by somebody else.

Jimmy's twin passions were poetry and pretty girls. The two were not unconnected, as most of his poems were about girls, or about the equal beauties of his native islands. He was inordinately proud of these literary gems (which in truth resembled the effusions of William MacGonagall 'The worst poet ever to come out of Scotland'). Jimmy however, was apt to recite his own compositions in the aisles of Jumbo jets on long air journeys, to the bewilderment of the fare-paying passengers.

None of this did Jimmy Mancham any harm with his electorate. If anything they were rather proud of him. Indeed the main electoral drawback of his principal opponent, Albert René, may well have been the rather chill air of normality with which he seemed to be surrounded.

When René tried to make political capital out of Jimmy's tempestuous affair with a beautiful Jugoslav (while his wife Heather was on holiday in Britain,) that too backfired. Jimmy called a mass meeting in the centre of Victoria. In his delightful, but ultimately sad autobiography, he described the outcome with pride.

'"Is it not true," I asked, "that our forefathers made it our tradition to be honest and candid in our personal lives, and that we are proud of this tradition?"

"It is true," they shouted, "it is true."

"And did not our forefathers teach us to love beautiful things," I asked, "the men to love the beautiful ladies and the ladies the beautiful men?"

"Yes, yes," roared the crowd, "it is so."

"And you have heard," I went on, "that I fell in love with a beautiful girl, who was married and now my wife is angry."

There was silence while the crowd digested this confession. Then an old lady standing near the platform gave the lead.

"Poor Chief Minister," she said with feeling, "poor Chief Minister."

The late Philip Mondon, a close friend and political colleague, was always quick to seize such opportunities.

"Long live our Chief Minister," he bellowed.

"Long live our Chief Minister," they echoed.

"And three cheers for his honesty," added Philip getting into his stride.

The crowd responded heartily. Politically the subject of my affair ... was dead.'[1]

And René too was no saint, though his excesses were sometimes less naive than Jimmy's. Just before I arrived on the scene, a rather half-hearted bomb was set-off in the newly-completed lobby of the first tourist hotel. A close associate of René's was convicted and

---

1. *Paradise Raped: Life, Love and Power in the Seychelles* by James R. Mancham
   Methuen 1983.

sentenced to ten years, but the Governor decided not to make a political martyr of René by prosecuting him personally. The true reasons for the explosion were never revealed, but René's followers in the Seychelles People's United Party were certainly less enthusiastic than the Democratic Party about British tourists and indeed about the whole British connection.

René had some reason for his concern. The completion of the airport soon set off an explosion of hotel building all the way round the coasts of Mahé and soon spreading to the neighbouring islands of Praslin and La Digue.

The first result was a huge increase in male employment and wages, as the construction gangs frantically recruited labour. But this seller's market did not last. As the prime beach sites filled up, hotel building soon tailed away. The construction gangs were paid off and the men returned to sit in the sun. For a while there was a good living to be made, selling fish to the hotels from their small dug-out pirogues. But the insatiable demands of the tourists soon fished out the inshore waters, and the building of a cold-store encouraged large sea-going fishing boats, which relied on technology rather than men.

Soon virtually the only people who could get jobs were the women and girls, who were recruited by the hotels as chambermaids and cooks (this was indeed the main drawback to Seychelles tourism; on the whole the Seychelloises were charming but not notably efficient at domestic duties.)

At the same time the affluence of the tourists meant that food prices soared beyond the local pocket and the shortage of cultivable land meant that the seemingly inexhaustible supplies of pineapples, breadfruit, bananas, avocadoes, mangoes, pomegranates, paw-paws, limes, oranges and melons disappeared from Market Street in Victoria. It is small wonder that Albert René and his friends were able to exploit the vague unhappiness of the Seychellois.

For his part Jimmy Mancham was in a dilemma. By the 1970s it was no longer fashionable to attend meetings of the Organisation of African Unity draped in the Union Jack. Despite his status as the elected head of the Seychellois, he sometimes found himself left to cool his heels in the antechamber of the OAU, sadly reciting his poems to the international press, while inside, René, with no such democratic credentials, was regaling the leaders of Africa with the standard anti-colonial rhetoric.

Siren voices among the non-aligned nations reminded Jimmy that, if he clung too long to the coat-tails of the British, they might come away in his hand. 'One day,' they said 'Either the British will abandon you, or you will lose an election. Then the SPUP will take control, and go for Independence and you will be out of power for ever. Do it now yourself, then, like us, you will be the head of an independent country and able to call the shots.'

And as far as Britain was concerned they were quite right. The Seychelles was the last remaining British colony in the African area. Britain was withdrawing from East of Suez. Officials were told to draw up a strategy paper assuming that the Seychellois would be independent within five years whether they liked it or not.

I did not like this much. It seemed to me that, if Self-Determination meant anything, it implied that, if the people of Seychelles were determined to stay British, we should not actually kick them out. Somebody else, not me, was therefore deputed to hint to Jimmy that there might be something in what those siren voices were saying after all.

Jimmy was not the sharpest political brain in Africa, but he took the hint. Despite having very recently won an election on a platform of continued union with Britain, he announced that, as undisputed leader of the Seychelles, he would begin negotiations with the British Government for full internal self-government, followed by Independence.

Marlborough and Lancaster Houses, alongside the Mall in London, were once the stateliest of stately homes. Next door to St James's palace where the Queen Mother lives, they were now used by the British Government as an essential tool for dismantling the Empire.

At conference after conference – from East Africa alone, Uganda, Kenya, Tanganyika and now, Seychelles – the delegates had sat around the plenary table or retired to discreet committee rooms to hammer out an interim constitution for self-government and then for Independence itself.

The format was that all the relevant politicians, preferably from all strands of opinion in the about-to-be-ex-colony, would meet together with Foreign Office Officials, Legal Advisers and Aid

114

Experts, under the Chairmanship of a senior British Mandarin, to discuss a draft constitution, most of which had already been prepared in the Foreign Office.

Once a text had been agreed, a Minister would descend from the clouds, beam benignly on the assembled dignitaries and put his signature on the documents; (or her signature – in the case of the Seychelles our Minister was a fiery red-haired lady who was an expert in nursery education).

Then the delegations would go home to sell the new constitution to their people, who had rarely if ever been consulted. After a year or two of internal self-government (which meant that the British Governor was left with responsibility for little other than Defence and Foreign Affairs) there would be a final conference leading to Independence, with or without a final election.

In the case of the Seychelles all this did not go too well at first. As Chief Minister, Jimmy had five of his Democratic Party colleagues with him and a dozen observers. Albert René as leader of the opposition, had only two. But what the SPUP representatives lacked in numbers, they made up for in noise. Despite the fact that they had only two members in the seventeen member national assembly, René's party had a number of quite plausible grievances. The carelessness of the Seychellois about their family affairs meant that no-one was quite sure how many of them there were, where they were, or how many were genuinely Seychellois who should be allowed to vote and how many were foreigners, who should not.

One of the Seychelles delegates, with an attractive foreign wife, seriously told me that he had registered as Seychellois only those of their children of whose paternity he was certain. Those whom he was not quite so sure about were entered as foreigners. All this meant that electoral registers were unreliable, constituency boundaries uncertain and the possibilities of fraud and impersonation considerable. The SPUP claimed that they had been robbed.

René well understood that, if the Seychelles went to independence with the current distribution of the parties in parliament, then he would lose all hope of power. But he was inhibited from pressing his demand for new elections too strongly, by uncertainty whether the SPUP could win a fairly run election the next time around. The year before, the sole independent candidate, whose

115

platform had been the same nationalist line that the SPUP were now adopting, had polled no more than eleven votes in all.

After two weeks of talking, we were no nearer agreement on the central issues. It was time for the smoke-filled room. I flattered myself, probably wrongly, in the belief that I got on rather better with both Mancham and René than did the current Governor, a cold and rather remote man who had succeeded the ebullient Bob Greatbatch and whose main concern seemed to be with his own self-importance. I took both the leaders separately aside and said that, if they did not come up with some sort of Government of National Unity, they risked leaving Marlborough House without agreement on a timetable for Independence, which they now both said they wanted. They retired to a committee room to talk seriously to each other.

A couple of hours later, they came out all smiles. In the interests of national reconciliation, they announced, the Democratic Party had invited the Opposition to join the government and the SPUP had agreed. For this purpose ten additional members would be coopted to the legislature, five from each party. There would be a new cabinet of twelve – eight of them from the DP and four from the SPUP. Jimmy would be the leader and Albert his deputy.

On the whole I approved of this blatantly undemocratic bit of power play. For all the rhetoric, there was really very little but personalities between the two parties. Something had to be done to rescue the conference. Jimmy did his best to look statesmanlike, Albert looked as if he had swallowed the cream.

A couple of hours later, however, René was back again. The DP's host of Observers could not see enough jobs for themselves in the eight proposed DP portfolios. They therefore demanded a change in the proportion of DP and SPUP ministers.

Albert asked me to intervene, so I went and talked quietly to Jimmy in the corner. A promise was a promise; the DP would still be firmly in control; it was really time that the Chief Minister exercised some influence on his party colleagues. After another tense hour they accepted.

The lady British minister came back and made a nice little speech welcoming the agreement and saying that it opened the way to a 'peaceful, united and prosperous Seychelles' – well yes, sort of. Anyway the Minister said she was delighted and Seychelles could proceed to full Independence the following year.

So, when the delegates got back to the Seychelles, they were able to inform a rather startled electorate that they were free of a colonial tyranny that, in truth, they had barely begun to recognise. René and his colleagues were formally cleared of having blown up the tourist hotel, and moved into their new government offices and quarters.

There was much to be done. The Independence arrangements had to be finalized under the headings of Constitution, Citizenship, Human Rights, the Head of State, the Cabinet, Parliament, the Judicature, the Public Service and Pensions.

But none of this was any longer my business. Immediately after the conference I was posted abroad again to Indonesia and ceased to be directly involved in colonial affairs. A year later the final Seychelles Conference therefore took place without me.

The government of national unity between Jimmy Mancham and Albert René had held together through the year of internal self-government and it was now agreed that it would continue after Independence, with Jimmy as the President of the new republic and Albert as Prime Minister. Everyone dared to hope for a peaceful future.

Jimmy wrote to Pat and me in Jakarta and invited us to come to Mahé for the Independence celebrations. We would have liked to go. It was impossible not to be fond of the Seychellois and Jimmy in particular had always been a friend, even if sometimes a surreal one.

Once before I had had to turn down his invitation to join him on a flight to the French Riviera, with a passenger list of his girlfriends and a private aeroplane provided by a Saudi arms dealer, who hoped to use Seychelles as a base for his operations. The Foreign Office, however, had felt this was too close to official corruption and anyway Pat would not have approved. This time, however, neither of us wanted to miss the party.

We were thwarted by the stuffed-shirt governor who said there would not be room for us. This was nonsense, but, as a serving civil servant, I could not ignore his advice. So instead, a few months after Independence, we travelled back to the Seychelles on a private visit, by which time the stuffed-shirt had gone and Jimmy was living in Government House.

Claiming after the event to have known that trouble was coming, is the oldest trick in the book. Diplomats do it all the time. But in the case of Seychelles I have the evidence of an account which I wrote soon after that post-independence visit, saying that I feared that the careful compromises on which we had worked so hard, were not going to survive.

On the last day of our visit I went down to the airport to meet Albert René and his wife, flying back from a visit to Mrs Gandhi and the non-aligned movement. He was visibly disconcerted to see me, mumbled a few words of embarrassed greeting and hurried off to get into his official car.

Six months later, while Jimmy was away at a Commonwealth Heads of Government meeting in London (a favourite moment for getting rid of heads of state in their absence), Albert René took over the Seychelles.

It wasn't difficult. A few dozen barely-armed policemen were all the military force that the Seychelles government possessed. Five British advisers, drawn from the resolutely civilian Metropolitan Police, had been seconded to train them in the year since Independence. Under their guidance the Seychelles police had become experts in traffic control, court procedure, the enforcement of public-health bye-laws and community police work. The police armoury, containing a scattering of ancient Lee-Enfield rifles, was guarded by a single policeman. He was the sole initial casualty of the coup.

Against this rag-tag force, René had assembled a group of young Seychellois, who had been trained in guerilla warfare in the liberation camps of Tanzania, backed up by regular Tanzanian forces lying in wait in a Zanzibar registered vessel the Mapinduzi, which was anchored off Port Victoria. It was all over in three hours.

Nobody much was willing to help Jimmy. Idi Amin was the first to recognize the new government, followed by France. And Mancham's London friends, including some shadowy advisers thought by him, probably rightly, to be members of MI6, proved tantalizingly elusive.

Hearing of all this in far-off Indonesia, I had a bad conscience. I had played a part in encouraging the original coalition between Jimmy and Albert René. It seemed, not for the first time, that we had been naive. And the sad thing was that it was all completely unnecessary.

Visiting the Seychelles before the coup it had been completely obvious that René was already running the government. Jimmy as

President was already doing what he did best, travelling abroad, bedding beautiful women, writing his excruciating poems, selling the Seychelles as the islands of love and tourism. Elections were due within two years under the constitution. I have no doubt whatever that Albert would have won them and taken over the government if he had stuck to the constitutional path.

Instead he chose the coup d'état and his initial use of force condemned the unfortunate people of the Seychelles to years of Marxist rhetoric, austerity, military domination, coups and counter-coups. They did not deserve such a fate and we, the successors of Mr Carruthers of the Colonial Office, cannot escape our share of the responsibility.

But however tragic and unnecessary the result of our simplicity, fortunately nothing in Seychelles is ever too far removed from farce. The next attempt at a counter-revolution in the Seychelles was disguised as a social outing by members of the Ancient Order of Froth Blowers.

Five years after Independence and four years after René's coup, forty-four convivial gentlemen landed at Mahé wearing blazers with a badge depicting an overflowing beer-tankard. The Froth-blowers is a British charity working for deprived children, so they displayed to the customs men five bags of toys for Seychellois orphans. As is the habit of such organisations, each of them also carried a large team holdall, emblazoned with the Froth Blowers' arms.

Unfortunately one or two of them had carried verisimilitude one step too far. Into the top of their holdalls they had stuffed innocent bunches of bananas. Unknown to them, however, bananas are a prohibited import into the Seychelles, lest they infect the indigenous crop. The customs officers turned the bags upside down and out of each tumbled an AK47 and thirty rounds of ammunition.

Fortunately for the conspirators, an Air India jumbo jet landed at that moment. Most of the would-be invaders, including their mercenary leader 'Mad Mike' Hoare, ran helter-skelter to the tarmac, hijacked the jet and flew off to South Africa, leaving a handful of their comrades behind to be rounded up. It had been a fiasco.

Jimmy Mancham has never clearly stated whether he spearheaded this bungled coup. Nor is it known who financed it. In his autobiography Jimmy fairly pointed out that if the counter-revolution had succeeded and he had been returned to Seychelles as President, no-one would have lifted a finger to condemn him, any more than they had René four years earlier. As it was, the Security Council denounced the 'aggression against Seychelles' and Jimmy ends his account by describing the UN bitterly as 'the Hyde Park corner of international politics'.

But it is never possible to dampen Jimmy's spirits for too long. Soon he was his old ebullient self. At Independence time in Britain's former colonies, it has always been customary to award a British decoration to the Head of the new government, to symbolize an amicable parting of the ways. And when the new country opts to become a Republic (that is, no longer one of the Queen's dominions), then the Foreign Office has often felt free to be quite generous, since foreign holders of British decorations are only honorary members of the order of chivalry concerned and therefore unable to add a handle to their name or embarrass the Order by inappropriate and foreign behaviour.

Following this precedent, at the time of Independence, Jimmy had been made an Honorary Knight of the Most Excellent Order of the British Empire. While, therefore, he was licking his wounds after the failed coup, a consoling friend pointed out that, if he accepted defeat and took British citizenship, he would at a stroke become a subject of the Queen and entitled to style himself 'Sir James R. Mancham KBE'.

And so he is to this day. He deserves it.

13

Diego Garcia: A Bet on a Bikini

Before I left the Indian Ocean, however, I also had at least to have a look at the Anglo-American base on Diego Garcia.

At the height of Britain's post-war influence, before the Suez débacle and before the decision to withdraw imperial forces from East of Suez, the whole of the Indian Ocean and the Gulf had been dotted with British bases. Kenya, Aden, Oman, the Gulf States and the Maldives all had a sizeable British military presence. By the middle of the 1970s these had been reduced to only two.

It became a truism that you could always tell when the British were about to leave a colonial territory. Just before it happened they spent millions building a major base for the armed forces. Sometimes within months, the facilities had to be handed over to a newly independent government, which seldom knew what to do with them. The bases in Nairobi and Aden were a glaring case in point. It seemed that, not for the first time, the British military and diplomatic establishments were not really talking to each other.

By the late sixties the two last British bases in the Indian Ocean were Masirah island off the coast of Oman and the jewel-like coral atoll of Gan, in the Maldives.

But the British were really only in Oman because we were fighting the Sultan's war for him, and the Maldive islands too were about to become independent. On Gan there was a half-hearted attempt by a group of local fishermen to separate the island off from the rest of the Maldives. No-one was killed in the attempt and beyond a shame-faced declaration of separate independence, nothing very much happened. There were no Maldives policemen on Gan and therefore no one much to rebel against or take prisoner. The rebellion petered out almost as soon as it began.

Had it succeeded, it is possible that the British might have made an agreement with the new government and might have stayed on Gan to this day. In those days of limited aircraft range the base was a useful staging post on the way to Hong Kong and a sought-after RAF posting, with its palm trees, star-lit nights and blinding white beaches.

But the British were certainly not going to risk a confrontation with the Governments of India and Sri Lanka, which disapproved of the idea of a coup d'état on their doorstep. When, therefore, the coup collapsed of its own inertia, Britain did nothing beyond removing its leader, one Afif Didi, to a place of safety in the Seychelles, and there providing him with a house and the kind of ludicrously small pension with which the British government is apt to reward exiled kings as a way of salving its own conscience.

In Seychelles Afif Didi joined an even more distinguished exile, President Makarios from Cyprus. That wily cleric was staying in a beautiful villa looking out over the harbour of Mahé and doing his best to maintain that he was extremely unhappy and living only for the day of return to his native land.

With Gan firmly back in the ownership of the Maldives, however, it was clear that the closure of this final British base there could not long be delayed. The British government then went on a shopping spree. The Indian Ocean is sprinkled with little rocks, most of them uninhabited and uninhabitable, but all of them claimed by one sovereign power or another. One or two of them, like Aldabra, with its giant tortoises, are a naturalist's paradise, but most of them contain, well, nothing very much.

A couple of years before I appeared on the scene, the British government got rather excited about all this. All sorts of hare-brained ideas bubbled to the surface of overheated minds. Why not moor an obsolete aircraft-carrier in Aldabra, fill it with radio equipment and broadcast the BBC World Service direct on medium-wave to the oppressed peoples of southern Africa? Why not put a tropical-latitude satellite launching base on the outlying Seychelles islands of Farquhar or Desroches? Above all, why not use the former Mauritius-owned atoll of Diego Garcia in the Chagos archipelago, as an Anglo-American military base? This would not only replace Gan, but also give the United States a secure foothold in the Indian Ocean and help them to some degree to recover from the trauma of Vietnam.

Diego Garcia: A Bet on a Bikini

At the time Britain still controlled both Seychelles and Mauritius and could doubtless have transferred the rocks without so much as a by-your-leave. But this was thought to be not quite cricket.

In exchange for the islets, therefore, Seychelles got its new airport and Mauritius got a cash sum in compensation, which included a million pounds or so to resettle the Islois, the so called 'transient' or 'migrant' workers from the small coconut plantation on Diego Garcia.

When I got there, Aldabra, Farquhar and Desroches remained undeveloped, and were, in fact, handed back to the Seychelles as part of the independence settlement. But Diego Garcia was very much alive.

The Chagos archipelago lies a thousand miles further to the east of Seychelles and about the same distance from the southern tip of India. There is nothing in between. It must be one of the loneliest places in the world. Most of the archipelago is just rocks and shallows, the home of sharks, sea birds and innumerable fish. The only habitable island is Diego Garcia.

And even Diego Garcia is not much to look at. Formidable drop-offs of broken coral rim the outer edge of the almost circular atoll. Long Indian Ocean rollers continuously pound the circle perhaps two miles across. Even ten yards off the coast, the water is so deep that no ship's anchor will ever find holding ground. The only gap in the circle is a narrow passage through the northern rim, where the rip-tide swirls as it rushes to and from the wide flat lagoon inside.

Virtually the whole of the western, northern and southern part of the atoll is bare coral rock. Nothing seems to grow there or want to grow there. Only on the eastern rim is a narrow strip of palm trees and a village where the Ilois used to live.

Nominally Diego Garcia remains a British colony to this day, part of the British Indian Ocean Territory. Its administrator is a British naval lieutenant-commander, bored out of his socks, but never failing to order one of the naval Regulating (disciplinary) Petty Officers and Seamen under his command to raise and lower the BIOT ensign at dawn and at dusk.

They have practically nothing to do, except insist, if they choose, on their residual right to drive on the left-hand side of the road, in imminent danger of death from the huge American lorries that prefer the right. To the Colonel in charge of the Americans, however, the British regulating staff are (or were in those unregenerate post-Vietnam days) extremely useful. They were just about the only people on the atoll who weren't up in the trees with the birds.

In theory it should have been possible to keep Diego Garcia free of drugs. Nothing came in or out except US Navy and Military ships and aircraft. But the demoralisation of the US armed forces at the end of the Vietnam war was then such that Marijuana was grown on naval ships' messdecks, which officers were debarred from entering; and the ground crews loading and unloading the huge air freighters were unimaginably well-paid for handling the lighter packets of heroin and LSD.

The US Base Commander could not trust his own staff to police this universal racket, supplying two thousand Seabees, all wrapped in inspissated gloom and longing to be anywhere except Diego Garcia.

But the British sailors were largely insulated from this disconnected environment. They had their own mess and a British club with English beer flown out courtesy of the US Airforce. Moreover when the base commander asked them to exercise a little gentle pressure on his disordered command, they were quite within their rights. Diego Garcia was after all British, goddammit, and the British navy had certain standards to sustain. With their help the Base Commander somehow managed to keep a modicum of order and devote himself, somewhat lugubriously, to his unrivalled collection of cowrie shells.

The Seabees were there to build an airfield capable of handling B52 bombers, to widen the breach in the north wall and to deepen the lagoon to provide a safe anchorage for the USS Missouri and her sister battleships and aircraft carriers. On land they were beginning to build huge port installations, oil storage tanks, barracks, offices and quarters and, who knows, perhaps deep bunkers for storing nuclear weapons.

To the best of my knowledge all that effort has now been brought to a triumphant conclusion; with the Americans it usually is. Certainly Diego Garcia and its stores, ships and aircraft played a major part in the build-up of the Gulf War in 1991. But it was pretty hairy at the beginning.

Nominally the superior officers of the Lieutenant-Commander, (who was known as 'The Administrator BIOT') were myself and my immediate boss in Whitehall. The Ministry of Defence also had an interest, not only in their sailors, but in the military aspects of what was nominally an Anglo-American base. But nobody from London had ever been to Diego Garcia in serving memory. We decided that it needed an inspection.

The difficulty was how to get there. The protocol mandarins ruled that it was out of the question for the British Governor of a British colony to roll up in a US Airforce freighter. The whole effect would be spoiled. And we must fly in from the West, the direction of Whitehall, not from the degenerate east.

Nor could we simply turn up in a long range RAF VC10 jet. The difficulty about building an airfield on a circular atoll is that, unless you can cut corners, your runway ends up with a sideways curve like a banana. It was impossible to build the landing-strip straight out over the outside reef. The water there was hundreds of feet deep. And while in theory it would have been possible to cut the corner, on piles over the shallower waters of the lagoon, the airfield would then be like a banana suspended only at both ends. I have no idea how the problem was finally solved, but at the time it meant that only propeller-driven aircraft with a short take off run could land at Diego Garcia.

It was therefore a rather apprehensive cargo of British diplomats, boffins, civil servants and military folk who took off from Mahé in a rattling old piston-engined Britannia aircraft, specially chartered for the occasion.

The only bright spot as we ground our way slowly across the Indian Ocean, was our young lady companion. Looking like something from a garage pin-up poster, she was nevertheless a senior civil servant from the Ministry of Defence. Though admirably serious in purpose, she had nevertheless brought with her a couple of bikinis and a wardrobe calculated to encourage her designer tan. Someone should have warned her – and us.

The Seabees were sent to Diego Garcia on an eight-months unaccompanied posting. There were literally no women around. Word of her arrival had got about. As our shameful aircraft ground to a halt at the end of the landing-strip, we could see the few remaining palm-trees bending under the weight of overfed Americans, struggling to get a better view.

As the doors opened a tidal wave of sound washed over us like a Tsunami. Frantic Seabees fought each other for the first glimpse. As she appeared at the door, something like a groan broke out, as two thousand seriously deprived young men struggled to cope with a vision which, in their hopped-up state, could well have been a mirage.

A phalanx of British sailors formed around us as we made for the makeshift control tower at a run. They seemed quite unreasonably elated.

Later the British Chief Regulating Petty Officer explained. All that the Americans knew was that there was a woman coming on the plane. The Chief, however, had inside information and, when someone made a book on how old she was going to be, the British had bet the low field, under 25. Most of the Americans, knowing that she was a senior civil servant and being anyway sunk in pessimism and dope, had bet the high field, above 50.

The Chief and his friends had cleaned up.

Later that evening, when we had fought off the determination of the shell-collecting base commander to house the young lady in his own personal quarters, the British went off to their own club to celebrate on beer – lots of beer.

Only twice in my life have I been quite unable, the morning after, to remember what I had been doing the night before. The first I prefer to forget. The second was that night on Diego Garcia.

The next thing I remember was waking up in a ditch full of coral dust. This was made even more confusing by the fact that I was apparently sharing the ditch with a donkey. Nobody had told me about the wild asses of Diego Garcia, its only indigenous inhabitants. And even if they had, I would have been surprised by the fact that the donkey appeared to be surrounded by a pink halo, that seemed to have its origin somewhere in the back of my head.

I coughed. The donkey sneezed sympathetically and ejected a bright stream of urine over my trousers. That seemed, however, to be the limit of our conversation and we lay and looked at each other for a while.

Suddenly an insufferably cheerful naval voice boomed out behind me. 'Wakey, Wakey, rise and shine. You've had your time and I've had mine. Sun's burning yer bleeding eyes out. Come on my sons – you know what sons I mean, sons of the f---ing ocean. Show a leg, show a leg; hands off c---s, on socks. It's kippers and custard for breakfast. Beg pardon Sir, no offence meant. I thought you'd like a cup of tea.'

The Chief seemed none the worse for wear and only the rumpled state of his uniform suggested that he hadn't spent the night in his hammock either.

I was grateful for the tea and not inclined to object to being thus rudely forced back to life. Gradually as the sun rose higher through the fluffy Indian-Ocean clouds, I started to take an interest once again.

One of the things we had agreed to do was to check on the old plantation at the other side of the lagoon. The Ilois from Diego Garcia had indeed been resettled in Mauritius, allegedly with the help of the grant from the British Government. But they claimed that none of that money had ever reached them. And anyway they said that it was quite untrue that they were merely migrant workers, brought in annually to process the coconut harvest on Diego Garcia. Some of them asserted that their families had lived on the atoll continuously for over three generations and that they had as much right to the land as anyone else. An international scandal was brewing.

We needed to see for ourselves, so the Administrator had arranged for an American landing-craft to take us the couple of miles across the lagoon to look at the Ilois village. The landing craft's bows grounded on the bright sand. The ramp opened and the crew competed officiously to hand our young lady ashore 'because of the sharks'. She thanked them prettily and adjusted her bikini, followed by a thudding noise that sounded like the boat's cox'n banging his head on the wheelhouse bulkhead in an agony of frustration. We trudged up through the silent avenues of coconut trees.

To an unbiased eye, the settlement looked like a fully fledged village, complete with church, neighbourhood store and permanent boat sheds. It did not look like the sort of place whose inhabitants came there only for a few months before returning to their permanent homes. I felt depressed by this evidence of a community destroyed.

When we got back to London I told my masters so, and I am glad to say that a substantial further sum was eventually provided for the Ilois, in recognition both of their lost paradise and the fact that most of the money originally subscribed seemed to have gone astray in the bureaucracy of Mauritius.

We flew back to Seychelles in a sombre frame of mind, though not half as sombre as the Seabees we left behind. Our lady companion looked distinctly smug.

14

New Hebrides: Condominium in the South Pacific

Three years later I was working in Indonesia. We hated the overcrowding and filth of the capital, Jakarta, but revelled in the beauty and culture of the rest of those incomparable islands.

Out of the blue came a letter from John Champion, my first boss in Uganda so many years before. John had left Uganda and joined the Diplomatic Service shortly before I did. I knew him to be one of the best and most humane of colonial administrators, that attractive blend of honourable gentleman and sensible practitioner, whom those who knew the old Colonial Service had no difficulty in recognizing, but found it difficult to describe without inviting derision.

John's career in the Foreign Office had not, however, been all that successful. The diplomats found it difficult to cope with someone of his rocklike integrity and he had not risen as far, or as fast as he deserved. Now in his last posting before retirement, he was the British Resident Commissioner in the Anglo-French Condominium of the New Hebrides. He was not happy. His letter began, 'There are moments when we think that this is undoubtedly the most detestable place on earth.'

The Condominium was indeed a curiosity, almost a monstrosity. The eighty tropical islands of the New Hebrides lie in a Y-shaped chain 500 miles long, to the north-east of Australia between Fiji and New Caledonia. Unlike the Polynesian atolls still further east, the islands of the New Hebrides are not formed from the growth of coral reefs around an inner lagoon. Instead they are violent volcanic outcrops, created by huge underwater disturbances as the Australian and Pacific tectonic plates grind against each other across the fault-lines of the world's greatest ocean. Sometimes fierce cyclones come whirling down out of the Pacific carrying all before them with their 100 mile-an-hour winds and surging tidal waves. Then the islands can be an awful place, far removed from the bland vision of the smiling Pacific.

Smoking volcanoes along the line of the chain occasionally erupt in fury, causing the terrified inhabitants to flee for safety in their dug-out canoes. Deep forests and sharp lava rocks discourage all access to the islands' misty interiors. Only along the coastline, straggling coconut plantations and low built grass huts lie behind a bright ribbon of white sand and the endlessly pounding sea.

Five hundred years before Christ, the first inhabitants had begun to arrive in tiny settlements along the island coasts. Coal-black, sometimes almost plum-black Melanesians, far deeper in tone than most of the Africans we had grown up with, these earliest inhabitants had spread out from the great island of New Guinea to the north and west.

No-one knew for sure how they got to their new homes. In all probability it was by mistake. Small groups of canoes on a coastwise trading voyage, or on a fishing expedition in the teeming waters of the Coral Sea, had perhaps been blown away from their homeland by untimely winds from the north-west.

When they came to shore in the unnamed islands to the east, these groups set up camp wherever they landed through a gap in the fringing reef. The tiny settlements never coalesced. Partly, this must have been because of the hostile terrain of the interior, but almost certainly also because they were cannibals (a habit which persisted in Papua New Guinea into the 20th century). If an inhabitant of one of the settlements strayed into the territory of another group, he, or she, was liable to be eaten. It must have been a powerful deterrent.

As a result each little group lived in virtual isolation for over a thousand years. One consequence was that almost every village developed a distinct language of its own, often incomprehensible to everyone else. At the last count there were nearly 130 of these Melanesian dialects which, with a total population at Independence of 112,000, meant that, on average, every 1,000 New

Hebrideans had a separate and mutually incompatible language of their own. The smallest linguistic groups were sometimes made up of no more than seven or eight families. This was to have drastic consequences for nation-building after the arrival of the colonial powers.

The first Europeans to come to the islands thought that they were somewhere else. In that pre-scientific age they believed that there must be a vast southern continent lying at the Antipodes on the other side of the world from Europe. The logic behind this quaint theory was that if there was no such continent to balance the European land-mass, they believed that the whole world would wobble, like an ill-balanced motor-car tyre. The fact that the amount of land sticking above the sea in even the largest continent was only an infinitesimal fragment of everything that lay below, does not seem to have occurred to them.

When therefore, in 1606, the Spanish explorer Pedro Fernandez de Quiros first sighted one of the northern islands of the New Hebrides, now called Santo, he was sure that he must have discovered the great southern continent which he named Australia del Espiritu Santo. But his piety in naming the new land mass after the holy ghost was ill-rewarded, when the infuriated inhabitants chased him away almost immediately, accusing him of killing their sacred pigs.

The Melanesians and their pigs were then left in peace for another 150 years until the French sea captain Louis de Bougainville 'rediscovered' the islands. He was closely followed in 1774 by the incomparable navigator, James Cook. Cook soon realised that far from being a continent, what Quiros had found was a small crescent shaped island, part of a chain of no vast significance except to the people who lived there. Once that diminishing fact had been established, Santo could then be left in decent international obscurity until, in the middle of the 20th century, it became the hinge of the titanic struggle between the Americans and the Japanese for the control of the world.

Cook then went on, as was his wont, to discover practically everything else of importance in the islands, which he named, with a touch of whimsy, the New Hebrides. This has caused confusion ever since. When I myself was posted to the New Hebrides, a friend wrote and said that he hoped we would not be too depressed by the North Atlantic gales pounding the outer Scottish isles.

But, give or take the coconut plantations and ten or twenty degrees of temperature, it would not, in fact, have been too bizarre to compare the old Hebrides with the new. The smoking volcano of Lopevi has the same air of mystery as the Black Cuillins, as they soar into the mists above Loch Corruisk on Skye, and the isolated rocks of Futuna or Ambrym in the New Hebrides can without stretching the imagination too far, be compared with the rugged outlines of Rhum or Eigg.

Even though the islands had acquired a European name, however, they were still left alone to bask in the sun for another fifty years. Not until the middle of the 19th century did traders and missionaries begin to vie for local influence with the roving ships' captains of the great colonial powers, Britain and France, and with the latest invader of them all, Imperial Germany, newly united under Bismark.

The French and the British did not at first want much to do with those unprofitable shores. Unlike France's colony of New Caledonia, three hundred miles to the east, there were no great mineral deposits to be exploited in the New Hebrides. And Britain was preoccupied with the development of Australia and New Zealand a thousand miles to the south. At first the navies of the two powers contented themselves with sailing in and burning down a village or two whenever the inhabitants seemed too unwelcoming to white-skinned settlers, who claimed the right to buy their land for a few dollars or a handful of beads.

Then it became more complicated as British naval captains made the mistake of burning down villages to which their French counterparts had granted their protection, and vice versa. Eventually, to avoid these mishaps, Britain and France agreed in 1886 to set up a Joint Naval Commission, charged with the 'common protection of the lives and property of the subjects of the United Kingdom and France.'

Nobody, of course, troubled either to protect or to consult the original inhabitants of the islands, before creating this joint authority. In practice all it was apt to mean, from the indigenous population's point of view, was that, since British and French officers were in alternate command of the joint naval force, the French and British dominated villages were usually burnt in rotation, rather than simultaneously.

And even from the imperial viewpoint, the policy of sea-borne control by arson was less than satisfactory. It did not stop violent quarrels springing up between the British (in fact usually Australian) and French settlers, nearly always about land. The trouble was that, without some sort of joint legal authority to adjudicate land claims, no-one could settle down and enjoy his dubiously acquired estate in peace.

So gradually the two powers became more and more involved, not in the interests of the inhabitants, who indeed remained technically no-one's responsibility until the end of the Condominium three quarters of a century later, but solely to stop the British and French colonists from quarrelling with each other.

The normal colonial logic would have been for a trade-off to be agreed in Europe, by which hegemony over the New Hebrides would be ceded to one or other of the two imperial nations in return for an equivalent concession to the other one, somewhere else in the world. But this all happened at the beginning of the 20th century when the Entente Cordiale had temporarily convinced the British and the French, for the first time in centuries, that they actually liked one another.

Moreover, while Britain and France were still the main colonial rivals in the Pacific, the one thing they were both agreed on was that Germany must be kept out of it. So, for the first and hopefully the last time on history, London and Paris agreed to create, not a Colony, but a Condominium.

This term, in itself, has caused endless misunderstanding. To North Americans a condominium is not a state, but a city apartment building shared in common by its tenants. Americans have therefore always had difficulty understanding why a block of flats, built presumably somewhere on a coral atoll in the middle of the South Pacific, should have acquired two governors and two different systems of administration.

The reality, however, was hardly less bizarre. The first Condominium, established in 1906, simply put down two entirely separate governments in the same country, relating to each other in no way and claiming no jurisdiction except over their own subjects. This could never work and in 1914 a new Anglo-French protocol established the monstrosity which soon became known, with a touch of affectionate exasperation, as 'The Pandemonium'.

Under the Protocol, instead of two governments, there were now three, a British administration, a French one and a joint Condominium authority. Where their own subjects were concerned, the British and French Governors, known as the Resident Commissioners, could and did act independently. This meant that each had their own police force, their own schools, hospitals, public works department, treasury, marine department, their own prisons, civil service and courts. To the very end of the Condominium, when foreigners arrived at the ramshackle terminal building of the wartime airfield on the outskirts of the capital, Port Vila, a courteous policeman enquired of them whether they were British or French. When a visitor replied that he, or she, was neither, but, say, Swedish, he was politely told that, for the duration of his stay in the New Hebrides, there were only two alternatives, he must be British or he must be French.

If, tossing a coin, he chose to be French, then he was ushered towards the French immigration queue and given a document to say so. This may well have seemed to him odd, but the full implications probably did not strike him until, perhaps, on his way into town, he was knocked down by a passing lorry. As he lay bleeding on the sidewalk, a constable, dressed in the neatly pressed khaki and blue of the British colonial police, would come up to him and enquire, again with exquisite Melanesian politeness, whether he was British or French. If, in his last breath before lapsing into unconsciousness, the Swede admitted to being a temporary Frenchman, the British policeman would leave him alone and pass by on the other side.

Being a humane person, however, the constable might well step outside the bounds of his authority to make contact with one of his counterparts, an equally Melanesian, but French-recruited gendarme, wearing an equally well-pressed khaki uniform with different buttons and a red French fore-and-aft forage cap instead of a peaked British police hat.

Unless the French-directed policeman was in sight of the accident, however, communication between the two would be no simple matter. Language was not the problem. In speaking to each other they would use neither French nor English but Bislama, or 'Pidgin', the lingua franca of the Melanesian islanders. If they were out of sight, however, and even if the British constable had a radio, he could not simply call up his colleague. They were on entirely different networks. He could try, if he wished, using his radio to speak to British police headquarters, which was at one end of the town. There the officer in charge, if he had nothing better to do, could pick up the public telephone and speak to his French counterpart at the other end. The Frenchman could then, in turn, get on his radio to his own policeman and instruct him to proceed, on a French bicycle or in a French police truck, to the scene of the accident.

All this would, of course, take time, but assuming that French authority arrived before the unfortunate Swede expired, a French ambulance would then be summoned to take him to the French hospital. There French doctors and nurses would look after him until the time arrived for him to sue the lorry-driver in a French court under French law. Finally, if the lorry-driver was convicted and sentenced to a term of imprisonment, he would serve it in a French prison (where discipline was notoriously stricter than in its British counterpart – a notice outside the British jail in Port Vila read, 'Visitors are not allowed in prisoners' cells without permission').

This duplication was repeated throughout the islands. Certain services had been amalgamated and placed under the Condominium authorities. It would have been madness for the two Resident Commissioners to insist on driving on their opposing national sides of the road (we drove on the right because it mattered to the French), and there could be only one authority to produce electricity or control the airfield, but on the whole the British and French administrations kept themselves to themselves, except when they found it necessary to quarrel with each other.

The most visible symbol of this separation were the two Residencies where the respective Governors had chosen to live. The French Resident Commissioner lived on a hill at the edge of the town in a white villa that exuded a certain 'Je ne sais quois'. The food was better than in the British Residency – much better. The cars in the drive were Citroens and the domestic arrangements too, breathed a certain Frenchness (it was not until almost the end of the Condominium that I discovered that my colleague had a mistress).

By contrast the British Resident Commissioner lived on an island. Forty acres of tumbled wilderness in the middle of the harbour was crowned with a shambling colonial bungalow. Whenever there was a cyclone, the windows shattered; whenever it rained they leaked; whenever the mast of a passing yacht swept away the overhead electric cable across the harbour, the creaking air conditioners gave up the ghost and the bungalow lay sweltering in the tropical damp until they could be repaired. Clothes hung in wardrobes grew mildew within days, or caught fire when they touched the bare electric bulbs hung in the cupboards to dry out the air.

In the kitchen, Mangu, the huge black Solomon Islands cook, turned out roast beef and suet pudding to feed to the sweating guests, while John and Columbus, the two stewards, kept shovelling ice into the drinks; assuming that is, that the icemaker was working and that the glasses had not already slipped from our sweaty hands.

In the unkempt garden loomed the shaggy presence of Golden Boy, the charolais bull and his harem of nondescript cows. Better than any lawn-mower, they also provided milk and dung to fertilise the parched roses.

Between the house and the jetty, where an ancient but immaculately-kept harbour launch lay with its blue ensign flapping idly in the Pacific trade winds, was a concrete staircase with exactly one hundred and seventy eight steps. When the Resident Commissioner gave up his unequal struggle with the roast beef and decided to make his way back to his office, he had either to negotiate that staircase (going down was all right – it was coming back that killed you) or climb into a rusty Land Rover with no brakes and grind his way in low ratio down a dirt track which became a water-shute in the rains.

On the launch, the bearded figure of John, the Melanesian cox'n, dressed in spotless Naval whites that yet barely concealed his formidable beer-belly, threw his boss a tremendous salute, before grinding the ancient motor into life and inching across the hundred yards of bright blue water to the town quay, with the Resident Commissioner standing in the stern, gravely acknowledging the waves from passing dug-out canoes.

Once landed, the Queen's representative climbed aboard the oldest Jaguar in the world, which was confined to the half-mile or so of township tarmac, because its shock absorbers had long since given up the ghost. With the Union Jack fluttering bravely from the front bumper, he made his way to the 'British Paddock' where, in a white-shuttered office with an uneven linoleum floor, he had to deal with the latest crisis, usually in Anglo-French relations.

All too often, in the early days of the Condominium, these crises were of unbelievable banality. When I arrived, the thickest file in the Residency had to do with a new flag pole which the French had put up outside their office, three hundred yards away. It went without saying that the Tricolore and the Union Jack both had to fly and they both had to be exactly the same size. The trouble was that the top of the new French flagpole was a metre higher than the top of the old British one.

How this could have been detected without a theodolite I was never quite sure, but the issue had clearly occupied a quite inordinate amount of my predecessor's time. The idea that things might be evened up by flying the French flag a little bit down from the top of the French mast-head, had been met with the scornful rejection of half-masting the Tricolore as a sign of distress. Equally a tentative suggestion of shortening the French flag pole by three feet, had prompted the indignant inquiry whether the British were proposing the destruction of the property of La Belle France?

Eventually the problem was solved by fitting the British flag pole with a new three-foot concrete plinth at its base, but the pettiness of these frequent squabbles only served to underline the maxim that, if democracy is indeed the least worst system of government, then condominium colonialism must be, at most, the least best.

All this was hard on the respective administrators and their hard-working staffs. But it was hardest of all on the original inhabitants, the overwhelming majority of Melanesians who, if they wanted anything at all, must have wished that the metropolitan powers would just go away and leave them in peace.

This was not because the condominium system was positively oppressive. Indeed there were certain advantages in having two different colonial masters, both competing fiercely for influence in the same territory. Once national elections had been introduced in the last years before independence and the competing Melanesian political parties had, as was almost inevitable, divided themselves along the fault lines of anglophony and francophonie, the two Resident Commissioners became extremely busy distributing goodies to ensure as far as they could that their clients remained loyal, or at least did not go and vote for the other side.

Before the last elections of all, my French colleague, Inspector General Jean-Jaques Robert, went whizzing around the islands doling out a dispensary here, an electric generator there, an access road somewhere else. The fact that the British Resident Commissioners were, on the whole, less pro-active, was partly because they had smaller funds available for community development, but it owed more to the fact that, (thanks largely to the missionaries, rather than to the British Government), there were more English-medium bush schools than there were French-speaking ones and hence more English speakers in the population and more natural voters for the Anglophone parties, Q.E.D.

Nor, on the whole, were the native New Hebrideans oppressed with the burden of condominium taxes or over-officious interference with their daily existence. To the end of the Condominium there were no personal taxes whatever in the New Hebrides, and on the whole the Melanesians were left to get on with their own lives. If anyone meddled with their 'Kastom' it was more likely to be the missionaries than the Metropolitan authorities, who had each other to worry about.

No, the main driving force of Melanesian unhappiness was land. Land was the main reason why the white-men had come to the New Hebrides in the first place, along with the natural resources which they found already in place on that land.

The first lure of all was the aromatic sandalwood, for which 19th century Chinese Buddhists paid good money, to sweeten the air of their temples. As the opium trade into China declined, sandalwood became more and more important to balance Chinese exports of tea and silks. The first commercial voyagers into the New Hebrides found huge stands of sandalwood trees on the islands of Erromango Aneityum and Santo.

Then, as the sandalwood forests were cut down, with no thought of regeneration, it was the human product of the land that became more important to the roving traders, who were, in truth, little better than Buccaneers. In the second half of the 19th century and before the start of the white Australia policy in the 20th, the 'Blackbirders' and their human cargoes of 'indentured labourers', taken off to work in the sugar plantations of Queensland, became the main point of human contact (and friction) between the Melanesians and their white invaders.

But though these incursions were a nuisance to the inhabitants they were not so very different from the tribal disputes that had plagued the islands since the first canoe that had tried to land on an already populated shore. What really upset the Melanesians was the alienation of their very land itself.

The lure of the South Seas has always attracted adventurers with visions of an easy living to be made, believing that they will gather the abundant fruits of the earth on a palm-fringed shore, while dusky maidens minister to their every need. From about 1850 onwards the first of such beachcombers began to arrive in the islands of the New Hebrides.

By that time the Melanesians, who owned the land in a system of common tenure that was clear enough to them, but totally mysterious to the incoming whites, had already become accustomed to making small parcels of land available to the early missionaries for specific use. But they had no concept of permanent alienation, or of contracts of sale or value for money. When therefore the incomers produced a piece of paper with mysterious markings on it and, in exchange for some more equally mysterious markings at the bottom, handed over trade-goods, axes, nails, tools, cotton cloth, fish hooks, and even sometimes the illegal rum and firearms, the Melanesians were delighted to let them squat on some unused part of their land, even in the so-called Dark Bush of the interior, where they could grow their coconuts and tend the first herds of cattle ever seen on the islands.

At first this made very little difference to the quality of life in the New Hebrides. The white settlers were few, poor, disorganised and soon became disillusioned with the constant battle against malaria and debilitation.

From about the 1880s onwards, however, the settlers started to get organised. John Higginson, an Irishman who loathed the British and assumed French nationality to get even with them, decided to take over the land of the New Hebrides in the interests of France. It took him no more than a total of twelve days, spread over a year, to 'purchase' 100,000 hectares of land, almost ten percent of the total cultivable area of the islands, both from the Melanesian inhabitants and from the settlers already in possession, who were mostly relieved to get rid of their dubious claims.

It was Higginson's actions that finally spurred the Metropolitan powers into creating the Condominium. The French on the whole were glad to do it. The acquisition of the New Hebrides would assure a labour force for their mining and penal settlement in New Caledonia and consolidate the chain of French islands across the width of the Pacific, ending in the east with Muroroa, of evil 20th century fame.

The British on the other hand would probably have been willing to bow out. They did not relish having to deal with Higginson and did not really need any more land. But, just as had happened in Uganda, the missionaries would not let them. The Presbyterians were both strong and strident in Britain and there was a public outcry when the British Government threatened to withdraw.

So the Condominium was born from a competition for land. And it was land which remained until the end both the main source of misunderstanding with the Melanesians and the main bone of contention between the Metropolitan powers. From Higginson onwards the planters were mainly French, or Francophone, or French half-castes; the missionaries were mainly British, or Australian and protestant (the Roman Catholic church had made valiant efforts to establish itself, but was frustrated by the requirement of celibacy for its clergy, which struck the Melanesians as not so much onerous, as boring and impracticable).

Thus, until by a strange twist of history not unrelated to the aforesaid goodies and the need for votes, the French administration managed to make themselves the patrons of the 'Kastom' movements in the islands of Santo and Tanna, the Melanesian struggle for Land and Independence came to be seen largely as a struggle against France, with the British as well-meaning but largely ineffectual observers, with their hearts in the right place but not the guts to skin a rabbit.

And this contrast was underlined by the different French and British attitudes to Independence. By two-thirds of the way through the 20th century, the British had, on the whole, had enough. Apart from Pitcairn, with its tiny and unviable population of the descendants of the Mutiny on the Bounty, the new Hebrides was the last remaining British Colony in the Pacific. British forces had withdrawn from east of Suez and the British Treasury could no longer sustain the policy of grants-in-aid for unprofitable colonies.

140

New Hebrides: Condominium in the South Pacific

More respectably, since Harold Macmillan's 'Wind of Change' speech and before, the British had grown accustomed to the idea that it was up to colonial peoples themselves to choose their own destiny. The new generation of colonial administrators honestly believed that it was their job to prepare the colonies for Independence. Thus John Champion and his predecessors had been sent to the New Hebrides to negotiate themselves out of a job, provided only that they did so in concert with their French colleagues.

And there lay the difficulty and the reason why the New Hebrides were the last in the line. The French are a logical people. They genuinely believe that to be French and to speak French is the highest state of human civilisation. It follows, therefore, that to become Independent, to cut the ties with France, is illogical and therefore wrong – a step from a higher state of civilisation to a lower one.

Moreover the French are perhaps the last subscribers to the domino theory that if you lose one colony, the rest will come crashing down with it. The New Hebrides' nearest neighbour, New Caledonia (also named by Cook) was an undiluted French Colony. Not only did it have those valuable mineral deposits; the French inhabitants, who made up almost half the New Caledonian population, were mainly ex-Algerian 'Pieds Noirs' who had already been turned out of one former French colony and had no intention of being displaced twice.

Moreover further to the East lay the scattered islands of French Polynesia, centred around Tahiti. Most of these, apart from the nuclear testing ground on Muroroa, were not really necessary to France, but the possession of the most beautiful islands and some of the most beautiful people in the world gave a lift to the French spirit that they badly needed in a 20th century that no longer seemed to acknowledge the supremacy of France. They had been humiliated in Indo-China; they were not going to lose control of another far-eastern colony if they could help it. And so the new Hebrides became for France a symbol and a bastion of French influence in the Pacific, if only the British had not been there with their weak-kneed babbling about self-determination and Independence.

And there precisely was the problem. Because there were more English-speakers than French-speakers in the population, in

141

election after election, after the democratic process had begun, the anglophone parties trounced the francophones. In French eyes, this was not only illogical, it was perverse and the French hate perversity. If opting for independence from France flouts the laws of Cartesian logic, then voting for an Anglo-Saxon form of independence is more than illogical. It is wicked and can only have been achieved by the cunning and deceit of Perfide Albion, in the person, usually, of its corrupt representative, the British Resident Commissioner.

His French colleagues did their best to counter this malign influence. It was not just the goodies. A decade before Independence but twenty years after the Presbyterian missionaries, the French government launched into a furious programme of primary school building. Whenever I travelled throughout the islands and came across a brand-new building, it invariably resounded with thirty or forty infant voices, raised in untuneful song, 'Allons enfants de la Patrie, le jour de Gloire est arrivé.' The Marseillaise. I couldn't really complain. They were usually built right next door to a much older and shabbier school where the same infants' brothers and sisters were practising God save the Queen in preparation for my visit.

Both schools were built in the same place, leaving huge distances before the next pair, on the same principle as the petrol companies, who all put their pumps together, in the name of consumer choice and superior additives.

But all this French educational effort was really too late. It takes eighteen years to train a voter. So the French Residency was reduced to gerrymandering on a mind-boggling scale. After each visit to the polls, election petitions had whittled down the Anglophone majority in the legislature. Special seats reserved for commercial interests and customary authorities mysteriously turned out to be filled with francophones that no-one had ever heard of.

After the latest elections a year or two before my arrival, the Anglophone parties had had enough. A massive majority of votes had been magicked into a meagre minority of seats. The French Residency manifestly rejoiced, the British seemed uncaring or impotent.

The Anglophone 'National Party' (having renamed itself the Vanuaaku Pati 'Our Land' – to emphasize that it owed nothing to the colonial powers), retreated into the areas which it controlled and set up what it chose to call 'Peoples Provisional Governments', with their own red and black flags and renegade parliament. Its leaders made it clear that they would stay there and sulk, until either new elections were held, or they gained an acknowledged parliamentary majority.

This was tricky. Police action against a clear majority of the country would not have been easy, but the French government was certainly not going to agree to the Vanuaaku Pati's demands. The first stand-off had lasted several months while everyone scratched their heads wondering what to do.

Then, unfortunately, the Vanuaaku Pati got impatient. They owned a building in Port Vila which they intended to make their headquarters, if and when they returned to power. In the latter part of 1977 they announced that they were going to march to the building to raise the PPG flag and dare the authorities to do their worst.

The Francophone parties, whimsically known, to themselves, as 'The Moderates', said they were having none of this. They would gather outside the building to drive the interlopers away. This was the time for the joint police forces of Britain and France to take action together to maintain and if necessary restore, order.

Unfortunately, not for the first or the last time in the history of the Condominium, the French police force found other things to do. There were none to be seen and increasingly urgent appeals from the British police commandant found the telephone lines inconveniently out of order.

The British police force therefore found itself alone between an increasingly restive crowd of 'moderates' who were starting to throw things, and the forces of the P.P.G. who in the Melanesian way, were keeping a prudent distance away while threatening to join battle.

It was then that the British police, perhaps, made a mistake. John Champion was not on the spot, nor, as the British Governor, would it have been proper for him to be there. But when the British police commandant and British administrator in local charge told John on the radio that things were getting out of hand, he authorised them to take action to disperse the crowd.

Unfortunately, since the Vanuaaku Pati were still out of range and it was the 'moderates' who were throwing things, this meant that it was mainly francophone eyes that were made to water by the British police teargas, and a Francophone youth who received a British rubber bullet in the stomach.

Huge emotion followed from the Moderates and the French Residency. Forgetting that their police had chosen to absent themselves, the French Government demanded the sacking of the British police commandant and the administrator, on pain of the immediate suspension of cooperation between the Metropolitan powers. John Champion himself, having been hastily summoned to the British Paddock, was confronted with a crowd of Moderates, still weeping copiously from the tear gas.

The French Mayor, always one for a dramatic gesture, threw his not inconsiderable bulk between John and the crowd, begging them not to do physical damage to 'Mon ami, Monsieur Champion'. Whatever the sins for which he and his perfidious government were responsible, he, Monsieur Delaveuve, was ready to die with him. It cannot have been easy for John to keep his dignity.

But the fall-out must have been even worse for someone of his shining integrity. Faced with the imminent breakdown of joint authority, he had no alternative but to suspend his two subordinates and send them both on leave to Australia to await events. Understandably, they protested their complete innocence, and he promised them a full and independent Inquiry.

But even this promise he was compelled to break. The Foreign Office brusquely told him that the priority was the restoration of relations with France. There would be no Inquiry and the errant two must be compelled to resign in absentia. And when John himself offered to go in their place, he was told to stay where he was and clear up the mess.

Small wonder, then, that his letter to us was full of gloom, describing not only the details of what came to be known as 'Les Événements', but also the darker side of island life, with its biting flies, unpalatable local food (which John described as 'looking, tasting and feeling like a foam-rubber cushion) and intolerable politics. We sympathised but had no idea that all this had anything to do with us.

As soon as John decently could, he resigned and took early retirement. I was appointed to replace him.

15

Resident Commissioner

Our first arrival in the New Hebrides was not auspicious. We flew there straight from Indonesia, where we were accorded an official send-off by the Indonesian government. As we left the VIP lounge in Jakarta to board the aircraft, the Chief of Protocol struggled after us with a parting gift from the Indonesian Minister of Foreign Affairs, a stuffed Bird of Paradise, complete with magnificent white, brown and red plumage, all in a massive domed glass case.

This was embarrassing. Birds of Paradise are highly protected, and the glass case weighed as much as a small trunk. As I staggered up the aircraft steps bearing this unlikely piece of hand-luggage, a disdainful French air hostess barred the way. 'Pas possible' she announced. 'C'est défendu.'

I explained that she could of course refuse to take the Minister's gift on board, but in that case I would have to return it to the VIP lounge and describe the circumstances. The airline would certainly lose its licence to land in Jakarta. The air hostess then thought it best to consult the captain and the upshot was that the Bird of Paradise was allowed aboard.

There it was strapped, still in its glass coffin, into a vacant first-class seat for the ten-hour flight to the South Pacific. Sitting comfortably, it did no harm to anybody except perhaps to a wandering Australian businessman who, having already dined well on the long flight from Europe, was clearly uncertain, when he caught sight of this unusual passenger, whether he was actually seeing what he thought he saw.

He started to comment, but then seemed to think better of it, as it occurred to him that he might well have lost touch with reality. So he decided to ignore the whole thing and spent the rest of the voyage in mournful contemplation of his toe-caps.

Nor was that the end of our troubles over that pesky parrot. I thought it might on the whole be undesirable and difficult to explain, for me to arrive in the New Hebrides carrying a large and illegal bird in an even larger glass case. Besides I was going to have to inspect a Guard of Honour on arrival and I needed my hands free to salute. So, without too much ceremony, I asked our elder teen-age son to carry the bird for me.

But James wasn't having any. He was on the lookout for birds of a different feather and thought the glass case might spoil his image. So observers of our first arrival in our new kingdom would have seen the Stuart family tumbling down the aircraft steps, quarrelling fiercely over a stuffed bird.

Nor were subsequent arrivals more successful. That first visit was only a reconnaissance. John Champion was still in post and we had to endure his agonised expression as his staff, soon to become mine, reproached him for abandoning his sacked officers. Three months later, after leave in England, I came back again on my own to assume the burdens of office. This time I flew west-about and changed planes in Fiji, having travelled, as is my wont, in jeans and a T-shirt.

I knew that on final arrival in Vila, I would have to inspect an even more impressive Guard of Honour, drawn from both British and French police forces and accompanied by the French police band – a tootling affair of drums, bugles and fifes that was apt, on no notice, to burst into a Melanesian version of 'Auprès de ma Blonde, Il fait bon, fait bon, fait bon,' possibly a tribute to my French Colleagues's unseen mistress.

I was also looking forward to my first meeting with that colleague, the formidable Inspecteur Général Jean-Jacques Robert, who outranked even the French High Commissioner for the South Pacific and had been sent to look after the interests of France in the count-down to Independence.

For this first crucial encounter I needed to be appropriately dressed and my white tropical Topee, crowned with the red and white cockatoo feathers of a Colonial Governor, was resting in its black japanned case in the aircraft hold. So too were my sparkling white uniform, sword and medals, ready for a rapid change of plumage during the stop-over in Fiji.

Unfortunately, however, the baggage-handlers neglected to unload all this finery in Fiji and it travelled serenely on to Australia, leaving me on the tarmac dressed in jeans, T-shirt and some beachcomber's rubber flip-flops, to await my final flight on to my new dominion.

I was furious. The airline officials did their best to placate me. 'Good news, Mr Stuart,' they announced after half-an-hour's futile searching. 'We've found your sword.'

Fortunately the image of arriving in Port Vila with a golden sword stuck through the belt of my jeans and with bare feet slapping the tarmac in rubber sandals, was too much for even my ill-humour. I sent a telegram ahead of us, cancelling the guard of honour and postponing the encounter with Robert until the following day.

That first meeting revealed further diplomatic rocks ahead. My colleague turned out to be a tough little Provençale, a good half metre shorter and five years older than I. He exuded Napoleonic self-confidence. He had once played Rugby for a French provincial team (and always managed to get visiting journalists to include this in their profiles of our contrasting personalities – much to my irritation, since I invariably failed to persuade them to give credit to my modest but international sporting qualifications).

Robert could speak English but normally declined to do so. This allowed him to assume a pained expression when my French subjunctives went astray, as they usually did. On the whole, though, his heart was in the right place. He recognised the inevitability of Independence and had indeed been sent there to make it happen. But he was determined to achieve this on terms honourable to France, and he was certainly not going to allow the wool to be pulled over his eyes by any effete, Cambridge-educated Anglais.

I was never quite sure if he had a sense of humour. Occasionally he would grin wolfishly at some unusually bizarre twist of Melanesian politics. Nor was he above making heavy fun of Pat as she laboured away in her schoolgirl French at the umpteenth dinner party, at which Robert and she were condemned to eternity to be seated in each other's company. 'Obbees' he would bellow down the table, as her desperate attempt to ask him about his leisure activities withered once more on the vine, 'Qu'est-ce-que c'est que ces "Obbees"?'

But the difference in our heights gave real trouble from the beginning. Just as with the earlier squabble over the elevations of our national flags, so it was not fitting for the head of France, in both senses of the word, to appear below the head of Britain. When we had an official photograph taken it was necessary on all occasions for us to seek out a staircase, so that he could stand two steps up from me and we could appear to be on the same level.

And my plumed topee only made matters worse. Eighteen inches of feathers on top of six foot seven of Resident Commissioner added up to a truly ludicrous total, alongside Robert's five foot something. Nor would matters have been improved if Robert too had worn his official uniform, since his headgear would then have been a flat French képi; which is perhaps why he preferred to remain in civilian dress.

The first time, therefore, that he came into the presence of what the local Bislama newspaper graphically described as my 'Hat mo grass blong arse blong Cock', Robert's understandable reaction was an expressive gallic shrug accompanied with an explosive 'Mon dieu. Ça c'est vraiment quelque chose'.

But I liked him, provided that I too was allowed to tease him from time to time. The surest way to do this was to invite someone to say Grace at one of our interminable working lunches. Robert could just about tolerate Priests. He had indeed little choice, since practically everyone in New Hebrides politics was ordained into one missionary church or another. But his whole Gallic anti-clerical soul revolted against what he regarded as mumbo-jumbo. He would sit at the bottom of the table spluttering away as God was invited, with great sincerity but at some length, to interest Himself in our deliberations. Robert's view was that we had enough difficulties to cope with as it was, without bringing outsiders into it.

And these difficulties did not seem to diminish as I began to settle into my job. The Condominium system was truly a monster. Nothing worked sensibly or, in many cases, at all. A supreme example was that High Court of joint jurisdiction which had been one of the main reasons for creating the Condominium in the first place.

Almost as soon as they had set it up, the two governments realised that a French and a British judge, sitting together, had about as much hope of reaching a consensus as Tweedledum and

148

Tweedledee. Even if their national interests had coincided, both were trained in entirely different traditions and accustomed to different laws. In criminal cases, French lawyers are accustomed to acting as both judge and inquisitor. Their job is to ask what questions they choose, in order to determine the truth and reveal the culprit. The British common-law judges, on the other hand, believe they are there to weigh up the evidence laid before them by counsel for the prosecution and the defence. This must be done in accordance with well defined rules, which give the benefit of the doubt always to the accused. No amount of willingness to compromise could obscure this basic difference of approach.

And in civil cases where the plaintiff was an angry French farmer asserting his right to land and the defendant an equally determined Brit; and where both of them were consummate liars with perjured witnesses, it was really too much to expect the two judges not to find from time to time in favour of their respective but opposite sides. With no president this was an inevitable recipe for impasse. Nor would it have been a solution to give either of them a casting vote, since he (it was always a he, no woman would have tolerated such a nonsense for a moment), might then as well have been sitting by himself.

Within five years of the creation of the Condominium, therefore, as the files of unconcluded cases piled up, some pesky bureaucrat in London or Paris came up with what must have seemed to him at the time a jolly clever wheeze. A third chair would be placed between the British and French judges, and on it would be seated a President of the court, to be nominated by the King of Spain.

There they all are, therefore, in the early pictures, the British barrister in his wig and gown, the Frenchman in his bands and an impressively bearded Spaniard between them, dressed in a sort of turban that may well have been part of his Moorish inheritance. In front of this formidable trio stands the Melanesian accused, dressed in nothing very much.

This troika system seems to have worked reasonably well for the first quarter-century of the condominium. At least it resulted in a single decision from which a judgement could be executed, gleefully by one side and no doubt reluctantly by the other. But things fell apart in the middle thirties when General Franco threw the King of Spain out of his home country. A sad ex-monarch, living in exile, was in no position to appoint Spanish judges to the New Hebrides or to anywhere else. So the chairman's seat in our Joint Court became vacant and remained so until Independence, more than forty years later.

A marked characteristic of a Condominium, however, is the ability to ignore reality. Things that have happened have not happened and things that have not happened are taken for real. There is no percentage in pointing out that the king is wearing no clothes. To the very end, therefore, the situation remained, at least in theory, that where a French and a British judge were sitting together, and where they were unable to agree, they would both turn to the empty chair between them and enquire (in French or English, or in Spanish if they knew it) '... and what is your opinion, Mr President?'

After waiting politely for the reply which perforce never came, since there was no-one there to give it, they would then adjourn the case for the Chairman's ruling. I was told, though I never had time to check it, that some such cases had been pending for forty years or more without a decision.

It was no wonder that we were all somewhat disorientated. And some of us were more disorientated than others. The ones I really felt for were the about-to-be citizens of the new state. For seventy years they had been technically stateless, since the metropolitan powers had been unable to agree on where sovereignty lay. But yet they were subject to the ludicrous Condominium system and obliged to conform to its always ambiguous laws. Small wonder, therefore, that one of the most able of the New Hebrides politicians, a former schoolmaster with a quiet dignity that shamed us all, should have written a despairing poem entitled 'Who am I?' I couldn't tell him. By that stage I rather wondered about myself.

When I arrived things seemed to be at an impasse. Having successfully gerrymandered the results of the last elections to prevent the Vanuaaku Pati taking power, the Resident Commissioners, under French influence after John Champion's prestige had suffered a catastrophic drop in the wake of 'Les Événements', had installed an allegedly joint Anglophone/Francophone government, under French influence, but headed by a pantomime ex-constable of the British Police, whose role, in the words of W.S. Gilbert, was to 'add verisimilitude to an otherwise bald and unconvincing narrative'.

This government was supposed to implement the 'Plan Dijoud'. Paul Dijoud was the French 'Minister of Overseas Departments and Territories'. An intelligent but overbearing man of colossal vanity, he had nevertheless endeared himself to us on his first visit after my arrival by disembarking with his mistress after a long overnight flight from Paris, with five livid scratches down each cheek, all still dripping blood. The image of his presumed night of passion made it difficult for me to avoid catching Robert's eye.

The 'Plan Dijoud' was what the French call a 'Projet'. This in itself caused problems. The assumed similarities of the French and English languages are in fact the cause of endless misunderstandings. To an English-speaker, a project is no more than a possibility, subject to debate, refinement and, if necessary, abandonment. To a Frenchman a 'projet' is a full draft, usually in writing and often worked out in minute detail, subject indeed to debate, but very often to be accepted or rejected as a whole. When, therefore, Dijoud produced the already-prepared text of his 'projet' out of his pocket, many of the anglophones felt pre-empted, when really all they needed was a better translator.

The same sort of misunderstanding arose when the French asked a question. 'Je demande quelque chose' is apt to sound to an anglophone like a threat, when really to the French it is no more than a mark of interrogation. Very often it seemed that we would all have got on better in Bislama. At least then the puppet Chief Minister might have understood what we were talking about.

Even had he done so, however, he was in no position to deliver an authoritative response from the people of the New Hebrides to the 'Plan Dijoud'.

The majority Vanuaaku Pati was still locked in the sterility of their People's Provisional Government. A disgruntled early settler in the new Hebrides had once written a book about the islands entitled 'The Isles of Illusion'. The PPG was an illusion which we nevertheless had to take seriously, like the Russian Empress Catherine the Great's 'Potemkin Villages', where cardboard cut-out shop fronts were required to be taken as evidence of a prosperous, even if non-existent, village.

Wherever the Vanuaaku Pati was in the clear majority (which meant in a major proportion of the islands) the PPG flag flew from makeshift masts to symbolize a no-go area for the Resident

Commissioners, for the Condominium Government and, above all, for the 'Plan Dijoud'. Not that the Vanuaaku Pati were hostile to the idea of Independence – far from it. But Dijoud's plan envisaged a decentralised form of Independence in which the islands where the Francophones might reasonably hope to form a majority, would be virtually independent of the control of the central government, though still subject to the influence of France. This was not at all what the majority party had in mind.

Although therefore, in true Melanesian style, the leaders of the Vanuaaku Pati still lived in Port Vila town and went about their everyday business as priests, teachers, civil servants, farmers or full-time politicians, they were nevertheless technically in revolt against the lawful government and liable to arrest and imprisonment for treason.

The first thing that had to be done, therefore, was somehow to bring the VP back around the negotiating table. There were certain factors encouraging this. The more intelligent VP leaders realised that they were in a dead-end. So did most of the ministers of the puppet government, of whom the most sensible was Gerard Leymang, a splendid Catholic priest, whose chuckle started somewhere around his clerical boots and who, despite his authoritarian background, knew what it was to compromise.

Besides, the ministers were fed up with trying to explain the situation to their nominal Chief and knew that the time had come for a change. For the Resident Commissioners' part, Robert's orders were to be conciliatory, while I was brand-new and therefore unaware of the complications and untainted with the problems that had bedeviled John Champion's latter days.

My first act therefore was to ask my engagingly sardonic deputy, Chris Turner, (who later became a Colonial Governor in his own right, but had been on the islands for years and knew everyone and everything) to call on the VP leaders and ask them to lunch.

At first they were hesitant and I put this down to a reluctance to engage in the political process (though I realised later that it probably had at least as much to do with a reluctance to engage with Mangu's roast beef). Eventually, however, the VP president, Walter Lini – another priest, though this time an Anglican one, who was later to become the independent country's first Prime Minister – said he thought they could perhaps venture across for talks to our island of Iririki, provided I realised that they recognized only the authority of the PPG.

To me it did not much matter what they recognized, provided they came to lunch, so a day or two later our steward John put an extra couple of leaves in the dining-room table and we all settled down to await Mangu's cooking, with what I had, by then, come to realise was the appropriate mood of grim anticipation.

First, however, we had to get over the hurdle of whom to ask to say grace, the Anglican priest Walter Lini or the Catholic Gerard Leymang – or even the Presbyterian pastor Fred Timakata or the ambivalent Chief Minister George Kalsakau. Robert refused to have anything to do with this and sat glowering at the bottom of the table. Eventually, in a spirit of compromise which boded well for the future of the discussions, the politicians agreed that Lini would say grace at the beginning and Leymang at the end. So it was that we began the construction of a Government of National Unity by asking a joint blessing on food that was certainly in need of help of some kind.

After that things went rapidly. There were more lunches at Iririki, until the delegates tactfully decided that they would prefer to eat elsewhere by themselves. And anyway by that time the presence of the Resident Commissioners was really superfluous. The islanders have always prided themselves on the 'Melanesian Way' of dialogue, compromise and mutual respect. To a certain extent this was a myth, like the assertion that all Englishmen sleep with hot-water-bottles and play cricket. But there was truth in the myth nevertheless and anyway the Melanesian politicians were really more comfortable speaking Bislama among themselves, rather than struggling with French and English, of which only Gerard Leymang spoke both with any fluency.

Besides the really unifying factor between the two delegations was that they all wanted to get rid of both France and Britain as quickly as possible, but were too polite to say so in front of the Resident Commissioners. In a surprisingly short time, therefore, the two leaders came to tell my colleague and myself that the Vanu-aaku Pati and the 'Moderates' had decided to form a coalition, which would be led by Gerard Leymang. This Government of National Unity's sole task would be to set up a commission to agree on a new constitution, followed by elections to choose the government of a new and independent Republic.

That suited me and my Whitehall masters fine, and it was not inconsistent with the 'Plan Dijoud' either. So Robert was soon able to convey the French government's consent, reserving only to the Metropolitan Governments the power to dictate the exact time-table of Independence. The G.N.U. could begin work.

However, before the new administration could be voted into office by a compliant legislature, there were still one or two hitches to be unravelled. Gerard Leymang had promised Lini the Ministry of Information as well as the deputy premiership. But some of his 'moderate' colleagues objected, primed, it was unkindly suggested, by the French Residency. They were shrewd enough to realise the importance of the media and particularly of the control of the national radio in the run up to Independence.

Faced with the intransigence of his extremists, Leymang tried to renege on his promise and for a while the negotiations were close to breakdown. Greatly daring, however, I ventured to quote, to the priest, the Sermon on the Mount, 'Let your yea be yea and your nay be nay' and he had the good sense to withdraw. This only increased the general respect for him, since few politicians, even priests, allow themselves to be guided by the precepts of the new Testament.

So, within a couple of months, the leaders of the New Hebrides sat down to plan themselves a new Constitution. It was a heady time. The negotiations made rapid progress, helped by advisers from Britain and from France (ours was an engaging Indian academic with a Finnish girl-friend, neither of whom could be accused of being in Whitehall's pocket).

Near the end of the process, we all went to a meeting of the South Pacific Commission in Tahiti to tell the other nations of the Pacific what we were achieving. To tease the conference inter-preters and to emphasise at the same time that we were the sole bilingual nation in the Pacific basin, we all insisted on mixing French sentences with English ones in our speeches, to the accom-paniment of hopeless clicks from the other delegates' earphones as they tried to keep up with what was happening. This helped to lighten the atmosphere, along with the departure of the chief Australian delegate, who, having opened the session with a fiery attack on French colonial policy, had been provided by the wily French High Commissioner with a beautiful Tahitian girl and a ticket to Bora Bora island and was not to reappear for the rest of the conference.

Back home in the New Hebrides, the new Constitution was all but complete. All it needed was the endorsement of the two Metropolitan Governments. Then it could be passed into law and we could move on to Elections and Independence.

But things were not that simple. They never were in the New Hebrides. The French and British Ministers concerned were due to come out to Port Vila to symbolise the consent of the Condominium authorities and together to sign the new constitution into law. But Dijoud arrived in a towering rage. It was evident that he had not read the text of the draft constitution until he had got on his plane at Charles de Gaulle airport. Immediately on arrival in the New Hebrides he summoned us all, including the team which had laboured so mightily to produce an agreed text, to denounce the constitution as a manifesto for a dictatorship.

When my own master, an inoffensive junior British Minister, whose main and understandable wish was not to quarrel with France, pointed out mildly enough that Dijoud's personal legal adviser had participated in the drafting and the consensus and had presumably kept Paris informed throughout, his protest was brushed aside. This, said Dijoud was a Fascist Constitution. He would have nothing to do with it.

Wearily we looked at each other. Everyone was dog tired. Gerard Leymang, who had kept the coalition together throughout the negotiations, said that, in that case, he too would wash his hands of the whole thing and go back to the Church. Unable to think of any new ploy I suggested that we should all adjourn to Iririki for lunch to talk things over. Presumably for both culinary and constitutional reason, this seemed only to deepen Leymang's mood of inspissated gloom.

Eventually, however, since no one could think of any better suggestion, we all forgathered around the familiar dining table, gloomily sipping tonic-water laced with Bisodol. My Minister invited his French colleague to explain his objections. Hitherto all we had heard was hissing noises, interspersed with explosions of 'Incroyable', 'Insupportable', 'Imbécile'. Now, however, Dijoud stopped hissing long enough to explain that we had not followed his 'Plan'. The draft constitution now before us was for a unitary state with federal add-ons, not the other way around as in the Plan Dijoud. Ignoring the fact that France is itself about the most centralised state in Western Europe, Dijoud again denounced the draft as 'fascist', 'a dictatorship', 'a charade' and an 'idiocy'. It must be entirely redrafted.

The next twelve hours were hideous. Redraft after redraft of the crucial passages was tried, considered and rejected. Everyone, including my Minister and all the New Hebrideans, attempted to be conciliatory, but Dijoud was not to be conciliated. At last however, exhaustion and jet-lag set in even there, and around midnight we reached a compromise.

As well as a sovereign Parliament, each of the main islands would have its own elected regional assembly, with substantial powers which it could invoke, if it so wished, against the central government. With enormous relief we all signed and went off to bed.

Fifteen years later someone asked me to write an article explaining how the French Minister Dijoud had 'rescued' the independence negotiations from certain failure. By that time I had left the Foreign Office and my reply is not to be printed in a book intended primarily for family reading. Still, we had our constitution and Robert and I could instruct our deputies to work on a law for the General Elections which would set the seal on the whole process. Even Jean-Jacques Robert permitted himself a wintry smile.

Again, everything went incredibly smoothly. Much of the credit for this must go to as hard working a bunch of expatriate and New Hebridean civil servants as I ever hope to meet . The British Colonial Service were never averse to working themselves out of a job, provided they were told exactly what they were doing and why. And even the French district officers, once Dijoud had blessed the constitution, buckled down to registering the population, constructing the polling booths, arranging the supervision of the count and declaring the results in the presence of the parties. A French TV journalist asked me the age-old Colonialist question. 'How do you know that the people are ready for Independence – do they really know what they are doing?' I could only invite him to go and see for himself.

On Election Day, November 14th, 1979 the two hundred and sixty-two polling stations throughout the islands opened on time.

Orderly queues formed outside the booths. One admiring journalist reported that, at a station in the main island of Efate, where the tradition of the separation of males and females had been maintained, 'the villagers had organised themselves so that women voted in the morning and men in the afternoon'. This, he wrote, had been so successful that 'the polling-station there was able to close by midday'. If true this would appear effectively to have disenfranchised the local males, but it did not seem to be borne out by the voting figures, so we took no action.

At the final count it became apparent that 90 per cent of the New Hebrides electorate had voted. There had been no disturbances and a visiting group of United National observers were satisfied that all was well. It had been a major triumph for the New Hebrides people. And as for me, I really felt that Mr Carruthers would have been proud of us.

Two days later, however, the tensions began all over again. As the results came in to the chamber of the legislature, Robert and I took it in turns to announce them, in English and in French (I suggested that, as a further gesture of solidarity, we should read them in each-other's language, but my colleague thought I was trying to be funny). As the declarations went on, it became apparent that all the assumptions of the Plan Dijoud and of Dijoud's own last minute intervention, had been overturned.

The independence constitution contained the usual provision that its central clauses could not be amended or deleted except by a two-thirds majority in the new parliament. The idea was to provide a period of stability during which the new constitution could bed itself down. When the counting was complete, however, the Vanuaaku Pati had won 26 of the 39 seats. They already had their two thirds majority and could do what they liked. Even worse, from Dijoud's point of view, the Regional Assemblies in the two main outlying islands of Santo and Tanna, where the French hoped to retain their hegemony, also had VP majorities. The elaborate midnight compromise to allow the regions to retain virtual independence from the centre had proved valueless to France, since the anglophone Vanuaaku Pati controlled them all.

My Colleague was aghast and his officials set about collecting material for election petitions against the results (which in the end came to nothing since, in truth, there was no substance in any of them). And I too, saw trouble ahead. The malign legacy of the condominium was not simply going to disappear. The VP leaders would need wisdom and magnanimity to see through the compromises that would be needed to keep the country together after the French and British left.

On the night the results were declared, the new Government threw a mammoth party. I attended it and was accused of triumphalism by a French reporter who saw me there. In truth, however, my purpose was to catch Walter Lini at a moment when he was relaxed and unafraid, to try to persuade him that the francophone Catholic priest, Gerard Leymang, who had served the Government of National Unity so well, should be appointed as the first President of the new Republic.

In accordance with the Constitution, the office of President was to be largely ceremonial and symbolic. Walter Lini, as Prime Minister, would control all the decisions of substance. But Leymang's presence as titular Head of State would reassure the French and the francophones, and his wise advice would help to keep Walter's somewhat volatile feet on the ground.

But it was no good. Lini had political debts to pay and the Presidency had already been promised to a party stalwart, who had also just about enough of a following of his own to have posed a challenge to Lini if he had stayed in active politics.

But, even if we had been successful, neither Robert's attempts to alter the electoral balance, nor mine to stabilize the political one, were in fact worth the effort we put into them. We could have saved our breath to cool our porridge. Things were stirring in Santo and in Tanna which, for a while seemed likely to upset everything and were eventually to lead to a combined intervention by the finest fighting troops of Britain and France.

16

The Land of the Holy Spirit

After Captain Cook's departure, the next great event in the history of the northern island of Espiritu Santo was the arrival of the American army during the Second World War. The terrible battles in the Solomon Islands, just to the north of the New Hebrides, marked the high water mark of the Japanese expansion into the Coral Sea. The base from which the Americans fought that battle was Santo.

A hundred thousand GIs, serviced by ten thousand New Hebrideans – one in ten of the total population of the islands, built a huge military base around the protected harbour at Luganville, at the southern end of the island. Wharfs, airfields, roads, buildings, ammunition dumps, PX stores, whorehouses, churches, and Chinese laundries sprang up in what had been Dark Bush, the tribal lands of the interior. The harbour was full of warships, tank transports, landing craft, troopships, pinnaces and fast patrol boats.

The author James Mitchener, who visited Santo during the war, wrote his story 'South Pacific' about the love of an American GI for a girl from Aoba (which he called Bali Hai), the nearby island that hung like a white cloud just across the horizon. Revealingly not a single character in that story, or in the Rogers and Hammerstein musical that gave it worldwide fame, was a native New Hebridean. Instead the girl and her mother, 'Bloody Mary' were Vietnamese, from the community of indentured workers who had been brought in by the French from their Indo-Chinese colony before the war. American dramas about racial integration could just about imagine union between a US soldier and a beautiful light-skinned Vietnamese. To write of a love affair between a whiteman and a black Melanesian was at that time clearly unthinkable.

159

Nor is it likely that, if the Japanese had got to Santo, their 'Greater East Asian Co-prosperity sphere' would have been any more tolerant. Fortunately for the New Hebrides, however, after ferocious battles on land, air and sea, the Japanese were stopped at Guadalcanal in the Solomans and thereafter pushed slowly back up the chain of islands towards their homeland. Santo was left to moulder in peace and, by the time I arrived, the crumbling jetties, decayed quonset huts and rutted airstrips were all the surface signs that were left of that titanic struggle.

But as in other places where the Americans had passed, 'Man Santo' – the custom people, found it impossible to sink back into what they had been before. Cargo cults, which were to find their most exotic expression in the island of Tanna to the south, sprang up as quasi-religions, to convince the people that the Americans would return to shower the islands with material goods as they had during the war. The returning post-war settlers, mostly French and French half-castes, found it harder than they had before to assert their absolute right to lands which Man Santo had always regarded as his own. The shortage of food after the war led to the introduction of cattle by the planters and the fencing-off of Dark Bush whose ownership had never been properly defined, and which Man Santo regarded as his own. As so often in the New Hebrides, the reaction of the people was to turn back to 'Kastom', the traditional values of the Melanesians, based on the ownership and sacrifice of curly-tusked pigs and the rejection of the whiteman's values.

In Santo, however, this reversion to the 'Melanesian Way' found itself a leader of genius. Jimmy Stevens, (a semi-illiterate who just as often signed himself 'Stephens') claimed to be the Santo-born son of a Scottish seaman and a Tongan Princess. Who the Scottish seaman was (and indeed who was the Tongan and whether she was really a princess) seems to be one of those mysteries of which great myths are made. All that is known is that, during the war, this charismatic little man of immense whiskeriness and charm, somehow, at the age of only sixteen, got himself taken on by the Americans as a foreman at the army hospital. There he substantially increased his prestige by doling out stores that probably did not belong to him, and subsequently, after the war, got taken on by the British as a bulldozer driver.

Jimmy, however, had ambitions. His heart was in becoming a Melanesian 'Big Man'. Fortunately for him, this status is accessible in the islands, even for people of such dubious background. All that is needed is a sufficient supply of pigs to be killed to mark each grade-stage in the gentrification process, and a substantial commitment to 'Kastom', allied to a ready tongue. Jimmy Stevens had all of these. He ended up as a 'Moli', which is something in standing between a Duke and an Earl.

But Jimmy was certainly more than an upwardly mobile rogue – though he was that too. Perhaps precisely because of his international background, he had from the beginning a clear understanding that what was needed was action to challenge the settlers in their occupation of land before they overran it all. Some twenty years after the war therefore, Stevens and his followers founded the 'Nagriamel' movement and by the 'Act of Dark Bush' announced that the extension of foreign-owned plantations must cease.

To back up this claim, Stevens established, in the disputed area, the domain of Vanafo (or Tanafo, or Fanafo). This settlement, twenty miles north of Luganville, was, he announced, to be the centre of the re-occupation of the ancestral lands. By a judicious mixture of his own dubious land-grants and promises, Jimmy there managed to attract to himself an excitable and growing population of converts, not just from Santo but from all over the northern islands.

Showing a clear grasp of dynastic politics, which the Tudor kings might have envied, Stevens also persuaded the various island communities settled at Vanafo, that their surest way to the ear of their leader was for each of them to provide him with a wife, ('Women given to the cause' as an official Nagriamel publication described them). He also successfully played on his supposed regal origins to found, like Henry VIII, an official church of his own to bless these unions.

'The Nagriamel Federation Independent United Royal Church', at first scandalised the missionaries. Nor did the plantation owners much like it when Jimmy, as the self-appointed descendant of Moses, quoted the Book of Proverbs at them 'Remove not the old landmarks and enter not into the fields of the fatherless'. But there was not much they could do about it and they soon learned to come to terms with Jimmy or to leave him alone.

Since Nagriamel's original quarrel had been with the French settlers, the British Residency, in the oversimplified way of the

Condominium, at first regarded Jimmy almost as an ally, while the French, if they considered him at all, thought of him as an enemy. But as the anglophone Vanuaaku Pati began to dominate the nationalist politics of the new Hebrides, Jimmy was quite shrewd enough to realise that his best hope of sustaining a feudal oligarchy in Santo lay in playing up to the federalist hopes of France.

In 1976 he went to Paris to propose to M. Dijoud's predecessor, Olivier Stirn, that Nagriamel should switch its support to France, in return for a school and a dispensary at Vanafo, economic and technical aid in setting up a cattle ranching project, and the establishment of a French naval base on Santo.

M. Stirn apparently agreed to all this except for the naval base, which would have been difficult to explain to the British. At all events he must have been sufficiently impressed with Jimmy to arrange for him to dine with the French President, Valerie Giscard d'Estaing. History does not relate what passed between the two potentates during that dinner, but I would love to have been a fly on the wall. Jimmy Steven's normal costume was a battered T-shirt and a greasy beret. He must have looked like a street urchin alongside the patrician Frenchman.

Unfortunately for Stevens, however, while he knew quite clearly what he wanted for Nagriamel and had sufficient experience of the two Condominium powers to understand how to play one off against the other, there were other forces becoming interested in Santo, which were quite outside Jimmy's experience and had private agendas of their own.

Most of these were American. James Mitchener's romance of the South Pacific had invested Santo with a mysterious glamour. While the Vietnam war was collapsing into chaos and humiliation, the tropical islands of the bright blue sea appeared to many American GIs as an impossible dream of indolence and peace. Some of them had married Vietnamese wives, or were reluctant to abandon their Vietnamese girl friends and coffee-coloured offspring. Advertisements that appeared in the Forces magazines, offering them on completion of their Vietnam tour, 'a place in paradise', seemed to them the fulfilment of that dream.

The dream merchant was an American property speculator based in Hawaii, Eugene Peacock. After stumbling upon Santo in 1967, Peacock bought up derelict plantations on the eastern coasts of the island, attracted by low prices, the absence of taxes and the prospect of quick and easy profits. To lure the romantic ex-GIs, Peacock split the land up into small, high-density parcels and then, when even smaller plots became possible, acted as agent for the first purchasers in yet further sub-divisions.

Most of the buyers put down their money without even coming to see the islands, which was just as well. Hog harbour (renamed by Peacock, for obvious reasons, 'Lokalee Beach') is a hot, dusty, fly-ridden place, sweltering under an unforgiving sun upon the infertile soil. Peacock's hotel, restaurant, golf course, lush gardens, coral reefs, white sands, coconut palms, soft music and dusky maidens, had shrunk by the end to a derelict café, a parking lot and ten ramshackle bungalows.

Nor did the lavish advertisements in the Saigon Post mention that even the title to the land was disputed by the Kastom owners. But the dream was strong and Peacock is reputed to have made five million dollars from his sales and subdivisions.

His most astute move, however, was to make a deal with Jimmy Stevens. Although the land which Peacock was purporting to sell was also the subject of conflicting claims by Man Santo, it was not in the centre of Jimmy's shadowy empire, and had, at least in theory, been alienated to foreigners for many years.

Moreover Stevens badly needed 'Cargo' in order to prove to his followers that he had something to offer them in exchange for his 'wives'. Peacock, with his materialist philosophy, understood this well. Bull-dozers and jeeps, cranes, ploughs, lorries, graders and machine tools were seen for the first time at Vanafo and although it was never entirely clear who they belonged to, they provided visible proof to Man Santo that Jimmy was the 'Big Man' he had always claimed to be.

Although Eugene Peacock himself probably never egged Jimmy on to declare Santo independent, it was inherent in his individualist philosophy that the new American settlers would expect as little interference as possible from the Condominium authorities 200 miles to the south.

Moreover Peacock certainly helped to strengthen the influence of the French in Santo and to alienate Stevens from the British administration. The latter were adamantly opposed to the prospect of a new American invasion. The British Resident Commissioner pointed out that, if Peacock's plans went ahead, there would in 25 years be more Americans in Santo then Melanesians and, as one of his staff acidly commented, 'I suppose there would be lots of jobs for black servants.'

The French, however, were more pragmatic. The land that Peacock had bought for his sub-divisions mostly 'belonged' to derelict French planters or to the 'Societé Français Des Nouvelles Hebrides (SFNH)', which had previously been the main target of Nagriamel's displeasure. The French Government were no doubt delighted to get their compatriots off their backs and, at the same time, to shift onto the Anglo-Saxons the responsibility for any friction between Man Santo and the incomers.

On the principle that 'Mine enemy's enemy is my friend', Peacock, Jimmy Stevens and the French Resident Commissioner formed an unlikely triumvirate in defence of Kastom, Francophonie and the right of every clean living American to find his own frontier and carry his own gun.

But Peacock did not last all that long. As the Vietnam war came to an end and the boys went home, so the flow of funds into the dream began to dry up. By the time of New Hebrides Independence his company was bankrupt.

Jimmy Stevens too was becoming disillusioned. His followers complained that Peacock's scheme was just another form of land expropriation. Few of those glittering machines were left in Vanafo, and Jimmy wrote to Peacock to complain that money owed to him had never been paid. Besides, by that time an altogether more powerful and sinister American group had become interested in Santo.

The Phoenix Foundation of Carson City, Nevada had had a checkered history. The founder, Michael Oliver, was himself a refugee from war torn Europe, who had made his fortune in America. There he became a champion of personal and political freedom, following the half-baked economic theories of the Austrian Ludwig van Mises, which Oliver equated with all the excesses of freebooting capitalism.

This ultimate expression of individualism rejected all forms of government or central direction, other than for the protection of persons and property. From this it was but a short step to announcing that America itself had become a totalitarian state, where Fascism and Socialism reigned side by side and which all red-blooded Americans should quit as soon as possible.

Oliver was a persuasive person and a wealthy one. He had tapped a rich vein in the individualism of the American far right. So he decided to found a new state, where like-minded souls could together live a life of unfettered liberty.

His first attempt was, on the face of it an unlikely venture for a citizen of the desert state of Nevada. He decided to build a four-hundred acre concrete raft anchored to the Minerva Reef, two hundred miles from the Pacific kingdom of Tonga. The ownership of this improbable kingdom had never been entirely clear. This was not surprising, as the Minerva Reef is four foot under water at high tide. But Oliver thought he could build on it a high-rise city of the sea. This did not, however, appeal to the King of Tonga, a massive twenty-five stoner, of whom one would think it unwise to make an enemy. He sailed to the reef in his royal yacht, tore down the flag of the embryo republic and that was the end of Minerva.

Oliver, however, was not deterred and tried again closer to home. Under 'General' Mitchell Livingstone Werbell III, an operation backed by Oliver tried to take over Abaco island in the Bahamas, but this scheme too collapsed in confusion.

The Phoenix foundation's next attempt was on Gaya Island in the New Hebrides, which Oliver had come across in the course of his wanderings. But that scheme too blew up, this time literally. Before the freedom-loving Americans could arrive, the volcano on Gaya exploded and all the inhabitants had to be evacuated.

A less determined person than Oliver might then have concluded that fate was against him and his plans, but at that moment a new, if unlikely, god-in-a-box appeared in the shape of Jimmy Stevens, whom Oliver met in Fiji during one of Jimmy's junkets, paid for by Eugene Peacock.

At first Oliver encouraged Jimmy to set up a movement for complete independence in Santo under the influence of the Phoenix Foundation, on the lines of its original plan for Abaco. A 'constitution' was drafted for the 'Republic of Vemarana', promising strictly limited government, full individual rights, a gold-backed currency and freedom from all taxation.

Very quickly, however, Oliver realised the parallel between his scheme and the 'Plan Dijoud', for substantial autonomy for Santo under the patronage of France. The failure of the Abaco coup d'état had also given Oliver a distaste for trying to create his new state by force of arms.

Accordingly, in 1978 his spokesman wrote to the French authorities urging them to defend France's interests against Walter Lini's 'communist threat'. In return for French recognition of Vemarana, he offered:

> 'Moli Stevens has agreed to co-operate with you in helping form an association with New Caledonia; thus while France could comply with the requirements of Independence, the key areas of the New Hebrides would still maintain a close association, administratively and otherwise, with France.'

To back up this bizarre proposal, Oliver and Jimmy Stevens went to see Paul Dijoud in Paris and handed over copies of Vemarana's draft 'constitution'. This was, however, too much for even Dijoud to swallow, (though he later described Jimmy Stevens to me as 'Our Best friend in the new Hebrides').

Besides Oliver had already damaged his credibility by supporting a proposal to settle 100,000 Vietnamese Boat People in Santo (as many as the whole population of the New Hebrides put together), as a means of establishing the economic infrastructure of the proposed new state.

Asked to justify the plan to settle the Vietnamese on land whose ownership was already fiercely disputed, Jimmy Stevens announced that they would be set to work by Man Santo planting peanuts, cocoa and coconuts, raising cattle and building houses. This vision of the industrious Vietnamese, with their ancient civilisation, becoming hewers of wood and drawers of water for Jimmy Stevens carried little conviction and Dijoud turned it down out of hand.

Nevertheless Oliver pressed on to provide Jimmy Stevens with at least the trappings, if not the reality, of sovereign power. Work on the draft constitution was completed. He also wrote to Jimmy announcing the despatch of a powerful transmitter for Vanafo's clandestine radio, some Nagriamel flags, two hundred uniforms, a first consignment of a new currency engraved with Jimmy's head, and 25,000 blue and gold passports for the new state (part of the Phoenix Foundation's fund raising effort involved a promise of

Nagriamel citizenship to anyone who would subscribe $1,000 to the cause). Unfortunately the passports never reached Santo. They were somewhat naively consigned via Port Vila, described as 'travel documents', and were confiscated by the authorities.

All this was, however, heady stuff for the former bulldozer driver, and when I went to call on him in Vanafo, Jimmy met me with unaffected hospitality, but an assumption of at least equal status. Looking rather like a moth-eaten Father Christmas, he invited me to inspect his ceremonial guard, most of whom were also in need of a good tailor, and announced that on his next visit to Vila, he would be sure to look me up.

This cordial stand-off, however, could not last. Once the country-wide elections had returned a Vanuaaku Pati majority in Santo as well as in the rest of the country, Jimmy had to act. He denounced the elections as fraudulent, the result of the introduction of people from other islands illegally enfranchised in Santo, and marched his army from Vanafo to Luganville township, with the declared intention of taking over the administration.

Much the same thing had happened four years before. On that occasion the incipient rebellion had evaporated as soon as eighty New Hebrides policemen of the French and British mobile forces arrived in Luganville from the capital. The British Police Mobile Unit was a splendidly disciplined body of armed constables, under the command of a British officer, Ian Cook. Apart from 'Les Evénements' which had proved the last straw for John Champion, the PMU had hardly ever had to fire a shot in anger. Despite their bloodstained past, the Melanesians are on the whole a peaceable people and the total number of casualties in all the tangled events leading up to and after Independence was two. I had little doubt that, once the joint Franco/British police force was deployed on the streets of Luganville, Stevens would go home.

But it would have been no good for the British police to arrive in Santo alone. Apart from the fact that the Condominium required the French and British Resident Commissioners to act together in all matters concerning security, Stevens' main allies in Santo were Frenchmen, or French half-castes, or Francophone New Hebrideans. The idea of British policemen hitting Frenchmen on the head would have seriously rattled the bars in London and Paris. In any case, 'Les Evénements' had shown that unilateral action by me would have led to a, perhaps final, breakdown of my relations with Jean-Jacques Robert.

Fortunately, however, the earlier successful precedent of joint action made it really impossible for my colleague to refuse to act when faced by Jimmy's announcement that he was in Luganville to stay. So, that same evening, the British PMU were loaded into the *Euphrosyne*, the rolling old tub that doubled as the British Resident Commissioner's official yacht, and the French police into a coastal steamer under Robert's control. Together they set sail for Santo.

With hindsight I should perhaps have insisted that the French and the British contingents should be mixed up on both boats. But it is doubtful whether Robert would have agreed and anyway the PMU were used to the *Euphrosyne*, whose captain, Leith Nasak, (splendidly arrayed in naval uniform, as were his crew, down to the roly-poly cook, Stephen) had sailed the Coral Sea for years and knew the islands backwards.

Anyway, having sailed separately, when the ships were half-way to Santo, Robert's radioed orders turned the French command around and brought his unit back to Vila. In the dark, neither Nasak nor I at first knew what had happened. When I did find out, we were enjoying a leisurely wine tasting with friends, with the feeling that the die had been cast and there was nothing more we could do. On being summoned to the telephone by the British Commandant of Police to give me the bad news, I was angrier than I have ever been before or since.

When I contacted Robert, however, he was unrepentant. He had been trying to get hold of me, he said, but had failed because I was out drinking. We had sent representatives by air to Santo the day before to make a last attempt to persuade Stevens to return to Vanafo, and Robert had heard from his man that evening that Jimmy had said he would probably withdraw within two or three days. So to send our police forces on to Luganville, said Robert, would have been unnecessary and provocative. He had therefore told his ship to come back.

There was nothing I could do. Stevens did not withdraw and I guess he never had any intention of doing so. But the moment for sending the police had passed and Santo had to be left to look after itself.

17

Rebellions and Taboos

We had promised to hand over the district administration to the new government. As in Uganda the whole improbable structure of local government had, since the foundation of the Condominium, been held together by tough and resourceful young expatriate officers, known locally as District Agents, with a handful of policemen, and sometimes a doctor and an agriculturalist. Each of the District Agents had been at the same time administrator, judge, tax collector, builder of roads and harbours, public health officer, jailor, and political mentor to the local population.

The difference in the New Hebrides was that in every district there were two of them, one French and one British. They lived in separate compounds, usually separated by a mile or two of coconut plantations. There they held separate court as independent potentates, sometimes friends, sometimes rivals, always wary of each other and always jealously guarding their own influence and clientele. As with everything else in the New Hebrides it was improbable and chaotic, but it worked, after a fashion.

There was, however, no way of handing over such a system as a going concern to the fledgling government of Vanuatu. In Uganda it had been relatively easy. As Independence approached, more and more of the District Commissioners there were already African. Where British District Officers were still in place they simply carried on, under the orders of the new government, until they were no longer needed.

In the New Hebrides, however, with its dual system, such a tidy solution was impossible. Clearly there could no longer be two different officials administering the same District for a single

Government. What would be the point? Nor could the British District Agents stay and the Frenchmen leave, or vice versa. Obviously there would have, by the time of independence, to be a single New Hebridean Government Agent in place, who would take over the power and the functions of both Agents of the Metropolitan governments. Or so we thought.

Jean-Jacques Robert and I had agreed with the Prime Minister a timetable for the installation of the new Government Agents. There was even agreement, of sorts, as to where they would live, either in the former British or the former French compound, and how they would take over and combine the powers and personnel of the departing expatriates. It was planned that some of the new Government Agents would, although all nationals of Vanuatu, be former servants of the French administration and some of the British.

As Independence approached, however, and the two largest Districts of Santo and Tanna became increasingly disaffected, Robert decided to renege. He announced that the former French District Agents, all of them French nationals, would remain in place as his 'Personal Representatives'.

This meant that in practice they carried on exactly as they had before, in direct communication with the French Residency in Vila, with French policemen wearing French uniforms, still occupying the French district offices and raising the Tricolore each morning.

These Personal Representatives continued at their posts throughout the rebellions in both Santo and Tanna. While elements in both islands were at some sort of war with the central government and, by extension, with the Condominium Authority, the French District agents and the French population of the Islands blandly carried on their everyday lives. They even, so it was rumoured by ill-intentioned people, exercised a certain degree of authority and control over the rebellions.

One consequence of this, which Robert surely cannot have intended if his purpose was to back the new government, was that the New Hebridean Government Agents installed by the Prime Minister, came to look entirely like the successors and the allies of the British. Since the French were not participating, the new Vanuatu Agents had to be drawn exclusively from the junior ranks of the former British service. They occupied the houses and the offices of the former British D.A.s and they had to rely for the enforcement of their orders, on a handful of New Hebridean constables and sergeants from the former British police.

Nevertheless we persevered, Walter Lini, Robert and I, with the fiction that the new Government Agents were to be put there with the agreement of all and with the full backing of the retreating Franco/British Condominium administration, as well as of the new government of Vanuatu. So when Jimmy Stevens announced on his radio that, if the new Government Agent dared to set foot in Santo, he would be driven out within the week, I managed, in Robert's absence in Paris, to persuade the French Deputy Resident Commissioner, an honourable man, that this would be an intolerable challenge to our joint authority.

There was not, however, much that we could do to prevent it, since I had been unable to get the P.M.U. to Santo, and it was now too late to remount the operation, even if the French had been willing to agree to it. There was no other force available which could impose a solution.

Meanwhile Jimmy and his boyos were still whooping it up in Luganville town. More sinisterly, they appeared to be supported by a group of unofficial Frenchmen and French-speaking half-castes, with an assortment of explosive weapons. These, though they might be as dangerous to their owners as to any enemy, were certainly capable of inflicting a nasty flesh wound. Furthermore, somewhere in the bush was a couple of hundredweight of dynamite that had recently been imported to Santo under a French Licence for 'blasting purposes' and had been extracted, by a person or persons unknown, from the unguarded corrugated-iron customs store.

It seemed to us that we must do something. The newly installed Vanuatu Government Agent, certainly thought so. A peaceable man by inclination, he had not joined the government service to be blown up, or even to be insulted. He suggested to the Prime Minister on the radio that, since he wasn't doing any good, sitting in his office in Luganville under threat of expulsion, with no-one paying any attention to his orders, he might as well withdraw.

The Prime Minister, however, was made of sterner stuff, and anyway he was two hundred miles away in Vila. He therefore reminded Peres, the Deputy French Resident Commissioner and myself of our joint responsibility for law and order, and sat back to see what we would do.

171

Ever since the episode in Uganda with the prophet on the rock, I have recognised in myself an unfortunate Carruthers-like tendency, when I haven't the faintest idea what to do, to let phantasy take over. I then find myself doing, not what prudence and common sense would appear to dictate, but what seems the 'right' thing, in accordance with a code to which I by no means subscribe and which seems to derive from a mixture of the Boys' Own Paper and Kipling's 'If'.

I therefore proposed to my French colleague, that since we had no police to stiffen the sinews of the Government Agent and protect his office, we, the Resident Commissioners, must ourselves go up to Santo to reason with those who would do him harm. Even, if necessary, I urged that we must be prepared to interpose ourselves between his shrinking body and the would-be rebels. 'Nobody', I remember declaiming to the astonished Frenchman, 'Would dare to defy our authority'.

Peres, however, had never heard of Kipling and rather doubted whether our presence would do much good. He was also in something of a dilemma. Robert's 'Personal Representative', the former French D.A. was still living peacefully in Santo town, going about his daily business with his own contingent of French police. My ever-logical French colleague could not see much mileage in travelling to Santo to the former British headquarters to protect the official whom everyone regarded as the successor and agent of the British.

Nevertheless he was, as I say, an honourable man and he reluctantly agreed to travel with me to Santo on the date which Jimmy Stevens had announced as Expulsion Day. Peres' only stipulation was that, to maintain his freedom of movement, he would fly up in his own aircraft (Robert had by that time, as befitted a full Inspector General of the French Government, the unfettered use of the French High Commissioner in Noumea's executive aeroplane – I had to travel by chartered hedge-hopper).

We landed together at Santo to find an uneasy calm. Jimmy Stevens, who had by this time taken to using quasi-military terminology to underline the steel and precision of his rag-tag army, had announced that the expulsion would take place at 'Thirteen hundred hours precisely'. When we touched down at eleven, we found nothing stirring between the airfield and Luganville town.

172

The 'British Paddock' a rather seedy collection of Public Works Department bungalows and paint-peeled offices, lay between the two.

Escorted by half the available ex-British police-force in one Land Rover, we came to a dusty halt in front of the Government Agent's office, which appeared to be empty. The shutters were down and there was no sign of the usual crowd of litigants, police, prisoners on cleaning duty and general hangers-on.

Inside, however, was the New Hebridean Government Agent, sitting at his official desk in his darkened office, reading a week-old newspaper and humming a protestant hymn-tune to himself in a distracted way.

We sat down to wait. It was hot. The flies buzzed lazily across the verandah. From the township half a mile to the West came a parallel humming noise that might or might not mean that Jimmy Stevens and his platoons were forming up. We suppressed the urge to go down to the hotel to have a beer. Nothing happened.

To fill in time I started to write my Annual Report to the British Secretary of State for Foreign Affairs. This was probably not a good idea, I was not in the state of judicious calm appropriate to the drafting of this official document, which is normally circulated to Ambassadors throughout the world. Nor had the Foreign Secretary, Lord Carrington, done anything to deserve being the receptacle for my irritation. On the contrary, he was by some way the best Chief I had had throughout my official career. But I was tired and cross and I needed to let off steam.

'My Lord', I wrote 'As I write this Report in January, I am sitting with my French colleague in the Government Office in the Northern District of Santo. We are here without any effective Police presence. We hope that just by being here we can prevent the separatist Nagriamel movement from driving the Government Agent from his post. I persuaded, or rather shamed, my French colleague into joining me here, because his Government has vetoed any use of the Joint Police in a protective role, saying that this would provoke the Nagriamel leader, Jimmy Stevens, into a violent reaction which we could not contain. However, we judged that whilst Stevens might be able to intimidate the unprotected New Hebrides Government Agent and with him expel the last symbol of the authority of the elected New Hebrides Government on Santo, this would be difficult for him in the presence of the Resident Commissioners. My colleague and I await the threat feeling rather like "The Boy stood on the burning deck, whence all but he had fled." Diplomats are expected to take oddities in their stride, but it all seems a strange way to run a Condominium.'

At ten-past one, however, Peres said it was clear that the news of our presence must have done the trick. Jimmy Stevens had not kept to his deadline and had lost face. Meanwhile he, Peres, had work to do and, if I had no objection, he proposed to return to the airfield and fly back to Vila. I couldn't think of a good enough reason to make him stay, so we parted amicably. I pondered a wasted trip, but did not feel it would be sensible to abandon the Government Agent quite so precipitately.

Fortunately I had come prepared to fill-in yet more time. In Luganville harbour, eighty feet down, lay the wreck of an American troopship, the President Coolidge, that had struck a mine during the war and settled gently to the bottom. No lives had been lost, but the wreck was crammed with vehicles, guns, and military equipment of all kinds, as well as interesting pictures, cutlery and fine china that had survived from the ship's peace-time profession as a luxury cruise ship.

Moreover, just round the corner from the President Coolidge, was Million Dollar Point. When the Americans left at the end of the Pacific War, they had for disposal the usual vast stocks of Jeeps, lorries, bulldozers, prefabricated buildings, bridging materials, furniture and refrigerators. There was no point in taking this material back to the States, so they offered it all to the Condominium Government at a dollar an item.

But somebody (I hope it was not the British) was too greedy. They calculated that, even if they paid nothing, the Americans were going to have to leave all the stuff behind anyway. The condominium would therefore get it for nothing. The Americans however said 'Nuts' and pushed everything into the sea. Hence 'Million Dollar Point'.

Anyway with a million dollars' worth of junk lying around on the seabed, plus a large and virtually complete ship-load of goodies lying within easy diving distance, Santo was a Scuba fanatic's paradise. I had therefore brought all my diving paraphanalia with me. If Jimmy Stevens was not going to march I might as well make a more agreeable use of the journey.

I should not have been so naive. I was down by Million Dollar Point, kitted up in wet-suit and flippers and about to lift the Scuba tank onto my back, when a young policeman skidded to a halt beside me in his Land Rover. 'Quickly Sir,' he said, 'They're coming'. On the way back to the district office he told me that the hum in the township had risen to a roar. A plain-clothes man had bicycled down to have a look-see and had found a motley platoon of bowmen being prodded into marching order.

There seemed little doubt of their intention. Jimmy Stevens himself was not to be seen (it was not his habit to lead from the front), but the policeman had recognised a number of Jimmy's henchmen, plus a scattering of French half-castes. The noise they had heard was the shouting of orders, whose intent seemed as much morale-raising as executive, since they had little discernable effect. But it seemed unlikely that some sort of move would be long delayed.

Still not fully changed out of my diving gear, I checked in at the district office, to find the Government Agent looking even more apprehensive, but still sticking gamely to his official desk. Then I made a mistake. The Kipling myth was still running strongly and I thought I had better go down to the outskirts of the township, to try to judge for myself whether Jimmy's troops meant business.

When I got there, it was clear that they did. I asked them their intention and they politely answered that they were about to march to the British Paddock. I enquired why and they replied that it was to chase away the 'so-called Lini Government's so-called Agent'. I asked them in that case to give me a couple of minutes to get back to the office myself, and this they courteously agreed to do.

I realised my mistake when I got back to the office. The Government Agent was nowhere to be seen. I asked an embarrassed policeman the reason and was told he had 'Gone for bush'. In other words he had scarpered. I contemplated evacuating myself too, but it was obvious that Jimmy's platoon wanted to expostulate with someone, and, in the Government Agent's absence, it had better be me. I sat down on the verandah to wait.

Up the road they came in a wobbly column of route, armed with some desultory bows and arrows and the occasional spear, their near-nakedness contrasting oddly with the wet-suit top that I had not had time to remove. Their apparent leader, George, one of

Jimmy Steven's lieutenants, brought them to a ragged halt. We looked at each other.

Finally, when the silence was becoming embarrassing, I asked him their business. 'To chase away the so-called Lini Government's so-called Agent' he repeated, with a rather half-hearted flourish of bows from the troops behind him.

'I'm afraid you can't do that' I replied.

'Why not?'

'Well he seems to have gone already.' That stopped him in his tracks.

'Excuse me a moment,' he said 'I need to discuss this.'

George then went into a huddle with his N.C.O.s and it was evident from the agitated whispering that they were not fully prepared for this unexpected turn of events. Eventually, however, one of his brighter sergeants came up with an idea that seemed to satisfy everybody. There was a general murmur of assent. George turned back to me.

'We want you to bring him back' he said.

'What for?'

'So that we can chase him away.'

I was sorry to spoil his neat solution. 'I'm afraid I can't do that either' I repeated.

'Why not?'

'I don't know where he is.' This brought him to a halt again and there was further urgent whispering. Finally the same intelligent sergeant hit on another bright idea.

A bowman was sent trotting down the road to fetch a hammer and nails. I suppressed the thought that the most probable place to get these was from the French District Agent's store. Eventually he came back again with the hammer and some long leafy branches from the Namwele trees that grew in profusion by the roadside.

'We are going', said George, 'To show him who is in charge here. When he comes back, he won't be able to get into his office.'

George had a point. Namwele leaves are a powerful taboo. No New Hebridean, however westernised or christianised, would willingly cross a threshold whose door had been barred by Namwele branches. The bright sergeant had a triumphant look in his eye as he took the hammer and nailed the crossed Namwele leaves to the door beside me.

With my six policemen it did not seem prudent to take any measures to try to stop him by force. However he had overlooked one thing. Such taboos do not apply to Europeans and have no power over them.

'If you do that' I said 'I shall take them down again' and started to do so. This provoked a growl from the assembled platoon and it seemed prudent to revise my plans slightly.

'All right' I said 'I'm not in a hurry. I shall wait here and take them down when you've gone.'

There was then a prolonged pause. I sat on the verandah trying to look nonchalant. George and his platoon, who were standing in the sun, but too polite to invade my space, began to look hot. Eventually they drifted away as the time for the evening drink drew closer.

After they had gone I took down the Namwele leaves realising, however, as I did so, that it was no sort of victory. I had to get back to Vila before dark, my small plane was not equipped for night-flying. I knew that as soon as I had gone they would be back and so would the Namwele leaves.

The Government Agent was still missing. He would have to take his chance and if necessary, assuming he did return and seek to resume his office, would have to operate from his house if he could not find the courage to ignore the Namwele leaves on the office door. And so, in the event, it proved. He stayed in the bush for several days and thereafter remained totally inactive.

I next saw him a fortnight later, when the French Resident Commissioner's sleek mediterranean-style launch (in which he never travelled, as it rolled horribly in the Pacific swells), glided into Vila harbour in front of our house. Robert's 'Personal Representative' in Santo had secured the Government Agent's release. I was relieved to see him, and had not the heart to question him about his hasty departure from the office.

But one question haunted me, and haunts me to this day. What should I have done? What would Carruthers have done?

18

John Frum's Cargoes

Tanna is the largest island at the southern end of the New Hebrides chain. Like virtually everything else of note in the Pacific it was revealed to the outside world by Captain Cook in the course of his second voyage in 1774.

In a group of islands that live off magic, Cook, if anyone, had the right to the title of Master Magician. Again and again the track of the Endeavour's course wanders off into the vast spaces of the Pacific Ocean, but then turns abruptly round and points directly at some hitherto undiscovered island, often hundreds of miles away, where Cook then made the first foreign landing.

How he did it, no-one knows, maybe land-birds drifting downwind; maybe vegetation bobbing on the surface; maybe only the smell of the land, fresh in the face of the supreme master-mariner. But I prefer to think it was magic.

Certainly nothing stranger can ever have met his eyes than his arrival off the south coast of Tanna. The first thing you see on the horizon is a puff of smoke, then a rapid succession of smoke balls, like a lunatic red indian, signalling to warn of the coming invasion. Cook approached by day, but at night he would have seen a strange glow in the northern sky.

Twenty miles from the coast all this would have been explained by the sand-heap summit of Yasur volcano pushing its dirty nose above the horizon. Then the usual palm-fringed coral beaches, and behind them a strange open high plateau with wild horses and, nowadays, unexplained crimson crosses on sinister-looking humps of rock and sand.

There is a picture of Cook's first landing, drawn by the expedition's official artist. The calm figure of the leader in white breeches and three cornered hat, is confronted by a weird assembly of islanders wearing nothing (if they were male – the women were not in evidence), but a penis-sheath, known locally as a Nambas, supported by a wide belt that today is made of leather, but in those days was probably plaited pandanus leaf.

No one knows for certain why many Melanesian tribes have such a preoccupation with protecting and adorning the penis (though the anthropologists of course, have plenty of theories). It is certainly not modesty, nor any attempt (like the bearskins of the British foot-guards) to terrify the onlooker with the implied threat of gigantic size.

There are distinct tribes further north in the New Hebrides known as the Big Nambas and Small Nambas. But as far as I can tell the distinction is ethnic and political and does not indicate any degree of size on the one part, or humiliation on the other.

Certainly some of the purpose of the Nambas must be purely decorative. There are tribes in New Guinea much given to the use of small dried and lightly polished gourds for the purpose, often with attractive curlicues at the front. In the New Hebrides, however, where gourds are scarce, the main construction seems (I have never examined one closely) to be the sort of raffia basket tatted by maiden aunts.

At the very least the Nambas, which kept the appropriate member in a permanently erect position, must have served the essential purpose of preventing it from dangling on the ground, as the wearer squatted comfortably during the nightly kava drink – the other feature of Tannese life that must have struck Captain Cook most forcibly on his arrival.

The Tannese are a warlike bunch. Their history is full of wild rages and sudden massacres, but everything stops for kava and, to quote the official slogan, which on the whole approves of the habit, or at least does nothing to prevent it, 'Kava brings peace'.

Kava is the root of an unassertive indigenous plant *Piper methysticum* which is prepared by the women and boys (who, however, are strictly forbidden to drink it. For them it is taboo, and therefore unthinkable). The method of manufacture is simple. Healthy white teeth grind up the Kava root until it produces a greenish yellow pulp liberally mixed with saliva. As each gobbet is fully chewed, it is spat out onto what Jim Biddulph, a fascinated BBC reporter, described as a 'scrupulously clean banana leaf'. Then the viscous yellow fluid is strained through a coconut fibre mat, mixed with dubious water and finally offered in a half-coconut shell to the avid drinker or the somewhat less avid, but highly honoured guest. The taste, as Jim Biddulph explained it, is 'as of something long dead, but with horrid intimations that it may soon come alive again.' More prosaically, to me it tastes like mud.

The effect, though not immediate, is like being buried in the self-same mud. Kava is a mild anaesthetic with an effect like having been to the dentist, but spreading, apparently, to every nerve and muscle of the body. Kava habitués wisely attempt neither mental nor bodily exercise, but are apt to sit for hours at a time, staring placidly into space. Less sensible foreigners try to swim against the flow, and Jim Biddulph unwisely allowed himself after a kava session to be filmed by a BBC cameraman, staggering slowly into the sunset like a giraffe in treacle.

Maybe it is the strain of trying to remain in a state of permanent erection; or possibly the result of the condition of numbed unreality induce by extended kava drinking; but whatever the reason, life in Tanna has to this day an element of charmed unreality that makes the Tannese inexpressibly attractive, even when they are at their most exasperating and incomprehensible.

And all too soon after Captain Cook's visit, the Tannese needed all the protection this inconsequential fuzziness could give them against the harsh realities of an unforgiving world. When James Cook first came ashore there were perhaps forty thousand Tannese, living in moderate prosperity off wild pigs and the taro pits that had been brought by their Melanesian forefathers from the mainland of New Guinea. By Independence in 1980 there were no more than ten thousand of them.

In between had come the missionaries; harsh Presbyterians who ruled their flock with the nineteenth century equivalent of whips and scorpions. As in the rest of the South Pacific, many of the Tannese, deprived of their customs, their Nambas and even their kava lost much of their reason for living. Even those who learned to bow before the missionary storm could not protect themselves from the whiteman's sickness. Thousands, even tens of thousands died of measles and venereal disease.

And, as if this was not enough, the curse of the Australian Black-birders, the unsung form of Pacific slavery, swept whole villages clear of their men and turned brother against brother as surely as the British slave traders of Bristol or the Arabs of Zanzibar.

Workers were needed in the sugar plantations of Queensland. The Blackbirders, the traders who procured these 'indentured labourers', were, in reality, little more than pirates.

They knew the New Hebrides chain well, having scoured the islands for their diminishing stocks of the aromatic sandalwood. They had no difficulty in working their way through the dangerous reefs of Tanna to lure the unsuspecting islanders away. At first they enticed with riches and promises of a return to their own homes after two years; and later, when their promises had been shown to be the lies that they were, with naked force and, where necessary, a few salutary deaths.

But the people of Tanna were cleverer than many other Pacific Islanders, who simply lay down and died under the combined assault of all these destructive forces. The Tannese invented John Frum.

The anthropologists have had a field day with the significance and origin of this, the granddaddy of all the Cargo Cults of the Pacific. Usually they ascribe it to the coming of American soldiers in the Second World War. The impact of these same soldiers when they landed in Britain, with their apparently inexhaustible supply of Jeeps, refrigerators, chewing gum, silk stockings and expansive good humour, was shocking enough. To the South Pacific islanders, who owned nothing but their Nambas, their fishing nets and a few pots and pans which they had made themselves, the Americans must have seemed like gods walking on Earth.

According to this account, the name John Frum, was thus a corruption of 'John From America', derived also doubtless from the universal American greeting 'Hey Johnny. Have some gum, chum.' The only trouble is that chronology is against this picturesque explanation. There is plenty of evidence that the John Frum cult started in Tanna before the war, initially as a reaction against the crushing weight of Presbyterian disapproval of all native 'Kastom', and later as a way of trying to forget about the Anglo-French administrators and avoid paying their absurd taxes.

Another earlier explanation of the cult's name therefore has it that it was taken from the John the Baptist Mission, together with a symbolic 'Broom' (many South Pacific Islanders have problems with their Bs and Fs) which would sweep away those bothersome spiritual and temporal tax collectors.

The gum-chewing American John Frum is therefore probably a rationalisation as well as an anachronism, but anyway it makes a good story and there is no doubt that the appearance of these god-like creatures, who were swarming through the New Hebrides in the 1940s as the tide of battle with the Japanese swung to and fro in the Solomon Islands just to the north, must have given the cult an enormous boost.

One of the less attractive characteristics of the early Presbyterian missionaries was that if you did not toe the line you were out – out of the Christian villages, out of the Christian schools, out of social contact with the community in which you had been born. The early John Frum settlements around Sulphur Bay in the east of Tanna were therefore created by outcasts who founded their own schools and rejected all contact with the missionaries and administrators. Such social misfits were suckers for a good Messiah and a number of these soon appeared.

One of the first was described by Reverend Bell, a Presbyterian Minister:

'Strange happenings at a place called Green Point. Roughly twelve month ago meetings were called secretly and took place in a clearing cut out of the bush, with a huge Banyan tree over all to shut out the light from the sky. They took place at night and no light was allowed, not even the glow of a cigarette or pipe.

'Chiefs and Elders and others were given positions befitting their rank, near to John Frum. A few bold spirits tried to peer into his face, but it was well hidden by a big hat.

'When he spoke it was in a falsetto voice and he said little. He was said to have told the chiefs they were fools to work for the government for nothing. Wondrous tales spread like wildfire – He lived before Noah but ascended above the clouds during the flood and had never known death. He, too, served God and was sent by him. John Frum was said to have visited the Government Agent and punched his nose, drunk beer at one trader's and driven a golden car to another.'

Not surprisingly the idea of punching the Government Agent on the nose did not find favour with the authorities. Nor did the fact that the cult members seemed likely to starve themselves to death. A twist of the John From America story was that he would only come with his bounty if his followers first purged themselves of all pre-existing worldly goods. Money was therefore thrown away, pigs were sacrificed, and fields and coconut plantations remained uncultivated.

In the middle of trying to fight a world war, neither the British nor the French had the means to sustain a programme of famine relief on Tanna. They therefore moved in to arrest the cult's leaders, starting with one called Manevi, who admitted readily enough that he was the original John Frum with the squeaky voice.

Unfortunately, as is often the way with cults, the John Frum figure turned out to be a many-headed hydra. No sooner was Manevi arrested, than others appeared, some of them, according to one account, claiming to be his son. These had a satisfactory and profitable reign as John Frum substitutes, until one of them was caught and imprisoned on charges of adultery and incest.

By this time the connection with America was well established in the confused minds of the cult. John Frum was the man who would lead an American task-force of ships and airplanes, loaded to the gunwales with goodies of every kind. These cargoes would be the reward for his followers' faithfulness. Each successive John Frum was therefore a man much to be curried favour with. What were the purity of a few daughters or the surrender of a curly-tusked pig to be compared with the life of perpetual ease that was to come?

The next John Frum to appear was, however, a local Tannese. This man, called Neloig, had first to overcome the problem, not unknown even in more soundly-based religions, that he was known locally as an illiterate and a drunkard, and therefore initially a prophet without much honour in his own country. He overcame this neatly by revealing that he was also King of America and could therefore be expected to know how to tap the resources of his U.S. homeland.

Neloig must have had some idea, perhaps derived from a period working for the Americans in the northern islands of Santo or Efate, of how jeeps and refrigerators would actually be delivered. Parachutes would do for small packets of goodies, but the heavy stuff needed transport aircraft and aircraft needed a landing ground. He therefore set his already somewhat emaciated devotees to building an airstrip on the flat ground below Mount Yasur.

Again this did not appeal to the authorities and Neloig and his main henchmen were arrested and taken away to a place of safety on another island. His story does not, however, have a happy ending. Neloig was eventually certified insane, which seems a bit harsh. Given the weirdness of his original premise, his subsequent actions seem not mad but eminently logical.

Other John Frums soon followed, a useful additional twist being added to the legend in the claim that he was invisible and undetectable by whites or women, and therefore protected both from arrest and from charges of adultery. But such anonymity did not protect the last of the line, who found himself arrested for bigamy and assault, but then returned to Tanna from jail three years later and raised the American flag at Sulphur Bay.

The John Frum cult had therefore been a running problem for the authorities for many years when I appeared on the scene. Mostly, it has to be said, it was a problem for the British. The French authorities seemed to believe that an American John Frum was largely a matter for the Anglo-Saxons to sort out between themselves. Moreover, as happened with Jimmy Stevens and the Nagriamel movement in Santo, what had started as an indigenous protest against all authority, seemed, to the logical French mind, an opportunity to make themselves the good guys and to ensure that, if there was any trouble, the British would have to take the blame – and the action.

An odd feature of the John Frum meeting ground on a dusty coral flat overlooked by the belching volcano of Yasur, was therefore that the Tricolore and the Stars and Stripes flew on either side of the crimson wooden cross of John Frum, but never a Union Jack in sight.

As the political problems of the New Hebrides increased, I was therefore inclined to let the John Frum severely alone, despite increasingly peremptory messages that they had something to complain about and wished to see both the Resident Commissioners forthwith at Sulphur Bay. I felt I had enough on my plate as it was.

My colleague Jean-Jacques Robert, however, had different ideas. He may have wanted to rub my nose in the fact that the British were not too popular in Sulphur Bay. More charitably he may have felt that the John Frum had genuine grievances and that we should attend to them. He therefore proposed a joint visit to Tanna to talk to them.

The next day we therefore flew the hundred or so miles down to the Tanna airfield at Isangel, in one of the bumpy yellow Britten-Norman Islanders of Air Melanesia, past the even more hair-raising airstrip on the sheer-sided island of Futuna, which was so short that the runway was on a steep slope; uphill on landing to stop the aircraft before it hit the cliff at the end and downhill on departure to give the plane some extra impetus before it took-off, in a still stalled condition, hoping to have achieved flying-speed before it hit the sea.

At Isangel it was clear that this was to be very much a Gallic operation. My colleague had assembled a convoy of light-blue French police Toyotas, the first of which carried a large Tricolore and a rather smaller Union Jack (those damned flags again). The British District Agent's Land Rover was right at the back of the line. I pondered insisting on bringing it to the front, but decided that that was just silly. Robert and I had arrived in Tanna together, we might as well travel on in the same vehicle.

On arrival at Sulphur Bay we were saluted by an immaculate French gendarme and a French police bugler, evidently flown down in advance from Port Vila for the occasion. We were ushered into a French-built meeting house, designed completely windowless to accommodate the John Frum preference for conspiratorial darkness. In the gloom I could barely distinguish the faces of the John Frum elders, marshalled by constables of the French Police, who came quiveringly to attention as Robert entered ahead of me.

The almost total darkness was not much to my liking, or to that of a BBC film-crew, who had hitched a lift to the meeting in the hope of some local colour but who could not even read their camera's light meter. Robert, however, brushed aside all comment and opened the meeting, speaking in French and translated into the John Frum dialect by one of his local constables. This frustrated the BBC even more, since they could speak neither French nor Tannese.

Behind the meeting-house the ever-present bulk of Mount Yasur could be heard but not seen, seeming to commentate on the proceedings with belches, rumbles and the occasional roar of approbation or rage.

I am bound to say that I too couldn't understand a word of what the John Frum elders had to say, not because I couldn't understand French, but because it was almost impossible to know what they were on about. It seemed that they wanted to complain about some property which the last of their John Frums, Nakomaha, had left behind (or not left behind) in the British prison in 1957. Nako-maha himself did not seem to be present. Perhaps he was in America – or even dead. But a number of old men were obviously extremely agitated on his behalf after more than twenty years later.

At the end of an hour and a half of what might equally well have been Chinese, Robert turned to me with what, if I could have read it in the dark, would probably have been a somewhat smug expression. 'Well, mon cher collégue' he said, 'it seems you have a problem. I have told them you will sort it out for them.'

As we left the meeting house, blinking in the unaccustomed sunlight, to be greeted by a final disgusted rumble from Yasur, I asked the BBC cameraman, who had seen action from Vietnam to Central America, what he thought of it all.

'Bit difficult to know' he said. 'You see I can't speak Volcano.'

19

Prince Philip's Paradis

The John Frum at Sulphur Bay were not, however, the only Cargo cultists in Tanna. A breakaway group at Iounhanan village, nearer to Isangel, had in the early 1960s established their independence from the Jon Frum for reasons that were as obscure as the Sulphur Bay lot's grievances about Nakomaha.

Originally the Iounhanans had seemed as volatile as the others in their attitude towards the authorities. But in 1962 the then British Resident Commissioner, Mr A. M. Wilkie CMG, evidently did his best to placate them. At all events, he came away from a meeting with the Iounhanan chiefs bearing a circular tusk from a Tanna pig.

No-one knows for sure why a pig's tusk that has grown into a complete circle should be an object of such reverence throughout the Melanesian islands. Certainly it must have been a matter of extreme discomfort to the unfortunate pig, since it could involve the tusk growing right back round again through the pig's jaw or cheek. Some anthropologists have suggested that the reverence for pigs in Melanesian custom may be a substitute for the cannibalism from which they were weaned by the early missionaries.

At any event Mr Wilkie was obviously highly honoured by the Iounhanans' gift. But unfortunately he seems to have done nothing about any return present.

As a result, my immediate predecessor, John Champion, was confronted during a visit in 1976 by an indignant gathering of Iounhanan's chiefs complaining that they had been insulted. Just as in Sulphur Bay, it had taken them a decade and more to get around to protesting, and by that time the details of whatever Wilkie had promised had long been forgotten. John, however, seems to have had a more fertile imagination than I, and he decided that the way to placate the Iounhanans was to give them a picture of the Duke of Edinburgh.

That did the trick in a way that nobody can fully have foreseen. The devotion of the Iounhanans to the Queen's husband was later the subject of a secret French memorandum, commissioned by my colleague Robert shortly before Independence, which, like so much else, was carelessly left behind when the French evacuated their offices in 1980. Perhaps because they were busy doing it themselves, the French always seemed ready to sniff out a cunning British plan to increase their influence at the expense of France.

The memorandum read:

'Subject *A new cargo cult in Tanna*

'The British are about to succeed in a master stroke (coup de maître) on the island of Tanna by promoting a new cargo cult around Prince Philip, the Duke of Edinburgh.

'*The preparation of the ground*

'In 1962 the British Resident Commissioner, Sandy Wilkie on a visit to Tanna, had himself presented by the village of Ionanen with the gift of a pig. Mr Wilkie promised in return a present from Prince Philip of England. But he [presumably Mr Wilkie, not Prince Philip: Ed] suffered a heart attack two years later and the exchange gift never arrived.

'Nevertheless it seems that, from that moment, the villagers began to create their mythical ideas about Prince Philip. This veneration seems to have been carefully nurtured (soigneuse-ment entretenu) by successive British Resident Commissioners and by the Australian trader Bob Paul (a rough-diamond merchant living in Tanna with no high regard for any government, but perhaps least of all for the French).

'*The visit of Prince Philip*

When in March 1971, the Duke of Edinburgh came to the New Hebrides he visited the island of Aneityum (Near Tanna – actually in 1974 on a Pacific tour in HMS Britannia when the passengers enjoyed an Aneityum picnic). The legend goes that he there declared that "Tanna was his native country and he would return there before Independence to give strength to his brothers."

'We must also remember that since his transit of Malekula

(another island in the north of the New Hebrides) he (the Duke) is the only European to have achieved a high grade in local custom. The people of Walla-Rao have nominated him "Lokorimal Buvanten wenu", that is to say "Great Chief of all the Islands".

'*The actions of John Champion*

'When he took up his post as Resident Commissioner in 1975, Mr Champion visited Tanna and heard of the prestige enjoyed by the husband of the Queen. After having had enquiries made by an anthropologist, Dr Sorenlund, he asked his predecessor as Resident Commissioner M. Roger Du Boulay (then Head of Protocol Department in the Foreign Office) to send him a signed portrait of the Prince for presentation to the people of Ionanen.

'On his final tour of the archipelago in 1978, M. Champion landed in Tanna on the 28th October and went directly to Ionanen where he delivered a four-page speech on the subject of Custom. Then he offered four tobacco pipes to four chiefs of the region, of whom one was Tuk Nao, member of the national Assembly (where he was prone to wear his Nambas on formal occasions, to the consternation of visiting female dignitaries). A fifth pipe was destined to be displayed in a "cultural centre of Kastom".

'He explained that these pipes, which were very old, symbolised the Kastom of Great Britain and would seal a rapprochement between the two kastoms of the Melanesians and the British.

'Then he (Mr Champion) offered two photographs which had been specially framed (apparently a heinous addition) by the Public Works Department of the British Residency. One portrayed Prince Philip in uniform alongside Queen Elizabeth. The other was a portrait of the Duke himself and bore his signature. M. Champion publicly displayed this signature to the assembled population and confirmed that it was truly in the hand of Prince Philip and addressed to the people of Ionanen.

'He added that Prince Philip owned a ship and intended to come in it to Tanna within a few months.'

'*Conclusion by the Research Department*

'One cannot but admire the way in which the British are making political use of the credulity of the Custom people of Tanna. They know that if the Custom people take part in the forthcoming elections then the "Moderates" (the French party) will get 80% of the votes of this island of 10,000 inhabitants. They only got 60% in 1975 because of the abstention of the Custom people, and the Moderates missed another trick when Tuk Nao was appointed to the Legislature in 1977.

'Thanks to the legend built up around Prince Philip, the British are on course to re-establish themselves, with a view to increasing abstentionism in Tanna during the forthcoming Elections.'

Poor John Champion. He had already resigned in total disillusionment with everything to do with the New Hebrides, including the policies of the British Government. It is indeed true that he had heard the legends surrounding Prince Philip and that he had asked the Palace to send him a portrait to present to the Iounhanans. The records in the British Residence show that he had done so out of sheer embarrassment at the original alleged slight by Sandy Wilkie, and that when the picture arrived, soon before his own departure from the islands, he judged that it would give further offence in London if it was not delivered.

But the indefatigable researchers of the French Residency had not finished with the Iounhanan story. Their account goes on:

'*The New Cargo Cult*
'Here, verbatim, is what the MP Tuk Nao told us today:

'One day Prince Philip will come back to Tanna, just before or just after Independence, and that day will usher in Paradise (Paradis) to the New Hebrides. The promises of the Vanuaaku Pati or the Tan Union (two of the main political groups) are as nothing beside the Paradis which the Prince will instal when he touches down in Tanna where he was born.

'In due course his son Charles will govern the whole world. There will be no more old age, for when men come

to advanced years, they will become young men once
again. This period will last for three years. Paradis is not to
be found in the sky as the Bible tells us, but in the New
Hebrides (Hebridis). The proof of this is that both the
words have the same ending, "Pa-ra-Dis" and "New-Heb-
ri-Dis". We are four persons who bear witness to this
truth' (the same four who received their pipes from M.
Champion).

'The Island Legend'

'"One day a nambas-wearing Man-Tanna went on
board an English man-of-war that stopped in Tanna.
Arriving in England he attended a ball and gave a ring to a
young girl. The British were jealous and attacked him but
he succeeded in escaping them.

"At another ball he found the young girl once again and
they spent the whole evening tête à tête. But at the end of
the party the English arrested him and threw him in
prison.

"For the young girl's name was Elizabeth. She was
destined to become Queen and the stranger claimed to be
American (the Jon Frum theme again). The British did not
want their Princess to run away to the Americas.

"The Man-Tanna was chained up and guarded by two
soldiers.

"Came the day when the future Queen must choose her
husband. She passed in revue all the sailors and soldiers
from among whom the chosen one must come. But at the
end of the rank one man sprang up to meet her. Elizabeth
understood at once that she loved him. Immediately the
name of this man, Philip, was spread abroad throughout
Britain.

"The stranger who crouched in prison was therefore no
longer a danger to the state, but when they went to release
him, to their astonishment they found that he had gone.
This turned to stupefaction when they discovered that 'The
American' and the husband chosen by the Queen were one
and the same person. But it was too late, there could be no
reversing the Royal Choice.

"In the end Philip admitted to his wife that he was no

American but had been born in Tanna. Elizabeth demanded to know her father-in-law, but when the latter arrived in England the Queen was asleep, so Philip took a photo of him and sent him back to Tanna.

"When she awoke, the Queen was bitterly disappointed to see the photograph of her father-in-law wearing a Nambas and sorely repented of her marriage. But what was done was done.""

This is the stuff of all good folk-tales and its provenance by Tuk Nao has the ring of truth. I doubt anyway if the solemn French researchers would have had the wit to invent it.

As for their other assertions, I do not know whether John Champion really told the Chiefs that their presentation Dunhill pipes were an ancient symbol of British Kastom that would seal the reconciliation between our two great nations. John sadly died not too long after his return to England.

It may be that the researchers had got a bit confused with pre-US Independence memories of the peace pipes of the American Indians. But when I myself visited Iounhanan I was intrigued to see a reassuringly chestnut coloured British pipe-bowl poking through the wide belt above an otherwise totally naked pair of Chiefly buttocks. So maybe there was something in the pipe story after all.

Nor does it make much sense to claim that the dastardly British had been preparing their coup as far back as Sandy Wilkie's tour in 1962. At that time the Duke of Edinburgh's visit was still twelve years in the future and it would have taken a clairvoyant Resident Commissioner to have foreseen that innocent picnic on the beach at Aneityum. But it does at least demonstrate the feverish atmosphere of the Condominium and our common human tendency to attribute fiendish cleverness to foreigners.

What is also interesting about the French analysis is their assumption that, if the Custom people had been persuaded out of their traditional unwillingness to support political parties, for whom they felt no sort of sympathy or affinity, then they would all have voted for the francophone 'Moderates'. Possibly Robert's largesse, so much more tangible than a few pipes of peace, might have had something to do with that.

As before in this improbable tale, however, the saga was not yet over. If we had not all been preoccupied with larger affairs, the busy researchers in the French Residency would have had cause to write yet another half-admiring secret paper about the machinations of Perfide Albion.

In the last months before Independence, I too returned to Iounhanan to present a portrait of Prince Philip to Chief Jack Naivo. The trouble with this business of reciprocal gift-giving is that 'cursed be he who first cries, Hold. Enough.'

When John Champion had handed over the first princely portrait, the then Chief Kalpapung was so overcome with the honour that he gave John one of the tribe's chief treasures, an ornamental pig-killing club, to be sent to the Royal Duke as a token of Iounhanan's thanks and fealty. By that time it was not surprising that John had pretty much run out of imaginative ideas, so he promised to forward the club to Buckingham Palace and to return once again with yet another portrait of the Duke holding it in the correct ceremonial attitude.

This caused further difficulty. The Duke – a true sportsman – was game, but nobody in London could tell him how such execution clubs were supposed to be held. Someone suggested that the correct posture was what the British army calls 'Resting on your Arms, reversed'. But since in England this is a sign of bereavement it was feared that this might inadvertently give offence in Tanna. After my arrival in the New Hebrides, telegrams on the subject therefore flew to and fro the Foreign Office, mixed up with rather more weighty ones about the possibility of war in Santo.

In the end someone sensibly suggested that we ask the Duke to stand with the club in several different poses. When the photographs arrived we could then make discreet inquiries as to which one would be most appropriate.

When the press got wind of this, some journalists impertinently assumed that the Duke had been asked to don a Nambas for the sittings and one went so far as to head his story 'They're changing gourd at Buckingham Palace'. This was not only lèse majesté for which he deserved a spell in the Tower, it was also grossly unfair to the Duke, who submitted to the whole absurd process with great good humour.

All this, however, took some time, and it was not until things in Tanna were getting really tense, that I was able to take the latest portrait down to Iounhanan. Hoping to avoid further tension between the metropolitan powers, I asked Robert to accompany me, which he equally politely declined, no doubt judging that it could only result in some lowering of French prestige. At this, since the press seemed to know everything that was going on, the cartoonist Dickinson published a picture of two French Gendarmes in tropical dress saying to each other, 'Our job is to persuade the natives that it's not Prince Philip that's God. It's Giscard.'

I therefore presented myself alone at Chief Jack's headquarters, having been advised that it would not be a good idea to take Pat with me. She would not have been allowed to witness the ceremony and might well have been consigned to the back quarters to chew kava.

Chief Jack was in a genial mood, although, in fact, it was not a particularly opportune moment for the visit. This was the time of year when the young boys of the tribe were confined in huts hidden in the forest undergoing initiation ceremonies that were never explained, and no doubt hypnotising themselves into the state of numb insensibility which would be necessary for them to face the blunt instruments of the circumcisers without crying out. It was a nervous period for the whole tribe.

But the new portrait of the Duke would bestow immense prestige on its possessor, as would the evidence provided by the pig-killing club, that the Duke of Edinburgh was truly Man-Tanna. Chief Jack therefore made it plain that he was very pleased to see me. I was not, however, permitted to make a long speech (which was just as well as I did not have John Champion's putative four pages on kastom to deliver). The Tannese are men of few words. They do it much better with their feet.

Tanna dancing is repetitive and hypnotic. The men stand in a circle in the middle, starting off with a few experimental drones, like a badly tuned bag-pipe. Then, at an invisible signal they are off, round and round, faster and faster. The droning grows louder, more insistent. There are no words, just a wild and syncopated rhythm that sounds like,

'*Oh* my God, I'm *bloody danc*ing. *Must* I *do* it *all* my *life*?
I'm fed *up* with *all* this *pranc*ing. *Want* to *get* home to my *wife*.'

In the background those self-same wives, dressed in grass skirts and glaringly nothing else, stand in a row, at first a bit self-conscious, uttering little yips of encouragement and swaying in time with the rhythm of the men. But soon, as the pace hots up, they abandon themselves into full fledged ululations, just like their far-off sisters in Africa or at a Western pop concert.

Meanwhile a new and insistent pounding shakes the ground. Flat feet slapped down in unison on the baked earth pound out the rhythm. Faster and faster goes the circle, testing the stability of every nambas almost to collapsing point. The dust rises until it obscures everything except the bobbing heads.

And then, just as suddenly and equally without warning, a little falsetto shriek from the dance leader brings the whole merry-go-round to a halt. The dancers turn outwards with embarrassed grins as if to say 'There you are. That's what we do for all our tourists' and you are made to understand that the time for the presentation has come.

Chief Jack Naivo received the club-holding portrait with great reverence, holding it gently before the people at such a level as to conceal his nambas, which seemed to be in a state of some agitation. One by one the chiefs came up to touch the picture, carefully, gently, with a rapt expression. A solitary woman, Jack's chief wife, approached timidly, but was shooed away, but lovingly and without offence.

I felt a fraud and could only hope that Chief Jack (and Prince Philip) would forgive me. Not a word was said about politics and I have no idea how the Iounhanans voted in the elections, if they did at all. But it was clear to me that something very important in the history of the tribe had occurred.

I was not, however, permitted to brood for too long. It was time for kava and kava meant starting off by sitting on the ground (there was no furniture) lest paralysis of the limbs lead to the falling sickness later (perhaps Julius Caesar was a secret kava addict?) I remember the next twenty minutes, but very little thereafter.

20

'The Pandemonium'

Alll this, however, was no more than an interlude. There are copycats in the South Pacific, just as in more conventional parts of the world. Jimmy Stevens' success in driving the Santo Government Agent from his office put the same idea into likeminds in Tanna.

Reuben Tamata, the Government Agent in Tanna was, however, a tougher nut than his colleague in Santo. When the John Frum threatened to come and get him, he didn't run away, but stayed and argued. When force majeure prevailed and he had no choice but to allow himself to be taken away into the dark bush, by all accounts he made a considerable nuisance of himself, meeting the weirder flights of John Frum fancy with his own stalwart brand of commonsense. Meanwhile his office in Isangel town was closed and sealed with Namwele leaves, just like the one in Santo.

Moreover, there being no other representative of any government present, apart from the former French District Agent (who seemed content to ignore the whole thing), there was nothing to prevent the dissidents from helping themselves to a first instalment of Cargo, in the shape of refrigerators, cookers and light fittings from the Government Agent's house and office. They had no electricity to power these things, but that, they felt, would surely follow once the alien presence had been removed and the island swept and garnished for the arrival of Jon Frum and his cargo plane, whether piloted by the Duke of Edinburgh or not.

Once again I told Robert that we must, we really must, do something; and so did Walter Lini, who by that time was firing off daily despatches demanding that the Resident Commissioners take immediate joint action to restore order. He never got a reply, mostly because I couldn't think of anything printable to say and a subsequent book, by one of Lini's foreign admirers, cited this as one more sign of lamentable weakness on the part of the British authorities. A look at the draft of my nightly telegrams to the Foreign Office should have acquitted me, at least, of the charge of indifference.

And in the case of Tanna, where the Jon Frum, unlike Jimmy's more sophisticated style, showed no sign of even promising to consider thinking about withdrawal, it was more difficult for my French colleague to maintain that there was no need for any police presence to restore order.

Accordingly he agreed, without too much difficulty, that the French and British Police Mobile Units should both fly down to Tanna in the Britten-Norman Islanders of Air Melanesia, to rescue the Government Agent and to restore the authority of the central government in Tanna.

And this indeed is what happened, at least in so far as the physical movement of the two police forces was concerned. But before they could arrive the Jon Frum, warned of our secret plans by malevolent persons unknown, tried to blow up the airfield. The thing about earth strips, however, is that, although you can make a hole in them quite easily, they are almost equally easy to mend. When therefore, some purloined sticks of French dynamite exploded in a culvert under the airfield, the morning the police were supposed to arrive, Bob Paul, (whose contempt for the condominium authorities was becoming daily more vocal), took a gang of his plantation workers and filled the hole up again without too much difficulty and then rang me up and said that the police could come, if they had the guts to do so.

As soon as the Islanders had landed, however, the French force disappeared, picked-up by the Toyotas of Robert's personal representative, leaving the British police, under the indomitable Ian Cook, to walk into town. When they got there, they found the Government Agent's office in a mess, with papers strewn all over the grass and crudely scrawled messages of general defiance.

Clearly, in the absence of the French police, there was no chance of joint action to restore order, but Tanna was different from Santo in that there were virtually no French citizens on the island, against whom action by the British police would have been imprudent.

Consulted on the radio in my office in Vila, I therefore told Ian to secure the situation at Isangel and then, if he thought it practicable, to go and look for Reuben Tamata.

Ian was the last person to think anything impracticable, and so he and his PMU set off within the hour, in a couple of government Land Rovers which, because machinery was not their strong point, had defeated the Jon Frum's attempts to remove them. After that we heard nothing until, around midday, a worried police sergeant, left behind to man the Isangel base radio, came through to say that he had heard a huge explosion somewhere up in the hills.

I thought 'Oh God – I've killed them all' and pestered the sergeant for more news throughout a long afternoon.

Just before dark, however, an ever cheerful Ian Cook came through on the radio himself to put an end to our worries. The bang that the sergeant had reported was indeed the explosion of a quantity of dynamite under the lorry track through the dark bush, and this had stripped away a surprising amount of the forest cover about a hundred yards short of the Jon Frum HQ. But, whether by accident or design, it had gone off well in front of the leading Land Rover and the drivers had had plenty of time to stop and take cover behind their vehicles, against some rather desultory sniping by .22 rifles and the occasional whizz-bang. These, however, seemed to have frightened the attackers more than the police, as, after one last explosion, the Jon Frum had run away.

Ian therefore had needed to do no more than round up a few stragglers and bring them down to the jail at Isangel. His only failure was that he had had to leave the Government Agent to walk back to headquarters by himself, as Reuben had taken advantage of the confusion to break out of his own makeshift jail and make for the bush, from which he duly reappeared next morning.

I was greatly relieved, but Ian seemed, if anything, to be no more than slightly exhilarated. At all events I congratulated the PMU on a job well done and asked them to stay at Isangel until matters had settled down. There they put on display a selection of captured devices which Jim Biddulph the BBC correspondent, described as 'sweating gently in the sun, looking as if they would explode if anyone so much as coughed'.

Nevertheless, despite the risk, this show of decisiveness on the part of at least half of the authorities, so heartened the supporters of the government (who were, after all, as the recent elections had shown, the large majority in Tanna as everywhere else) that they too began to be quite brave. They took to swaggering around the single main street of Isangel, boasting of what they would do to the John Frum if they came down from the hills.

Unfortunately, however, whatever the oddities of the Jon Frum mind, lack of courage was not one of their defects. A few nights later, before their captured friends could be moved to a safer jail, they came out of the bush and swooped on Isangel once more. Ian Cook's tiny detachment could not be in every place at once and a confrontation developed between some government supporters, (who had also taken the precaution of arming themselves with .22 sporting rifles), and a group of the Jon Frum, trying to infiltrate around the back of the prison. In the exchange of shots one man fell.

When morning broke this was found to have been Alexis Yolou, a prominent francophone member of the legislature, whose body was recovered by a French government Toyota and taken off for post-mortem examination at the local hospital. There it was found that the shots that had killed him were .22 bullets in the head and chest, not the antique .303 Lee Enfields of the British Police, nor the more modern weapons of the French.

The rest was mystery. Some on the government side said that Yolou had been shot by the Jon Frum, when he tried to dissuade them from storming the prison. The Government's opponents, on the other hand, claimed that Walter Lini's friends had surrounded this strong critic and treacherously murdered him in the dark. A joint police investigation, the first combined action of this unhappy episode, failed to establish the truth.

The fact that this was the first (and, as it turned out, the last) casualty of the pre-Independence pandemonium did not make it any easier to bear. Someone had murdered a leading citizen. And besides, we had no means of knowing that there would be no further deaths.

That afternoon I broadcast on New Hebrides radio, appealing for calm and saying that we must all examine our consciences. No-one could escape their share of responsibility for Alexis Yolou's death; the Jon Frum because they had attacked the prison; the government supporters because they had taken the law into their own hands; the British police because they had failed to prevent what had happened; and the French police because they were not there. It was a sombre moment.

But a more sombre one was to follow. Yolou's body was returned by the French police to Port Vila and a solemn Requiem Mass held for him in the great Catholic church there. The Prime Minister elect insisted that, since the government had done nothing wrong, he, albeit a Priest of the Anglican Church, must be present and must take a full part in the Catholic memorial service of a member of the central legislature. Jean-Jacques Robert and I naturally had no choice but to accompany him. When Walter Lini rose to receive Communion, taking advantage of a rare local dispensation that allowed non-Catholics to receive the Host from a Catholic priest, a subdued mutter of hatred ran through the mainly francophone and hostile congregation.

Robert, as a declared unbeliever, was exempt, but I felt that it would be too pointed to stay in my place and thus publicly to disown Walter, the country's elected leader; so, reluctantly, I went to the altar too. The crawling feeling between the shoulder-blades was almost like a blow, both then and afterwards, as we came out on the steps of the church and the congregation fell back in sullen acquiescence. I have seldom felt more uneasy.

The disturbances in Tanna might be over, but unfortunately all they achieved was to set Jimmy Stevens in Santo yet another target of misbehaviour to aim at. Although he had succeeded in driving out the Government Agent, he had not, at the time of Alexis Yolou's death, formally declared the independence of his self-styled Republic of Vemarana. He now proceeded to do so.

To signal his coup d'état, Jimmy needed some tangible sign of his new-found power. The expulsion of the Government Agent would have been a satisfactory symbol; so would the raising of the Vemarana flag. But Jimmy had already done both of these. Something more dramatic was needed. Accordingly he let loose his forces on the former government quarters and told them to rough up the inhabitants a bit and spread their belongings around for the television cameras. They did this with enthusiasm and then paraded through Luganville town dressed in a weird assortment of unisex clothing and the occasional pair of shoes.

This left a number of hard-working New Hebridean government teachers, agricultural and fisheries officers, community development specialists, health workers, post-office staff and accountants sitting disconsolately in the mud. There were also still a number of foreign nationals in Santo for whose safety I was ultimately responsible, on the ground that, even if not British, they had opted for British protection under the condominium system. Some of these had lived in Santo for years and had a fair idea of what was happening. Others were tourists who had arrived in all innocence at Luganville airport the previous day and were astonished to find themselves herded out of their hotel by a courteous gentleman wearing a brassiere on his head.

There was nothing I could do to protect them where they were. The British police were long gone. So I sent the Euphrosyne to a protestant mission station on the east coast of the island, where Jimmy's platoons had not yet penetrated and announced on the radio that, if anyone wanted to leave, they would be well advised to do so immediately.

At the same time the New Hebrides government chartered a number of small ships to bring off the Melanesian civil servants for whom they were responsible and their families. For three days a mini-Dunkirk armada ferried relays of bewildered, seasick and unhappy people down to the capital or across the narrow stretch of water to the nearest unoccupied airstrip on the island of Malekula, from where the same indefatigable Islander aircraft evacuated them to Vila.

Possibly all this was a mistake on my part. Jimmy's troops were then free to make hay in the abandoned properties. Moreover he was able, almost plausibly, to claim that the British had abandoned Santo of their own volition, and to contrast this with the French 'representative' who continued to sit peacefully in his Luganville office, apparently in cordial relations with the new regime.

But I did not feel able to put anybody's safety at risk for the sake of a policy of 'J'y suis, j'y reste', which even if it had been expressed in English as 'here I am and here I stay' would have seemed no more than a cynical assertion of political expediency at the expense of people.

Nor, when a French banker, whose staff had been instructed to stay put, approached me to ask us to evacuate a sick child and his mother, did I feel it my business to refuse. I therefore, since the main evacuation fleet had already sailed, sent a fisheries launch on a special voyage to Santo to pick up the ailing child.

Unfortunately, after I had informed my French colleague of this as a matter of courtesy, the launch was intercepted and turned back before it reached Santo, by a speedboat manned by a French half-caste with an automatic weapon, and the unhappy banker was given a dressing down for asking for help from the British. I then for the first time in my life, walked out of a meeting of the tripartite security committee that Robert and I had established with Walter Lini, afraid of what I might say if I stayed. It was not a happy moment.

But there was not a thing I could do about it. Independence was only three months away. The government's writ did not run in the largest island of the archipelago. The French and British Police Mobile Units, which might have restored the situation if they had been deployed in Santo months before, were back in Vila, practising their drill for the Independence Day parade.

Ian Cook did his best. By that time I had got him a second-in-command through the Foreign Office, a captain Dick Rouse of the Royal Artillery. Together, in the intervals of their ceremonial preparations, they trained the tiny, already highly-motivated PMU in jungle warfare, anti-riot procedures, crowd-control and survival. To them I attached my own eldest son, just about to join the Scots Guards. Less than two years later, he was to put to good use in the hard-pounding assault on Tumbledown Mountain in the Falkland Islands, the lessons he had first absorbed on the lava slopes of the New Hebrides. But, highly trained though they were, the PMU were two hundred miles away from where the action was, and even if I had been able to send them back to Santo, there was no way that they could go without their French counterparts.

The Pandemonium was in danger of going out, not with a bang but with the feeblest of whimpers. I felt a deep frustration.

And the unreal atmosphere was made even more bizarre by the fact that, while all this was going on in Santo and Tanna, the normal processes of colonial administration had still to be attended to in Port Vila. I still rode to my office each day in the moribund Jaguar. The courts still heard cases and either decided them or adjourned them for the opinion of the Spanish president. The civil servants were still being paid; the schools were still open; the Australian tourists were still decanted from the cruise ships to buy Melanesian artifacts and down prodigious quantities of Foster's lager at Ma Barker's Steak House in the main street; the duty free shops still did a roaring trade.

Even the representatives of foreign powers put in an occasional appearance. An American destroyer on a good will visit momentarily raised Jon Frum hopes that the age of Cargo had arrived, but her captain succeeded only in infuriating Robert by serving us hamburgers, french fries, apple pie and Coca Cola at an official luncheon, explaining that he wanted us to experience 'real Amurrican hospitality'. This was followed by an even greater miscalculation when the same captain reserved a hotel-room on shore after a return dinner on our island, in the confident expectation that our teen-age daughter was panting for a night in his arms. When Fiona declined, firmly but politely, he was most put out. He had assumed that was what was expected of him. Besides he had already paid the deposit.

Nevertheless, amid these alarms, we still thought it our duty to maintain an atmosphere of calm normality. This was particularly important when we were visited by an increasingly querulous stream of officials and ministers from London. Whitehall could not believe what was happening in this unheard-of colonial backwater and were more than a little inclined to assume that everyone in the islands must be mad, and not least of these, the British Resident Commissioner.

It was therefore important that, when they came to see for themselves, they be greeted with restrained but elegant hospitality. It was also important that this be as far removed as possible from the feverish impression conveyed by the increasing number of newsmen who, in a slack season, were swarming through the islands and interviewing Jimmy Stevens in the hope of quotes from his many wives.

Unfortunately everything seemed to conspire against us and to confirm, among other unfavourable impressions, that the British Representative had long since lost all touch with normality. When the Permanent Under-Secretary – the most senior Foreign Office civil servant, the mandarin of all the mandarins – made an unprecedented detour to the New Hebrides from the Chanceries of Europe and the corridors of Washington, to see for himself what was going on, an errant rope wound itself around the propeller of our harbour launch as we were taking him out to our island home.

John the boat boy could not swim and, since the trade winds seemed likely to blow us out into the limitless wastes of the Pacific, there was nothing for it but for the British Resident Commissioner to strip off to his underpants and dive beneath the boat with a knife between his teeth to cut the rope. The head mandarin was relieved, but not, I think, impressed.

Equally when our inoffensive Minister was still reeling from the impact of M. Dijoud's intransigence, Pat and I decided to take him out in the Euphrosyne for a swim and an elegant luncheon at a tropical islet an hour or so away across the bay. We invited Robert too and he said he would join us later in his speed boat.

Rightly mistrusting Mangu's roast beef, Pat ordered cold lobster and white burgundy from the best of the local restaurants. As we rounded the corner of the lagoon and came to anchor by the dazzling white sands of the palm-fringed shore, our Minister breathed a sigh of relaxation and pure relief.

'You know' he said 'I really appreciate what you and Pat have done for me. This has not been an easy posting for you, I know, but we are lucky to have you both here. Believe me the Office will not forget what you are doing for us.'

At that moment Robert's immaculate cream-coloured speedboat rounded the stem of the Euphrosyne and the French Resident Commissioner was piped aboard with a precision that would not have disgraced the flagship of the British Home Fleet.

The lobster, with all its trimmings, was laid out on a long white table on the upper deck, under a spotless awning. The wine was chilling nicely in its silver coolers. After a leisurely swim in the crystal-clear water, the sound of corks being drawn from their bottles, still dewy from the ice, told us that luncheon was ready.

Unfortunately it was also the signal for a ferocious tropical storm, which, in the way of such storms, sprang suddenly out of nowhere from exactly the opposite direction to the prevailing wind. Deprived of the shelter of the island, the Euphrosyne, as was her wont, began to roll horribly in the swell. Moored fore and after, neither anchor could be slipped, or we would have been swept immediately onto the shore, where the coconut palms were already thrashing wildly against the darkening sky. We were therefore broadside on to the rising sea. Within minutes the driving rain, mixed with spray and sand from the reef, dumped an unbelievable quantity of water onto the awning, which collapsed onto the lobster and then, as the wind caught it, flew up into the air and was whirled away over the back of the island. Robert's hat went with it and by the time we were able to shepherd my minister down the companion way and into the owner's cabin we were all drenched to the skin, chattering with cold, lunchless and feeling extremely queasy.

Robert was not amused. He hated the sea and had only come under protest because I had reminded him that we had all been dancing attendance on M. Dijoud throughout the previous week. He had lost both his hat and his dignity and refused to stay on board another minute.

With great difficulty his speed-boat was brought alongside and, without waiting to be piped ashore, my colleague fell rather than climbed down the accommodation ladder into his boat, where a rogue wave soaked him all over again and he was sick over the side, unfortunately to windward.

It had not been a success. Pat and I feared that Murphy's law had deprived us of the Minister's good opinion and had confirmed once again that the British Resident Commissioner was a Jonah who should be dumped into the mouth of the nearest whale. Fortunately, however, my Minister seemed, if anything, stimulated rather than angered by the fact that he had had no lunch and that the Euphrosyne seemed likely at any moment to be cast upon the shore, if she had not rolled herself gunwales under first.

The person who saved the day was the captain, the magnificent Leith Nasak. Appearing in his oilskins like the Flying Dutchman at the cabin door, he was followed by the cook Stephen, bearing a bottle of rum and three mugs of cocoa, which he had somehow managed to produce amid all the chaos.

As the storm began to pass over, Leith slipped anchor and we rolled our way home in the wheelhouse, the rum and the strengthening sun producing an equal warmth and the feeling that, really, it had not been so bad after all.

But it had been a close thing and behind it lurked the realisation that the problems of the New Hebrides were not likely to imitate the tropical storm and vanish of their own accord.

21

Soldier, Soldier

T hings were still not going well in Santo and Tanna. Jimmy
Stevens' ragged army was still in occupation of Luganville
town and he kept sending me rude messages (drafted in
immaculate French, which he did not speak), to the effect that since
the British had abandoned Santo and he did not recognise the 'Lini
Government of Port Vila', he would henceforth deal exclusively
with the French. The last of these messages was touchingly accompanied by a greetings card, picturing Jimmy himself and his large
family seated in polygamous bliss, with the altogether appropriate
motto, 'Be it never so humble, there's no place like home'.

In Tanna too, the Jon Frum were still unhappy. It was impossible
to guess what their continuing problem was, and whether they felt
any responsibility for the death of Alexis Yolou. Their pronounce-
ments still seemed to be couched in volcano-speak. At the same
time some of the more ineffable francophone politicians associated
with Jon Frum had formed what they chose to call the TAFEA
confederation, named after the southern islands of Tanna,
Aneityum, Futuna, Erromango and Aneiwa, which they affected,
on no evidence at all, to claim were all united in opposition to the
newly elected government.

More seriously, there were signs of the disaffection spreading to
the main island of Efate and the capital Port Vila. A rather half-
hearted fire bomb was exploded outside the government broadcasting station, and a few daring graffiti appeared on the streets
proclaiming 'Kafman (Government) blong Lini i bigfela mes(s)'.

I had no real doubt that the PMU could deal with any trouble
that might develop in Vila, but Walter Lini was by that time fed up
with both the metropolitan powers; with the British for failing to

quash the disaffection and with the French for doing even less. He summoned Robert and me to his office, reminded us that until Independence we were jointly responsible for security and demanded that we send for our respective armies.

To my amazement Robert agreed at once. There were French soldiers in New Caledonia two hundred miles away. They could be in Vila within the day. Lini turned to me. 'And what are the British going to do,' he asked ominously 'Sit on their hands as usual?'

This put me in a bit of a quandary. There were I knew, no British troops nearer than Hong Kong and they were presumably fully occupied. The British Government was busy trying to cut down its commitments all over the world. There was a new Prime Minister in Britain, Margaret Thatcher, who reportedly chewed nails for breakfast. But I had no expectation whatever that, in the current parlous state of the British economy, she would send UK soldiers right round the world to rescue Walter Lini, still less Andrew Stuart, who was clearly making a mess of the whole thing.

Fortunately I was not entirely without wise advice. A short time before, after the Santo Government Agent was expelled from his office, it had become obvious that at some stage someone was going to have to reason with Jimmy in a language he could understand, and that that someone would probably need to be carrying a bigger stick than I had available. My time as an Able Seaman thirty years before, and in chasing cattle thieves around Uganda, had not equipped me to deal with the implications of a possible opposed landing on hostile shores. And no one else in my administration was adequately experienced in such matters either. I needed some guidance and had called on the Foreign Office to send me a military adviser.

They came up trumps. A few days before Lini's abrupt request for troops, Colonel Charles Guthrie had arrived from London to survey the situation and report to me and to his masters in Whitehall. Charles had commanded both the Welsh Guards and the SAS (and since then has, indeed, become General Sir Charles, the Chief of the Defence Staff no less). We got on well. I could, usually, beat him at squash. He knew about soldiers, politicians and human nature. He was, and remains that attractive combination, a thinking soldier who knew his own mind and was not afraid to speak it.

He produced a report which demonstrated that a good infantry company could, if necessary, deal with Jimmy Stevens in short order, once the initial problems of landing in Santo had been overcome. So when Walter Lini asked for troops to assure the security of the government, I consulted Charles and together we drafted telegrams to our respective masters in Whitehall asking if we could please have some soldiers.

Amazingly the answer was positive. At that time (it was before the Falklands) no one had really taken the measure of Mrs Thatcher. But it was clear that she was not going to be pushed around by Jimmy Stevens. The next thing we heard was that elements of the Spearhead Battalion, Britain's finest, which happened at that time to be the Royal Marines, were on their way. I was ordered to make arrangements for their arrival in Efate.

Charles, with the help of my staff, then did a phenomenal job of arranging for the Marines to be quartered at the local anglophone secondary school and setting up the logistics and finances for their reception. All I had to do was tell a lie.

The Marines were coming from Britain in the RAF's four-jet VC10s. They were to be joined in Fiji by two lumbering Hercules, the RAF's transport plane that could land anywhere. But to depend on the Hercules to bring them on to Vila would have taken too long. The runway of Vila's wartime airfield was not designed to take large jets, though fortunately the VC10 had its engines grouped close in at the tail, so they would not blow stones all over the narrow runway. The trouble was that the certified strength of the tarmac was less than the landing weight of a fully loaded VC10.

Fortunately the New Hebrides Director of Civil Aviation, a less than onerous appointment, was British. Without telling anyone, we pored over landing weights and concrete strengths and forged the necessary documents. The VC10s could land. (When I went to observe the first troops landing, Robert, who by that time was hopping up and down with fury, observed that I seemed nervous. I did not tell him why.)

When all was ready and the Royal Marines were already in Hawaii, I told my French colleague that they were about to arrive, in accordance with our joint request for troops. He was aghast. The French contingent of Gardes Mobiles had arrived twenty-four hours earlier and were marching up and down the main street of Port Vila with determined expressions on their faces. It was therefore impossible for him to object to the arrival of the Marines by saying that it would breach our joint responsibility for security.

He retired furiously to think, (and presumably to burn up the wires to Paris). Their solution was to announce that the earlier arrival of the French force had so calmed the situation that the emergency was at an end. They were therefore being withdrawn immediately to their base in New Caledonia. It followed that the arrival of British Marines (however welcome in principle) was also unnecessary. Robert therefore proposed that they should be turned about in Hawaii and sent back to the United Kingdom, with the thanks of all concerned and the consciousness of a job well done.

At this the Foreign Office in London, who understandably did not want to irritate the French unnecessarily, asked whether I thought a compromise solution might be for the Marines to come on as far as Fiji, four hundred miles to the east of the New Hebrides, and stop there until the situation clarified.

I was not having any of that, nor was Charles Guthrie. By that time Walter Lini knew that the Marines were on their way. So did everyone else. It was quite obvious that Robert had miscalculated. When he had agreed to make a joint request for troops he too had underestimated Mrs Thatcher and had assumed that Britain would do nothing. French soldiers would be in Efate, thus effectively both controlling the situation on the ground and demonstrating the contrast between French power and British impotence.

If the Royal Marines actually arrived in Vila as well, we would in effect be demonstrating both that the incipient rebellions in Santo and Tanna needed to be dealt with, and that Britain, as well as France, took seriously our joint responsibility for dealing with them.

By a great and fortunate coincidence Mrs Thatcher was meeting the French President in southern Europe the next day. I sent them a personal telegram in the middle of the night saying I was quite clear what should happen. The French and British troops should come to the New Hebrides together and should jointly restore the authority of the new Government which we had both recognised.

This appeared to be well received. The Royal Marines came on and landed at Vila with a satisfying lack of damage to the runway.

As I stood at the terminal to receive them (unfortunately still wearing sailing clothes, having just come off the water – I always seemed to be incorrectly dressed at crucial moments), an immaculate French gendarme came up, saluted and handed me an official-looking envelope. It contained a formal note from my French colleague protesting at my unilateral act in allowing British troops to come to the New Hebrides without joint agreement. The statement had already been released to the press.

I thought this a bit rich. I drafted a reply in my suavest tones, which I showed to Robert and Lini that afternoon. I said that it was not for officials 'however distinguished' (a dig at Robert with his Inspector Generalship) to make policy, but to carry out jointly the decisions of our governments. I also pointed out that the Resident Commissioners, Robert and myself, had jointly asked for troops to be sent. I asked whether Robert would object to this being released to the press, as his had been (without consulting me). He found it difficult to object and stipulated only that I delete the reference to our joint request for the army.

I therefore read my statement, thus shortened, to an amused Jim Biddulph that same night, unfortunately adding, before the cameras were switched off, 'How's that for a really *British* statement?' I then implored him to delete that last remark, which, being an honourable man, he did.

So the Royal Marines arrived, settled down in their temporary quarters in Efate Island and started looking around for something to do. Unfortunately it then transpired that, linked to the French Government's eventual reluctant *non obstat* to their arrival, had been that while they could come (and the French troops would stay) in Efate Island, where there was no rebellion, they were under no circumstances to go to Santo or Tanna, where there was.

There then followed rather bizarre attempts by Charles Guthrie, Walter Lini and myself to justify the peaceful presence on this remote South Pacific Island of some of the most formidable fighting troops in Britain. And they were even more formidable than I at first realised. Four tough looking young men asked if I would take them diving on the wreck of a World War Two flying boat that was lying eighty feet down in Vila harbour. I was giving them fussy instructions on where to sit in the dive boat, when somebody whispered to me that they were members of the SBS (the elite Special Boat Service which is the maritime equivalent of the SAS). Realising that they knew more about boats than I ever would, I ceased being patronising on the spot.

In his attempts to be helpful, Walter Lini went too far. He was grateful to Britain for sending the Marines and he did not, at least to start with, want to embarrass us by implying that they ought to be in Santo fighting, not kicking their heels in Efate. He therefore instructed his press secretary to stress the positive role that the Marines were playing on the main island.

This gentleman, a newly-arrived British ci-devant politician, was a figure of fun to most of the assembled international press. With a penchant for loud ties, an interminable prose style and a tendency to under-estimate the intelligence of his audience, he was an easy target.

The French journalists in particular, got their own back at him by addressing him loudly and in public as Monsieur Baisant (a parody of his real name) and then falling about laughing. Fortunately he did not seem to know enough French argot to realise that this was the slang equivalent of the English F-word, and I certainly was not going to enlighten him.

But I liked him. He prevented an increasingly exasperating situation from leaving the plane of high farce that was the best way of preserving our collective sanity. He told the press that the Marines were being extremely useful clearing paths and building bridges on Efate, not to mention patting babies on the head and taking soup to old grandmothers.

The British press had a field day at the implication that the fiercest fighting troops in the world were really community developers and social workers in disguise, but fortunately the Ministry of Defence in London, under Charles Guthrie's guidance, retained their sense of humour and the Marines were content to wait and meantime make themselves as agreeable as possible.

Soon, however, it was the French who suffered a sense of humour failure. One of the Hercules troop-carrying aircraft had stayed in Vila to provide instant transport in case of need. The pilots had to go on flying to keep their statutory hours up, even when there was nothing special for them to do. By an unfortunate coincidence, they took off with a shattering roar right over our respectful silence at a ceremony for fallen French heroes at the memorial just outside the

Robert's Residence. He was not amused. I suspect he thought I had done it on purpose.

Then, the RAF offered to fly the new Government's Ministers around the islands, so that they could see their home villages from the air. It was a well-meant public relations gesture; but it was not, frankly, an enormous success. The back end of a Hercules is hot, noisy and uncomfortable. Many of the Ministers had little experience of travel-sickness and ceased to take much interest in the proceedings, as soon as the plane had taken off. Doubtless however, their constituents were suitably impressed as the huge plane dived to nought feet along the surf-fringed white beaches of their villages and they glimpsed vaguely familiar faces waving to them from the cockpit.

It was when they got back again that the trouble began. First I had to assure Robert that they had gone nowhere near Santo or Tanna. Then the opposition MPs, annoyed at having a session of the new parliament cancelled, asked the Ministers to explain what exactly they had been doing.

It may have been the fertile brain of Lini's Press Secretary which produced the answer that they had gone to check out reports of a French submarine that was said to be approaching Santo with relief supplies for the rebels. The RAF were greatly stimulated and painted the nose of their unarmed transport plane with the slogan 'Sub-Hunter'. But the French did not think it funny at all, and the reverberations went right back to Paris, and doubtless to London, there presumably adding to the general feeling that the British Resident Commissioner was an irresponsible lunatic.

All this time there was a constant series of meetings in Europe between the relevant British and French Ministers about which I was told little. The usual result was to send out yet another senior officer from London, who arrived with the clear but unspoken brief to 'find out what on Earth that man Stuart was doing and put it right as soon as possible.' Charles Guthrie was summoned (without me) to one such meeting in London, but was brusquely told to sit outside while the great men decided the issue, whatever it was. Soon, however, he was brought in to the Council chamber to clarify some point and, as he explained grimly on his return to Vila, '... found it necessary to put them right on one or two things.' He was too tactful to explain what those were, but I could guess.

Eventually however, commonsense must have prevailed. After one final Ministerial meeting I got a kindly oral message saying, in effect, that my prayers had been answered and the troops were going to Santo. This sounded like a pat on the head for a tiresome, if well meaning schoolboy, but in fact was probably a fair response to my increasingly plaintive telegrams saying that, whatever we did in the last three weeks before Independence, we couldn't just do *nothing*.

I did not, however, trouble to examine too closely the motives of London and Paris. It was enough that they had agreed to take action to end the rebellion. Palestine and Aden excepted we had never, to my knowledge, scuttled from a dependent territory leaving the newly independent country in a state of complete confusion, with half of its new subjects in open rebellion. I did not want to go down in history as the first colonial governor to do so. Even more importantly we owed it to the citizens of the new state, whom we had harried unmercifully for three quarters of century with the absurd Condominium system, to leave them with some hope of peace and unity. Now it seemed that there was at least some chance of doing so.

The troops were going to Santo.

22

The 'Coconut War'

Before the Royal Marines could go in to Santo however, with 100 equally tough-looking French paratroopers sent direct from New Caledonia, my colleague Jean-Jacques Robert flew himself to Luganville in his official plane. He didn't tell me he was going, still less what he was going to do. It would, I imagine, have surprised him that, if I had known what he was after, he would have had my enthusiastic support.

On arrival at Santo Airport, specially cleared for him by his personal representative, M. Pasquet the former French District Agent, Robert went straight to talk to the French, French half-caste and Francophone inhabitants of Luganville. At the meeting Robert adopted the avuncular and jocular tone in which he specialised; the tough ex-rugby player, speaking man-to-man with his cynical and Gaulloise-smoking compatriots.

The fact that he also told them some terrible lies may have caused him a moment's embarrassment later. A clandestine tape-recording of his remarks was produced at the post-Independence trial of Jimmy Stevens, as evidence that Jimmy was an innocent tribal leader duped into rebellion by the unscrupulous French.

I doubt, however, whether Robert was much worried about his post-Independence reputation in the re-named Republic of Vanuatu, though he may have regretted the necessity of incurring the eventual wrath of his audience, who claimed that he had betrayed them. But I am sure he consoled himself, with his expressive gallic shrug, that it was all necessary – and even with the benefit of hind-sight I agree with him, and take off my plumed topee to his unscrupulous devotion to the main objective.

He began by telling his audience that, within twenty-four hours, two hundred soldiers, half British, half French but all under his personal command, would be coming ashore at Santo. The officer in charge of both contingents would be Lt. Col. Vidal of the French paratroops. The Royal Marine commanding officer would be second-in-command to Col. Vidal, who in turn would be under his, Robert's, personal orders. The whole operation had been placed under Robert's responsibility.

So far so, relatively, truthful. It was correct, though London had not bothered to take my advice, that Colonel Vidal had been designated the commanding officer of the joint force. But if I had been consulted, I would again have enthusiastically agreed. The nominal opponents of the expeditionary force would be Jimmy Stevens and his rag-tag army; but the only real threat to the operation was always the French and half-caste colons, rough handling of whom by a force commanded by a British officer would have been imprudent.

Robert's address, however, then soared into the realms of phantasy.

'You see, our aim is to avoid a massacre by the 200 English Royal Marine Commandos, supported by the Papua New Guinea, Fijian, Australian and other regional expeditionary forces. This is because the countries of the Pacific Forum (the coordinating body of independent states in the Pacific) understand very well how crucial the Santo question is for them. As soon as one of the islands of the New Hebrides manages to secede, many other islands belonging to those countries would also follow suit. That they do not want at any cost and that is why they have decided to go the whole hog and really go to war here. We, the French, do not want you to be the first victims of this war. We had no choice about how to do this ... We had to take over the leadership by taking control of the operation ... I personally feel that this is the best thing that could happen from your point of view, given what *was* going to happen.'

Robert went on to assure his audience that they need have no fear of reprisals by the new government or the return of the British public prosecutor, because 'The law will be neither British nor French; it will be whatever I say, because, of course, I will be staying here with Colonel Vidal and the British Colonel, who will only be second-in-command of the joint force ... There will be no curfew. Again, it's me who will be taking the decisions.'

Lini's Government, he said, would have no authority and no power to react. 'That's not possible, they are much too far away.' The blockade of Santo would be lifted and a French ship would be arriving 'with certain things on board that I know you haven't got.'

Robert then went on to refer to Alan Donald, my colleague from the Foreign Office (who had visited Santo the previous week, one of the stream of officials who kept being sent out from London to clean up Stuart's mess) in patronising tones that would have made Alan squirm with embarrassment if he ever heard them. 'I think you made a very great impression on M. Donald. He swears by what you say. He will be coming to talk to you. I think that you managed to win him over completely.'

Finally, having urged his audience to receive the occupying force 'calmly and peacefully and with as many smiles as possible,' Robert went off to exercise similar blandishments on Jimmy Stevens in Vanafo.

They must have worked. The following day the Royal Marines and the French paratroops flew the two hundred miles from Efate to Santo ready for war. They were prepared if necessary for an opposed landing, to drop paratroops to clear the landing field and then to fight their way down to Luganville township. Instead they were greeted with smiles and garlands. Richard Shears, one of the journalists, who by that time were swarming all over the islands, described their arrival thus, 'At 11 am on 24 July the joint force left Port Vila ... The scene at Luganville was extraordinary. Hundreds of Na Griamel supporters waved garlands of bougainvillaea. Women sang and danced. The men laughed and cheered. The British and French troops, jumping from their aircraft in full battle-dress, were bewildered ... Regaining control of the airstrip was not a task that called on the highest standard of commando training. The troops simply walked over to the tiny cream terminal building and took over guard positions without even announcing they were taking it back. The rebels simply let them have it. Two soldiers stood guard over the airport's fire engine and others posted themselves along the airstrip and beside the military aircraft.'

This incident, with all that had gone before and was to follow after, was finally to persuade the world's press to treat the whole business as a ludicrous farce. Richard Shears' book is entitled 'The Coconut War'. Even before the Marines had flown to Santo, the press, in their boredom and having exhausted the supplies of most of the bars in Port Vila, had had T-shirts made for themselves carrying the slogan 'Coconut Commando'. This had nearly caused a nasty incident with some off-duty Marines, but it was understandably symptomatic of the attitude of many of the journalists. They thought they had come to cover a war, but instead had found themselves greeted by Jimmy Stevens with jovial laughs and offers of girls.

One or two of the journalists, however, notably Dennis Reinhardt of *The Times* and Jim Biddulph of the BBC always seemed sympathetic to the woes of the New Hebrideans and not overly inclined to pillory the British Resident Commissioner as a ludicrous figure of fun. But perhaps this was only because, with people like the Government's Press Spokesman around, there were much easier targets to shoot at.

Farce or not, however, I was immensely relieved that the Royal Marines had got ashore in Santo without a fight. Had I known what Robert was up to I'm not sure that I would have joined in his wilder flights of fancy, but I would certainly have applauded his underlying purpose. Although I never discussed this with him, then or since, I am quite sure that he was prepared to do and say anything that would ensure that the French Paras and the Royal Marines did not have a fight on their hands.

A cynic would say, and many did say, that if the joint force had had to fight its way ashore they could hardly have avoided carrying their invasion through to occupy Jimmy Steven's headquarters at Vanafo and put down the rebellion as a whole before Independence. That was not what the French wanted at the time, for the reasons I have already described.

More charitably, however, and I believe more accurately, I'm sure Robert wanted, as I would have done, to avoid or at least to minimize French and British casualties. As a result, not one French or British soldier was killed in the 'Coconut war'.

So Robert told his lies. Jimmy Stevens and the colons believed him, and back in Port Vila I congratulated Charles Guthrie and Colin Howgill, the Commanding Officer of the Royal Marines, on an operation that had gone without a hitch.

There was, however, a downside to all this. Robert's 'personal control' did not amount to much, indeed he returned immediately to Port Vila. But the implications of overall French command of the soldiers on the ground soon became apparent. Robert had told the colons that the joint force would be confined to Luganville township by Colonel Vidal, and so indeed it proved. Jimmy Stevens still lurked undisturbed in his hideout at Vanafo. His radio still poured out its daily stream of sub-Goebbels invective, introduced by an antipodean journalist who claimed improbably to be an agent of Australian intelligence and who still had the run of the bars in Luganville Town. His signature tune, dedicated to Jimmy Stevens, was the pop song 'Daddy Cool'. Somehow it lacked the universal appeal of Lili Marlene. Some of the Royal Marine technicians tried to jam Radio Vanafo, with, it has to be admitted, varying success. Robert was, however, most upset that this was done without his authority.

Soldiers of the joint force were also left at the airfield, outside Luganville, but their instructions from Colonel Vidal were similarly to do nothing beyond ensuring that that the landing ground was kept open. This upset the journalists, who, as always, considered themselves in the style of the old-time ambassadors, with their persons inviolable and exempt from the restrictions and hazards of ordinary men. When a group of them flew to Santo in a chartered plane, they were surrounded, within sight of the joint-force detachment, by a large crowd of Jimmy Stevens' supporters, who threatened to burn the plane, on the ground that they had given it no permission to land. The troops made no move to intervene.

More seriously Colonel Vidal's instructions for the control of Luganville Town seemed limited to say the least. The Vemarana headquarters office within the town remained open for business and the rebel flag flew unhindered within sight of the barracks of the joint force. When Robert and Alan Donald flew to Santo soon after the arrival of the joint force, for final talks with Jimmy Stevens before Independence, Donald, surrounded by the finest fighting troops of the British and French armies, told Stevens only

218

that he would not negotiate beneath the rebel flag. They must at least take it down before he would talk. I hope Jimmy was impressed by his firmness.

Indeed, after these final talks collapsed (in the morning Jimmy had seemed inclined to call the whole rebellion off, but returned after a long lunch with his supporters to say it was all on again), the matter of flags took on an unexpected importance. Colonel Vidal's instructions appeared to have dwindled to a courageous decision that the Royal Marines and the French Paratroops would defend, come what may and with their lives if necessary, the flag-pole on which the new flag of Vanuatu would be raised three days later on Independence Day. It was therefore fortunate that, on the night before Independence, the Marines were able to prevent one of Stevens' bulldozers from knocking the designated flag-pole down, particularly as Jimmy had already uprooted all the other suitable poles in the township. If the last one, at the old British Paddock, had gone down, the whole ceremony would have been a fiasco.

As it was, however, on the day of Independence and thereafter until the whole island was retaken for the government by some-body else, the flag of the Republic of Vanuatu, guarded by Franco-British soldiers around the clock, flew in lonely splendour as the sole symbol of the new Government's authority. At the same time, however, no official attempt was made to remove the flag of Jimmy Stevens' breakaway republic of Vemarana. It was the Condo-minium all over again.

The whole flag business must have been intensely exasperating for the Royal Marines, who proved less than two years later in the Falklands, as they had done worldwide for centuries, that they were capable of guarding more than flagpoles. But in the end when they finally left three weeks after Independence, they devised an adequate riposte. Richard Shears was close to the action:

'The official flag of the Vanuatu Government fluttered on the hill in the grounds of the former British District Agent's Office. The rebel flag of Vemarana was on a metal pole in a beachside park at the other end of town. ... The Vemarana flag had no guards, but the rope had been removed, the pole had been greased at the top to deter athletic climbers and it had also been covered with taboo (Namwele) leaves. During the night of Sunday 17 August, the handful of journalists staying at the Hotel Santo, which was just across the road from the Vemarana flag, thought they heard a loud bump in the night. The next morning the flagpole was found lying across the park, the two steel bolts that had held it in place having been sliced with a pipe-cutting tool. The flag was missing.

'At the airport shortly afterwards' continued Shears 'I wandered up to the British Royal Marines encampment. They were pulling out that day and they were busy folding up their tents and packing their camping gear.

'Did you know that the Vemerana flag was removed last night?' I asked a young officer.

'Well I'll be blowed' he said with just the faintest of grins, 'Just fancy that. Wonder who would have done a thing like that?"

So ended the involvement of the Royal Marines in the Coconut war. They had performed a most thankless task, for which nothing in their training could possibly have fitted them, with patience and good humour. One of them had even got married. Marine James had proposed (through an intermediary – they had no common language) to a local French girl and been accepted. I remarked to my French colleague that it sounded like Romeo and Juliet, but he was not sure what I was talking about.

The saga of the British and French involvement with the Santo rebellion did not, however, end with Independence. The reason why the joint force was still in Luganville at the time of the last flagpole episode, nearly three weeks after the end of the Condominium, was an acute attack of British diplomatic blindness.

Several weeks before Independence Day, there had, as Robert had explained to the Colons (albeit with embellishments) been a meeting of the South Pacific Forum. At that meeting, attended only by the independent nations of the South Pacific, and therefore not by Britain or France, the member states had unanimously agreed an informal resolution, drafted by Malcolm Fraser, the Australian Prime Minister, calling upon Britain and France to put down the rebellion within fourteen days.

Walter Lini had, however, no expectation that this would happen; at the time the Royal Marines were still in the capital and there was no sign of a breakthrough with Jimmy Stevens, or with the French. Lini had therefore opened negotiations for military assistance with Sir Julius Chan, the Prime Minister of Papua New Guinea and with the Chief of the PNG Defence Force, Brigadier Ted Diro, who had been secretly summoned to the Forum Meeting. However, they could promise nothing.

The Government and people of Papua New Guinea had an instinctive sympathy for the New Hebrides/Vanuatu, their fellow Melanesians. But the PNG army was a small self-defence force with little offensive capacity and no experience of operations overseas. It took time for the two parties to reach agreement (entirely without British connivance or assistance, which made nonsense of Robert's assertion to the colons that the Royal Marines were planning to lead a ravening force of PNG soldiers to murder them all.)

In the last week before Independence, however the PNG and New Hebrides Prime Ministers finally agreed (again without British connivance) that a PNG force would fly into Santo as soon as possible. This could not, however, be done before Independence, now only days away. When we heard of the agreement, Charles Guthrie and I therefore urged on the Foreign Office that, if the Franco-British force was to leave Santo with any sort of honour, it must be prepared to stay and guard the airport until the PNG troops arrived.

Otherwise they would have had to fight their way onto the ground over a blocked runway. This had been the nightmare scenario for which we had been prepared before the Royal Marines first went in and from which Roberts prevarications had fortunately rescued us. It would have been far worse for the PNG 'Kumul Force'. They had neither the equipment nor the experience to make an opposed landing.

Jimmy Steven's coconut army might be militarily negligible, with or without a reinforcement of colons. But a few trucks and oildrums blocking the Santo airstrip would have made it impossible for the lumbering PNG Dakotas to land. The PNG armed forces had no parachutes to seize the airfield by force and no landing craft to make an opposed sea-borne landing. The whole thing could have been a disaster.

Fortunately London agreed that, if the new government of Vanuatu asked us to stay, the Marines could do so for long enough to shepherd the PNG forces safely onto the ground, after which the Marines would leave. Once landed, fellow Melanesian soldiers could then dispose of the rebellion in their own time. With this concession from Whitehall, I was satisfied that we could leave the New Hebrides with enough honour intact to let me sleep o'nights.

But Walter Lini, within hours of Independence, had had enough. He was furious that the joint force had done virtually done nothing since their arrival in Santo. He wanted to see the back of us all as soon as possible. He did not wait to learn if the Marines would be allowed to stay after Independence. Instead he sent an official Note to Robert and myself demanding the immediate withdrawal of all foreign forces from the New Hebrides.

I knew that the continued presence of the Royal Marines was essential for the success of the PNG operation. I also knew that London had agreed to this, but could not yet tell Lini so. If I had officially received his ultimatum it could have spoiled it all. I had to find some way of not receiving it. 'I'm sorry', I said, 'I can't read your letter. I've lost my glasses.' I therefore insisted that the messenger take his letter back to the Prime Minister, since I was regrettably unable to receive it.

The next day, in official ignorance of his Government's ultimatum, I was therefore able to tell Walter Lini that the Royal Marines could stay if needed even after Independence and this he graciously accepted. Of such are the realities of the diplomatic quadrille.

So, the following month, the PNG force landed unopposed in Santo. The Royal Marines stayed long enough to see them safely on the ground and then took off themselves in the lumbering Hercules. With only one fatal casualty, Jimmy Stevens' son, who drove into a road block and refused to stop, the PNG Kumul force then swiftly restored order throughout Santo.

A few French citizens were deported, adding to the number who had been warned by the new French Ambassador to leave before the arrival of the PNG troops and who departed, cursing Jean-Jacques Robert who, they said, had deceived them. But Robert himself had long gone from Vila, as indeed had I. I only hope he read in the press the news of the safe ending of the revolt with as much relief as I did.

There was one final sequel which must have amused Charles Guthrie and I hope was not too offensive to the military pride of the Royal Marines. The Vanuatu government and people were understandably cock-a-hoop that their Melanesian brothers from PNG had disposed of the revolt with so little trouble and bloodshed. Their seventy-five years of colonial experience had left them short of ethnic self-confidence. Now, however, they were able to announce that the dreaded army of Jimmy Stevens, which had struck such terror into the finest European troops of Britain and France that they had been unable to move against him, had succumbed quickly and completely to the superior forces of PNG. This was proof, if proof was needed, that Melanesian soldiers were the best in the world and that Melanesia had come of age.

Who would he grudge them this triumph? Certainly not I.

And as for the major actor in this sad pantomime, Jimmy Stevens, he was brought to trial before the Supreme Court and sentenced to a total of 14 years imprisonment on charges varying from conspiracy to procure the secession of Santo to the illegal importation of passports. His own comment to the *Sunday Times* provided a fitting epitaph to a blip in history that had finally left him stripped of all pretensions.

'For me I think that everything will be buggered up. I do not see any good of this fourteen years. That's the way I look at it.'

23

The End of Empire

But all this was still in the future. Meanwhile the independence of the New Hebrides could no longer be postponed. We had already delayed it once after Dijoud threw his tantrum and there were uncomfortable signs that if we tried to put the date back yet again, Walter Lini and his government would go ahead and declare Independence anyway.

Six weeks before the appointed 'Freedom Day' of July 30, 1980, his Press Secretary announced in his best circumlocutory style, that 'The Government of the New Hebrides would wish to state that the date of 30 July for the attainment of Independence is not negotiable.' In other words, if we did not agree, they would declare UDI.

This rang alarm bells in my mind and in Whitehall. As the Press Secretary put it 'The British Resident Commissioner was clearly in a state of anxiety on the matter.' The Rhodesian Unilateral Declaration of Independence was still fresh in the British government's mind and I could think of no surer way of finally losing their sympathy than a repeat performance in the New Hebrides.

And the threat was not an idle one. With the Press Secretary's help, the Government had already drafted a proclamation declaring the Republic of Vanuatu a 'Free and Independent State.' 'Monsieur Baisant' had clearly got the bit between his teeth and increasingly began to move centre stage. As he commented in his subsequent book (not without a touch of self-satisfaction, though coyly refraining from naming himself) 'The daily press conferences held by Walter Lini's Press Secretary came to be regarded with an apprehension bordering on paranoia by the two Resident Commissioners'.

224

They were certainly a para-normal experience though 'paranoia' would, I think, have been overstating the case. They were the cream on my otherwise unappetising day. Nevertheless, something had to be done to appease London. Taking a leaf out of the press secretary's Manual of Ineffable Statements, I announced.

'The Prime Minister has assured me that his main aim is to make it clear that he hopes the metropolitan Governments will abide by their already stated acceptance of July 30th as the Independence date. He intended only to say that if this did not happen he would have to consider seriously all the options open to him.'

Fortunately this mealy-mouthed way of saying the same thing seemed to satisfy Whitehall and Lord Carrington announced in the House of Lords that the 30 July date would stand. After that the French government had, for once, little option but to follow suit. So, while Jimmy Stevens still rampaged around Santo and the Jon Frum continued to mutter into their Nambas in Tanna, preparations for the party to end all parties began in Vila.

With only a month to go before freedom day there was no time for elaborate preparations. Nor were there any precedents that we could follow. Over the previous generation the ex-British colonies had developed a more or less standard pattern for celebrating Independence. This had changed little since Uganda eighteen years before.

The centre piece would have been the midnight ceremony where the Queen's representative handed over the instruments of Independence to the new Head of State. Then the British flag came down on one flag pole as the new nation's standard rose on the other. The singing of the old national anthem, followed by the new, left hardly a dry eye in the huge crowd. Fireworks bursting across the sky heralded a party that mingled nostalgia and delight in an unforgettable cocktail.

In the New Hebrides, however, things had perforce to be different. In the first place there was not one single colonial authority to hand over its power, but two. The Queen's Representative, (in our case the entirely admirable Duke of Gloucester) had to share the stage with a political Minister from republican France (one of the best demonstrations of the abiding value of the British monarchy that I can think of).

Monsieur Paul Dijoud was no longer on the scene, though whether he had been replaced or simply did not wish to be seen eating so many of his own words, I have never discovered. Instead a less colourful figure, Oliver Stirn, represented the French Republic on what must, for him, have been a poignant and difficult occasion.

Whether symptomatic or not of a French belief that decolonisation from France is an act of self-destruction, not of re-birth, Paris had decreed that there must be no lowering of the French flag in public. Instead it was to be secreted away in the middle of the night, twenty-four hours before Independence.

Although, thereafter, M. Stirn participated with dignity in the ceremonies on Independence day, he refused to lend himself to any general celebration. Instead France's national holiday on the 14th of July, two weeks before Independence, had been made the occasion for a massive demonstration of French loyalty and pride. A procession through Port Vila was followed by an air and parachuting show and a fireworks display on the waterfront that entirely outshone the national celebrations at the end of the same month. It was all rather sad.

Nor were the British able to mount any great display of pomp and circumstance to mark our enthusiastic acceptance of the new Republic of Vanuatu. The Royal Marines were still chafing under French command in Santo and to bring them back to march in the Independence day parade would have been a cruel mockery of all that that ceremony was supposed to represent.

Nor, because of the shortage of time, could the Royal Navy spare a warship to lie in Port Vila harbour within sight of the parade ground on the old British Paddock. The only foreign ship that was present was therefore an Australian destroyer. The Australians were increasingly taking the new Republic under their wing and found no difficulty in agreeing with Walter Lini that the French were duplicitous bastards and the British feeble beyond belief.

The only symbol of British metropolitan majesty present (other than the Duke himself – who was no small symbol and an excellent guest to boot), was the band of the Royal Marines, who joined their fighting comrades in the New Hebrides on the day before Independence. The presence of the Band was by no means negligible and they added their inimitable touch of pride and nostalgia to both the final British ceremony and the national celebrations. But the effect was somewhat marred, on the Duke's arrival, by the fact that the band was with him on the same RAF VC10 aircraft. He therefore had to descend the aircraft steps to greet the assembled dignitaries, to a fanfare by the same tootling French police band that had greeted my own arrival two years before.

Those dignitaries too were a mixed bag. The Australian Foreign Minister and the Prime Minsters of Papua New Guinea and the Solomons, rubbed shoulders with the honorary Consuls for Venezuela and the Principality of Monaco. By an imaginative touch, the official representative of the United States was that same author James Mitchener who had written his romance about Santo and Aoba forty years before. But even the presence of the supreme story teller lacked something by comparison with the great officers of the most powerful nation on earth, who should have been there, but weren't.

It didn't really matter though. In the middle of all their worries about their divided nation and their concerns for the future, the Ni-Vanuatu were having themselves a ball. The first official item on the programme, which everybody wished to attend, was the Royal Marines Beating the Retreat on our island of Iririki on the evening before Independence.

I was determined that, come what may, the Union Jack would come down with dignity. All afternoon every boat in the former British Marine was pressed into service to bring the guests across from the town jetty to face the climb of our 178 steps. At the top Pat and I stood with the Duke greeting old friends and colleagues, not least the veterans of the Independence negotiations, who had survived both Mangu's cooking and the assaults of Monsieur Dijoud to prepare for this day. Earlier the Duke had presented both Walter Lini and Father Gerard Leymang with the insignia of the CBE to signal the part that anglophone and francophone Ni-Vanuatu had played together in making Independence possible.

The rough gardens and the building of our ramshackle Residence, were soon to be abandoned to anyone who wanted to lay claim to them (the ownership of the land, as usual in the New Hebrides, was disputed). We had not had time to negotiate any sort of hand-over, not just of the house and gardens, but also of the furniture, beds, carpets, glass, china, cutlery and equipment, all of them emblazoned with the Royal crest. Doubtless they are now embellishing some rustic cottage in the Solomon Islands, to which

Mangu and his family retired after our departure, to live on his pension and poison the neighbours. But the sense that the tradition of eighty colonial years was about to vanish in a puff of smoke, only made us all the more determined to mark the evening in a way that would be remembered.

As the sun sank over the harbour with a flash of green across the velvet sky, the Marine Band took up the Sunset hymn, with a solo-trumpeter soaring above the melody, as the flag came down. This truly was the last time and it was hard not to feel both sadness and the weight of tradition pressing around our ears.

But it was not the final act. It was only the beginning of the end. The next twenty-four hours were a kaleidoscope of impressions and thoughts, spoken and unspoken, of the future and the past. First, at midnight, in the absence of a joint celebration, we gathered at the Parliament building, where the President and the new government were sworn in and the Resident Commissioners relinquished their responsibility. For once the staircase arrangement had failed and Robert and I were left on an even footing, like a giraffe and a walrus, to read the instruments of our own deposition.

Some adventurous entrepreneur caught the mood of the occasion and the next day a T-shirt was for sale on the streets of Port Vila. On a yellow background a huge red sun sets over a tropical island where the palm trees are all bent and broken. On the left is a lanky and ungainly figure carrying a briefcase and wearing a pair of Union Jack shorts. On the right, looking angrily towards him is a squat gentleman in a Kepi, whose ample behind is clothed in the red, white and blue of the Tricolore. Above their heads are the words CONDOMINIUM 1980, and underneath, between their elongated shadows, is the apocalyptic slogan FINIS – FIN – THE END.

The next day was also a time of mixed emotions, exhilarated for most of us, no doubt sombre for others. The Duke, ever game, made a speech in broken Bislama, which was wildly applauded. Oliver Stirn muttered a few well chosen platitudes in French which, however, went little further than to wish the new Republic well. Walter Lini's speech, in its length and complexity, bore the signs of drafting by his Press Secretary, who appeared well satisfied in a new red tie.

Then the troops, mainly from Papua New Guinea but with some alert-looking French paras from New Caledonia and the British

PMU, which was not to be outdone by any of them in precision and turn-out, marched and counter marched to the immaculate music of the Royal Marines. The lumbering Hercules flew overhead with some ancient Dakotas from the New Guinea army that looked as if they were about to fall out of the sky. Finally, on the single flag pole, after some delay caused by a tangled halliard, rose the flag of the Republic of Vanuatu, black, green, red and yellow with a design of Namwele leaves within a curled pig's tusk, to symbolize Kastom and national unity.

The national anthem, at its first airing, had none of the complexity of its Uganda equivalent. A simple melody, starting with the opening bars of 'Oh parlez moi d'amour' (or 'Oh speak to me of love' – a final touch of the Condominium?) affirmed the people's faith in God and the brotherhood of all mankind.

'Yumi, Yumi Yumi i glad blong talem se
Yumi, Yumi Yumi i man blong Vanuatu
God i givim ples long yumi
Yumi glad tumas long hem
Yumi strong mo yumi free long him
Yumi brata evriwan'[1]

The visiting dignitaries looked uncomfortable, as they always do when confronted with the choice of either pretending to understand the language, or staying silent and looking vaguely disapproving lest the unknown words contain sentiments from which they ought to disassociate themselves. I have often seen the identical expression on English faces during the singing of the Welsh national anthem before a Wales/England rugby match at Cardiff. But it was only a momentary discomfort. We soon

---

1. 'We, oh we, yes we, are glad to tell it out
    that we are the people of Vanuatu.
    God has given us our country,
    And we rejoice in him.
    To him we owe our strength and freedom
    For we are all brothers.'
    (Bislama is lacking in plurals, so 'Yumi' means 'We' or 'us'. It was only the twisted minds of some of the tabloid press that suggested that 'Yumi, Yumi' might unconsciously be a reflection of the islands' cannibal past.)

adjourned for lunch, presentations and more speeches, this time tactfully in English and in French.

Again things went swimmingly. There was only a momentary hiccup when the new Prime Minister inadvertently referred to the West German delegate as 'the representative of the German Democratic Republic' and I unwisely caught the Australian Foreign Minister's eye. Nor, I am sure, was there any malice in the chance that, when the time came to present the visitors with 'Kastom' trophies, one of the officials from London, who had been involved in the abortive negotiations with Jimmy Stevens, was given a curly pig's tusk labelled 'Santo'. He however chose to take it personally and I found him afterwards gazing sadly at this symbol of ill-omen and muttering 'They hate me. I know they hate me!' He seemed close to tears, but that was after the ceremonial taking of Kava, which had worked its usual disorientating magic on the unsuspecting guests.

He could not, however, be left long to mope. There were still momentous decisions to be made about the future of British aid to the newly independent nation and about the timing and scope of our post-independence intervention in Santo.

From midnight the previous night, I myself had been in an anomalous position, with no official status left and no accreditation to any government. My successor had already arrived, travelling out in the Royal plane. His duties would be solely representational and diplomatic and he would have to live in a rabbit hutch in the middle of town, which was all the British Treasury could afford. All the trappings of power were gone; the staff; the Euphrosyne; the Jaguar (no great loss that) the island; the police force and the feathered hat. He would have to shift for himself.

On the other hand I was still there. The Duke of Gloucester was staying in our house; I was still getting alternately angry and anguished telephone calls from Walter Lini, usually reflecting the presence or absence of his Press Secretary; I still felt responsible.

In this situation the sensible colonial tradition is that the retreating Governor must leave immediately. Pat and I would have liked to stay, to travel around the islands and to say goodbye to friends. We would have liked to spend some time in the rest of the South Pacific to see those romantic places that were tantalisingly near but had remained out of reach as the crises of the New

Hebrides had ebbed and flowed. But we were needed elsewhere and anyway the Foreign Office had ruled that we must travel home on the Duke's aircraft and so save the cost of an airfare. So I ground my teeth and was silent.

That meant, however, that we only had twenty-four hours to wind up eighty years of colonial administration. We felt like A. A. Milne's shipwrecked sailor, of whom it was said that:

'And so in the end he did nothing at all,
 But just basked on the shingle wrapped up in a shawl,
 I think it's disgraceful the way he behaved
 He did nothing but basking until he was saved.'

I told my successor he would have to work out his relationships as best he could; I called on Robert's successor, the new French Ambassador (who, however, only lasted a matter of weeks before he was declared Persona non Grata by the new Government); I settled up a few bills in the town and had a beer at Ma Barkers. Pat, for her part, went off to say goodbye to a few friends and to worry about our daughter Fiona, who was staying behind for a few days to clear things up.

Meanwhile the Duke, whom we should have been looking after, seemed perfectly happy to sit in our garden in the sun and chortle over a book I had lent him called 'The Psychology of Military Incompetence'. He saved up the choicest bits for our farewell family dinner that night, to tease his ex-Scots-Guards-Colonel private secretary who, however, took it all in excellent part. As we retreated exhausted to an early bed, we heard the Duke, still engrossed, calling out, 'Come and look at this bit, Simon. Inadequate potty training – that's what it says. Inadequate potty training was what was wrong with General Haig.'

The last night in our home was followed by the last morning. This was a nightmare. Protocol demanded that we attend upon the Duke as he left our house. On the other hand the same protocol insisted that, since we were to travel on the same aeroplane, we must board the flight before him. In theory we had only the duration of the Duke's journey from house to airport in which to pack up our home and our belongings, say goodbye to our staff, board the harbour launch and the Jaguar for the last time and reach the

231

airport, say goodbye to our friends and the Government and be on the aircraft before the Duke arrived.

They say that if you can travel faster then the speed of light, you become younger and end up in the cradle. We, on the other hand, found that it had the opposite effect.

As the Jaguar turned into the airport approach road we could bear it no longer. Despite the growing excitement of the Duke's approach behind us, I stopped the car and walked down the crowded road, touching familiar hands, faces, waving to those at the back of the crowd whom we could not reach. Fiona, who was with us, was in floods of tears and, though Mr Carruther's first rule had always been 'Colonialists don't cry', we too were close to it.

I felt terrible at the thought of a job that seemed only half complete. As we climbed into the aircraft I felt exhausted with hopes, fears, regrets, negotiations, wars, justices and rank injustices. And yet, in truth, we were the lucky ones.

The people we should have felt sorry for were the leaders and ministers who were left behind. Somehow, out of the chaos of the Condominium they had to construct a country. And they had to do this with no respite at all. After our departure, Walter Lini went off to spend a couple of days in his village. But immediately thereafter he and all his ministers had to be back, negotiating with Jimmy Stevens and the government of Papua New Guinea; with Britain, France and Australia; with the John Frum, the Big Nambas and the Small Nambas; with the Francophones and the Anglophones; with the Anglicans, the Catholics, the Presbyterians and the Seventh Day Adventists; with Russia and America.

Small wonder that for a while they seemed to go off the rails. Not too long after Independence Walter Lini had a stroke, the Vanuaaku Pati broke up, the British and French governments largely lost interest in aid to the South Pacific, and the tourist industry virtually collapsed under the pressure of world recession and internal instability.

I only wish we had been able to do something to help, both then and now. But that is a different story.

Envoi
Brought to Justice

I had to be in Finland within five days of leaving the New Hebrides. The delay in Vanuatu's Independence and the imminent visit of the British Foreign Secretary for talks with the Finnish President, meant that the normal stately diplomatic process had to be absurdly telescoped.

There is considerable ceremony about the appointment of a new ambassador, much of it archaic and often faintly ridiculous. Official despatches are exchanged about 'A person of approved Wisdom, Diligence and Circumspection ... whom We do by these presents nominate, constitute and appoint ... for the promotion of relations of friendship, good understanding and harmonious intercourse, ... namely our Trusty and Well-beloved Andrew Christopher Stuart ... in whose discretion and faithfulness We repose especial Trust and Confidence.'

It is difficult by the end of these exchanges for the object of that Trust and Confidence not to feel like a pretty fine fellow indeed.

However, despite the press of all these great events, there was one summons which I could not ignore. A heavily stamped buff form required me to present myself at room no 325 in Customs House next to the Tower of London on the day before we flew to Helsinki.

I had no idea what it was about. Pat and I had had an elegant conversation with Her Majesty that morning and were feeling pretty elevated. I assumed that I would be met by the Chief Customs Officer with equal ceremony and some deference.

It was therefore a shock to find that room 325 was a cubby-hole at the end of a dingy corridor, into which I was ushered by a female wardress and told to 'Wait there until they're ready for you.' The

only furnishings were a desk and three grotty chairs. A single overhead light had a broken shade, stuck together with sellotape. I
waited.

After ten minutes, two grimly uniformed gentlemen came in and
started fiddling with their papers. They ignored me. Lest they
might be feeling over-awed by my presence, I decided to put them
at their ease with a gracious comment on the weather. But one of
them held up a restraining hand. 'You are not obliged to say
anything' he intoned 'but I must warn you that anything you do
say will be taken down and may be given in evidence.'

This seemed to be carrying deference too far. I did not really need
or expect my lightest comments to be recorded for the benefit of
posterity. Besides I was getting late for my next appointment. I
decided to cut short the formalities.

'So what can I do for you gentlemen?' I asked, pleasantly
enough.

The shorter one, who looked remarkably like Jean-Jacques
Robert, was clearly in charge.

'Is this your signature on this document?' he inquired, holding up
some sheets of paper, which on closer inspection turned out to be
lists of our heavy baggage, which had been packed up and sent
before us while I was still busy with the pandemonium.

'Certainly' I replied 'D'you need a counter-signature?'

A harsher note crept into his voice. 'Are you aware that by this
signature, you have formally certified that all goods and chattels
consigned by you in accordance with this manifest are used household effects and at least 12 calendar months old?'

I confessed that I had not previously given the matter any
thought. As he might have seen from the TV news bulletins, things
in the New Hebrides had been rather busy lately. I had simply
signed the papers that had been put before me.

'When you signed this certificate' he continued 'Were you aware
that electrical equipment labelled "Fiona and James' Hi-Fi" and
listed in the manifest, had in fact, as shown by the invoices
enclosed with the equipment, been purchased not twelve months
previously, but only ten months and twenty-seven days before the
date of your signature?'

I knew that James and Fiona had each used their Christmas
money to buy a Ghetto-blaster in the Japanese store in Port Vila,

but I could not, for the life of me, have remembered when. I replied, humbly enough, that I knew nothing of the matter.

My interrogator seemed unconvinced. 'I have to inform you' he said coldly 'that I suspect you of the illegal importation and avoidance of customs dues on dutiable goods brought into the United Kingdom, contrary to subsection 3 of section 45 of the Act.'

'I am, however, empowered under Section 54 to accept your admission of liability should you choose to make such an admission. In that event, and on payment of three times the import duty on the illegally imported article or articles, no further action will be taken against you.'

'Should you continue to deny liability, however, you will be charged under the relevant provision of the Act and bound over to appear in court on a date to be determined.'

I had a vision of excusing myself from the meeting with the Finnish President on the ground that I was due to appear in a London magistrate's court on a charge of smuggling. Bowing to the inevitable I took out my cheque book. Then a thought struck me.

'How about the Hi-Fi equipment?' I asked.

He softened momentarily.

'Who are Fiona and James?'

'My children.'

'How old are they?'

'Nineteen and Seventeen.'

'Are the articles in question their property?'

'Yes.'

'Were they an accessory to your commission of this offence?'

'No.'

'I am a father myself. It was you and not they who signed the form. I will consider releasing the equipment into their custody, if they will write to me, giving a solemn assurance that they are not a party to your unlawful act.'

Somewhat shaken, I got up to go. I was a convicted criminal.

On reflection, however, it seemed a fitting note on which to end my career as a colonialist.

But I'm not sure that Mr Carruthers would have approved.

"It is not our business to dominate anybody"